WILLIAM MAXWELL
TO ROBERT BURNS

THERE'S braw, braw lads on Yarrow braes,
That wander thro' the blooming heather;
But Yarrow braes nor Ettrick shaws
Can match the lads o' Galla Water.
Robert Burns

William Maxwell, c. 1810, possibly by John Allan.

Robert Burns, 1795/6. Miniature by Alexander Reid.

William Maxwell to Robert Burns

ROBERT DONALD THORNTON

But as for that the travelling there
Had worn them really about the same.
Robert Frost

JOHN DONALD PUBLISHERS LTD
EDINBURGH

ISBN 0 85976 052 9

Phototypesetting by Burns & Harris Limited, Dundee
Printed in Great Britain by Bell & Bain Ltd., Glasgow

Contents

List of Plates

Colour

1. William Maxwell

2. Robert Burns

Black and white

1. Map of Nithside

2A. Sweetheart Abbey

2B. Kirkconnell

3. Dinant

4. The Dagger Scene

5A. Mary Maxwell (mother)

5B. James Maxwell (father)

6A. John Syme

6B. James Maxwell (brother)

7. John Menzies

8. William Maxwell (silhouette)

Thanks go to the following for permission to reproduce plates: Mrs Bettina M. G. Maxwell-Witham: colour plate 1 and plates 2B, 5A, 5B, 6B and 8; the Scottish National Portrait Gallery: colour plate 2; the National Library of Scotland: plate 1; the Department of the Environment: plate 2A; Edit. Anciens, Bruxelles: plate 3; the British Museum: plate 4; and Dumfries Royal Burgh Museum: plate 6A.

Robert Donald Thornton

Introduction

Of course, Robert Burns is nowhere, yet everywhere in modern Dumfries. Some find him in the statuary all about town; some, in the gimcrackery peddled in the High Street and down along the White-sands, soiled with soot, paper, and broken bottles. Others seek him on Bank Street or Burns Street, at the Globe or Bridgend; in the Ewart Library or the Burgh Museum. An occasional solitary works his way out of shops and residences, through a gravel quarry, to the poet's view of abbey ruins at the confluence of Cluden and Nith, even as tourists scramble off a bus near St Michael's so that they can go up into the graveyard to take a snapshot of the Mausoleum.

Long a light in the eyes of staunchest supporters like Currie and Syme, William Roscoe and Maria Riddell,[1] this tomb could not be realized until the year of Waterloo. Irregularly maintained today, it still can impress: location, dome, figures of Coila and the poet, grave-stone itself. First words upon the slab read:

In MEMORY OF
ROBERT BURNS
who died the 21st July 1796
in the 37th year of his age
AND
MAXWELL BURNS

MAXWELL BURNS! Here the story, here the song. Not the poet's last child himself, not the baby pitiably born as the military slow-stepped his father's corpse to St Michael's, not the lad who lived less than three years, not the son named 'Maxwell'. Rather the young gentleman after whom that son was named. Who was this person so

1

honored by Burns and his family? How did he enter the poet's life? What was their friendship? Why was he appointed executor and how did he serve widow and children? In short, who was the 'Maxwell' of MAXWELL BURNS?

Robert Burns sought to make his children's names 'altars of gratitude':

> To name my child after any of the Great, with a view of their future beneficence, is quite foreign to my ideas: my motive is gratitude, not selfishness. Though I may die a very Poor Man, yet I hope my children shall ever boast the character of their Father: and as that father has some few in the upper ranks of life to whom he is peculiarly indebted, or whom he holds peculiarly dear, he wishes his children likewise to indulge an honest pride on that account; not only as a memento of these honors their father enjoyed, but as an incentive to noble action, he will call his children after the names of his illustrious friends and benefactors.[2]

From Brow Well, two weeks before his death, Burns wrote Alexander Cunningham that the child Jean was then carrying would be named after him, 'if the right gender'.[3] Burns died. On the Monday of his burial, Jean gave birth. The gender *was* right, but the baby was named 'Maxwell', not 'Cunningham'.

Did Jean defy her husband's last wishes? Was she ignorant of those wishes? Or, reasonably, had Burns and Jean, in those few days between his return to Dumfries and his death, decided that there was a man whom they should honor before Cunningham, to whom they both owed a debt of gratitude far beyond any they might owe Cunningham? That man was Robert's intimate. That man was Robert's and Jean's personal physician, who watched the father to death on Thursday and then watched the mother to her delivery on the burial Monday. Attending the exhausted mother at her bedside, he had caught with her the last strains of Handel's 'Dead March' as they had mingled with the first cries of her newborn son: Maxwell Burns.

Despite the fact that everybody who has written about Robert Burns has found it necessary to say something about Dr Maxwell, nothing better exists today than a footnote of Henley and Henderson based upon the earlier report of William McDowall:

> Dr. William Maxwell, son of a noted Jacobite, James Maxwell of Kirk-connell, was born in 1760. He was educated at the Jesuits' College at Dinant, and afterwards studied medicine at Paris. In 1792 he started a

London Subscription for the French Jacobins, and he is the Englishman said in Burke's speech (28th December 1792) to have ordered three thousand daggers at Birmingham. As a National Guard he was present at the execution of Louis XVI., and is reported to have dipped his handkerchief in the King's blood. When Burns wrote, he had just returned to Scotland and started a practice in Dumfries. Burns and he became fast friends. He attended Burns during the last illness, when the dying man presented him with his pistols. He died 13th October 1834.[4]

Clearly Henley and Henderson did some homework; at least they, unlike the twentieth-century Oxford editor of Burns's poetry, give the first name correctly.[5] But, just as clearly, what they give is rumor as well as fact, which together no more than hint why the bairn was christened 'Maxwell'.

Biographers and critics of Burns have never questioned that Maxwell was important to Robert Burns or that, apart from Burns, he was 'a man of somewhat singular character and attainments'.[6] Yet all have been content, more or less, to settle for 'popular report'[7] in lieu of fact; and each has helped contribute to a bedevilment not different from the confusions of Robert Riddell and James Currie.[8] Once in a while a Lockhart has evaded the issue by using no Christian name;[9] and once in a while a critic has found the right name, only to lose his wits among the three William Maxwells (a physician, a surgeon, and a nailer) and the one Mrs William Maxwell listed in the *Dumfries Diet Book*.[10] Less often an historian has candidly settled for 'William Maxwell was a doctor, but I can discover nothing of his parentage or early life.'[11] Standard procedure has become perpetuation of anecdote and surmise and downright error: that the doctor was 'Doctor James', that he pursued the study of medicine in Paris, that he dipped his handkerchief in the blood of Louis XVI, that he fell 'in La Vendée', that he enlisted with Burns and Syme in the Dumfries Volunteers, that he killed Burns, that he was born Dutch, English, German. Indubitably, as subject for a biography, Dr William Maxwell is no sitting duck.

Rather he is most difficult to approach. After all, he was born into one of Scotland's illustrious Roman Catholic families *after* the sixteenth century. Try, for example, to discover where a Roman Catholic was buried in Edinburgh yesterday or to penetrate the Stygian darkness of Edinburgh Catholic Archives today! What is more, one does not have a rich correspondence of Burns with Maxwell as with a George Thomson, a 'Clarinda', or a Mrs Dunlop. Why should Burns have *written* to anybody a street or so away? There is not a single extant letter to John Lewars or Thomas White who, like Maxwell, lived close at hand — and only one to John Syme across the Nith. What seems true, moreover, is that there are all but no private papers of William today because there were individuals who had reasons upon his death to make his oblivion complete.

For whatever remains — before it becomes too late — 'I haif inquyrit in mony a place,' but at no place with more satisfaction than at Kirkconnell House, where the family had invited me to work and where I have known the support of Mrs Bettina M. G. Maxwell-Witham's spirit and intelligence.

As facts mount, as searches continue like cells dividing, one concurs with Samuel Johnson, who opined while at work on his *Dictionary*:

> . . . I did not find by my first experiments, that what I had not of my own was easily to be obtained; I saw that one inquiry only gave occasion to another, that book referred to book, that to search was not always to find, and to find was not always to be informed; and that thus to pursue perfection was, like the first inhabitants of Arcadia, to chase the sun, which, when they had reached the hill where he seemed to rest, was still beheld at the same distance from them.[12]

Fortunately, for the biographer, understanding of his subject arrives before his last facts and must always be given without the final fact. Also, it is likely to arrive heralded with that confidence which derives from verification by facts gathered late of postulates based upon facts gathered early.

Robert Burns once wrote to his fellow reveler James Smith, 'There is no understanding a man properly, without knowing something of his previous ideas . . .' (*Letters*, I, 218). The first purpose of this book is to know William Maxwell of Kirkconnell, the man and his ideas; thereby and thereafter, one can know more of Robert Burns. Quite another purpose is to repay, at long last, an unpaid debt that has been accumulating interest for almost one hundred and fifty years; for this debt was contracted by the *Dumfries Times*, 22 October 1834: 'Scotland owes Maxwell a death notice.'

FROM ROBERT BURNS —

My Fathers that name have rever'd on a throne;
    My Fathers have fallen to right it:
Those Fathers would spurn their degenerate son,
    That name, should he scoffingly slight it.

        — 'To Wm. Tytler, Esq., of Woodhouselee'

    Yonder Clouden's silent towers,
    Where, at moonshine's midnight hours,
    O'er the dewy bending flowers
        Fairies dance sae cheery.

           — 'Ca' the yowes'

    Wha will be a traitor knave?
    Wha can fill a coward's grave?
    Wha sae base as be a slave?
        Let him turn and flee!

          — 'Scots, wha hae'

Worth, in whatever circumstances, I [ever] prize; but Worth conjoined with Greatness has a certain irresistible power of attracting esteem.

        — To John Ballantine

—FROM ROBERT BURNS

This country is charmingly romantic & picturesque in the whole; 'tis besides highly improving & improveable, & a cheap Country to live in — you will be within six miles of the third town for importance & elegance in Scotland — your neighbourhood will abound in 'Honest men & bonnie lasses'—

—To [—M'Leod]

Now a' is done that men can do,
And a' is done in vain,
My Love and Native Land farewell,
For I maun cross the main.

— 'It was a' for our rightfu' king'

My lady's gown, there's gairs upon't,
And gowden flowers sae rare upon't

— 'My Lord A-Hunting'

Setting my obligations to & respect for the Arbigland Family out of the question, any friend of a gentleman whom I value & respect as I do Mr Maxwell of Carruchan, may command me, nay would honor me with his or her commands.   — To Miss Helen Craik of Arbigland

CHAPTER ONE

Before Birth

Under which king, Bezonian? speak, or die!
— William Shakespeare

From the world of Sir Walter Scott's romances — *Waverley*, *Guy Mannering* and *Old Mortality* — we begin with three families: the Maxwells of Kirkconnell, the Menzies of Pitfodels, and the Riddells of Swinburne Castle.[1] Three families at three streams: the Nith, the Dee, and the Swin. Three families outside three towns: Dumfries, Aberdeen, and Newcastle. Three family seats deeply secluded from public view: Kirkconnell in Kirkcudbrightshire, away from the military road leading westward to Portpatrick and passage to Belfast; Pitfodels in Aberdeenshire, away from a road which, in fair weather at any rate, linked Aberdeen with Edinburgh, more than 130 miles south; Swinburne Castle in Northumberland, away from the Roman road joining Carlisle and Newcastle, above Hadrian's Wall but below the Border.

That there should have been ties among these three seats, that there should have been bonds to death among these three families might upon first thought be thought strange. But such ties and such bonds there were during the eighteenth century, continuing from generation to generation and involving cross and sceptre, book and bride.

In the tenth century a Maccus had been born son to the King of Northumberland; a century later, under Macbeth's opponent Malcolm Canmore, King of the Scots, the Maxwells (Maccus' well) held the Dumfriesshire side of the Nith estuary, while the old Celtic family of the Kirkconnells settled the Galloway side. Thus the owners of Caerlaverock Castle and Kirkconnell Tower became near neighbors; and thus with the marriage of the first Lord Maxwell's nephew to the Kirkconnell heiress Janet (?1430) began the Maxwells of Kirkconnell.

Deeply religious, both sides of the family were celebrated bene-factors of the Church. They had aided in the founding of Lincluden Abbey in the twelfth century; four hundred years later their heirs attended, on Christmas Day 1585, the last mass before Lincluden's destruction. They had supported the Cistercians at Sweetheart Abbey (or New Abbey) ever since Devorguilla, wife of John Balliol, had founded the monastery (1273); in the sixteenth century their heirs had received those monks as their tenants and had been entrusted with some of the monastery's own lands, and Lord Maxwell had refused to destroy the Abbey Kirk and the cloistral buildings 'quhair he was maist part brocht up in his youth'.[2] In the early seventeenth century John Maxwell of Kirkconnell had been one of three to insure that the last abbot would remain in Sweetheart Abbey and had been entrusted with all the books of the Abbey before Charles I put the premises into the hands of the Bishop of Edinburgh. For such devotion, the spot before the altar became burial ground for the lairds of Kirkconnell.

Strong men these lairds and their sons were, like the lairds and sons of other Maxwells at Braigh, Carnsalloch, Carruchan, Munches, Ter-raughty, and Terregles. They knew the truth of Dunbar's

> Gude rewle is banist our the Bordour,
> And rangst ringis but ony ordour,
> With reird of rebaldis and of swane;
> Quhilk to considder is ane pane.[3]

And some of them seem to have sat for Scott's portrait of Godfrey Bertram of Ellangowan's ancestors:

> His list of forefathers ascended so high that they were lost in the barbarous ages of Galwegian independence . . . They had made war, raised rebellions, been defeated, beheaded, and hanged, as became a family of importance, for many centuries.[4]

One would believe that SPERO MELIORA, the motto of the Maxwells of Kirkconnell, could never have had more meaning for that family than it had in the seventeenth century. If their hope for some-thing better in heaven was salvation and bliss, surely their hope for something better on earth was tolerance and freedom from persecution. These hopes they shared with the families at Pitfodels and Swinburne Castle.

That anti-Popery was the major factor in late seventeenth-century English politics is the theme of John Miller's *Popery and Politics.* The Scots Parliament, of course, had abolished the authority of the Pope in 1560. Protestant, whether Scotsman or Englishman, tended to believe that all priests, but especially the Jesuits, were subversive activists and that all Papists were potential traitors. No wonder that such a Protestant should charge a Robert Rig of Dumfries with having been married 'by a Popish priest, on a Sunday, at night, with candle-light, above the bridge of Cluden in the fields, in presence of four witnesses, to Elspeth Maxwell, an excommunicate Papist'.[5]

No wonder that Rig should be imprisoned in the Tolbooth at Edinburgh. In the Presbyterians' own 'Cameronian killing time', when a kirk session could order '20 lodds peats to burn witches', no wonder that fifteen women should be jailed in Dumfries for 'hearing mass'.[6]

Traditionally Maxwell sons like the Menzies's and the Riddells were educated abroad in the Scots College at Douay; also traditionally, a brother or two entered the Society of Jesus. These traditions had held true for Dr William Maxwell's great-grandfather James, who in turn educated his own sons in Flanders at Douay. The first of these sons, another James, was served heir in 1699; by the time of his death in 1705, he had managed to affront Presbyterian authorities from Dumfries to Edinburgh. In 1704, for example, he was cited to answer in Auld Reekie for contravening Acts of Parliament 'gainst hearing mass and harboring and concealing Jesuits and priests'.[7] A year later books of the kirk session of New Abbey stigmatized the Maxwells of Kirk-connell as a 'popish' family and warned Protestants not to take domestic service with them. The brother who was served heir to this James in 1706 was William; his grandson and namesake was Dr William.

A stalwart, William Maxwell of Kirkconnell, the grandfather, had been but a boy at Douay during the time of the Glorious Revolution; but he was more than old enough in 1715 to 'go out' with leaders of the other branches of Maxwells, strongly united, whether Catholic or Protestant, by the Stuart cause. Their union is the matter of Scott's *Tales of a Grandfather:*

> On the western frontier of Scotland, there were many families not only Jacobites in politics, but Roman Catholics in religion; and therefore bound by a double tie to the heir of James II., who, for the sake of that form of faith, may be justly thought to have forfeited his kingdoms. Among the rest, the Earl of Nithsdale, continuing in his person the rep-

resentation of two noble families, those of the Lord Herries and the Lord Maxwell, might be considered as the natural leader of the party.[8]

William may or may not have been with the Jacobite forces when they unsuccessfully assaulted Dumfries in October 1715 and again in November. It is doubtful, however, that he participated in the Battle of Sheriffmuir, on the thirteenth of the same November, where Robert Burnes, grandfather of the poet, may have served under the Earl of Mar and where Chieftain Gilbert Menzies of Pitfodels, John Menzies of Pitfodels, and Gilbert Menzies, junior, of Pitfodels valiantly fought on the right wing of Mar's army under their motto MALO MORI QUAM FOEDARI ('death rather thean disgrace'). Tam, the shepherd in Burns's ballad 'The Battle of Sherra-Moor', recalls the onslaught:

> I saw the battle, sair and teugh,
> And reekin red ran mony a sheugh,
> My heart for fear gae sough for sough,
> To hear the thuds, and see the cluds,
> O' clans frae woods, in tartan duds,
> Wha glaum'd at kingdoms three, man.

Sometime before this battle, Thomas of Swinburne Castle had been captured by troops loyal to George I and imprisoned in Lancaster Castle. He escaped this prison and lived to be indicted and then pardoned without having had any of the Riddell estates confiscated, perhaps because he had not as yet succeeded his father Edward.[9]

Having shared the experiences of the Jacobite uprising of 1715, the Maxwells of Kirkconnell, the Menzies of Pitfodels, and the Riddells of Swinburne Castle had become certain of each other so as to seek out each other during ensuing years of peace. Since 1706 William had been married to Janet Maxwell, eldest daughter of George Maxwell of Carnsalloch and, eventually, his heiress. Of the ten children, their eldest daughter married William Maxwell of Munches; their youngest daughter married John Menzies of Pitfodels; their second and third sons embraced the Jesuit priesthood; their eldest son, the cadet James, married Mary Riddell of Swinburne Castle. The pattern of these marriages traces abiding interest in heritage through entails of name and religion; a figure of the pattern circumscribes three families.

William Maxwell of Kirkconnell died on 13 April 1746, two days before Prince Charles Edward drew up his army on Culloden Muir while 'Butcher Willie' Cumberland celebrated his birthday. His son and heir James was not at the deathbed, but with the Young Chevalier at Culloden under his father's blessing. When he had been told that James would 'go out' in the Forty-Five, William had exclaimed that he was glad to hear it and that if James lost his life, it would be a sacrifice for a good cause.[10]

William had been given forty years as laird of Kirkconnell. Early years had been precarious with confiscations of property and anxiety for life itself; but after the pardons following the Fifteen, he as well as others of the landed gentry like the Menzies and the Riddells had steadily prospered. In addition to extensive properties west and south-west of the city, Menzies had heavier and heavier investments in the harbor at Aberdeen and in its fishing and trading; in addition to even more extensive lands, generally across the top of Northumberland, Riddell owned collieries all the way to Newcastle-upon-Tyne. Maxwell's advancement was due chiefly to land acquisition and management, although salmon fishing, woodcutting, and Nithside trade contributed to his successes. Each of the three appears to have been content to live in his home much as he had inherited it, leaving it up to his heir to improve and rebuild if he so chose.

Kirkconnell country has always been dominated by the mountain Criffell with its Loch Kindar underneath; by the Solway and its skies alive with the swift motion of black, grey, and grey-white clouds; and by the River Nith taking better than twelve-foot tides from the Solway Firth in order to wash her rich merselands. Ground rises with an alternation of hill and dale. River banks are wooded; pastures, green; and vales, well cultivated. The hardwoods are oak, elm, beech, chest-nut, ash, and red maple, dominated by an oak older than Magna Carta. 'Black cattle' and blackface sheep share pastures with the shelduck nesting in a rabbit burrow, the pheasant, and the mole. In the woods, the roe deer and the fox, which can bring down a lamb. In the road and on the shield of Terregles, the hurcheons (hedgehogs). In the streams, the brown trout. And in the Nith, the salmon heavy as forty pounds, speared with a 'waster' or caught with the stake-net and 'haaf-net' to be brained by the 'mel'.

The approach to the ancient Tower of Kirkconnell is along an avenue of oaks, one of which is said to have hidden Prince Charles. Across the Nith from this tower are Brow and the site of the Ruthwell Cross. At the side of the crow-stepped fort is the baronial house, second oldest inhabited house in Scotland; and at the side of the house, St Mary's Chapel: longer than the St Mary's at Swinburne Castle, but not so beautiful; higher than the Queir at Terregles, but never so jewel-like.

William gave his eldest son James thirteen years to grow stronger at Kirkconnell before sending him to the Scots college at Douay for the next eight years. In Scotland his education had been at the hands of the family chaplain; fellow students had been his brothers and sisters. At Douay his education was at the hands of the Jesuit brothers; fellow students were the cadets of Scottish and English families like his own together with their younger brothers, seasoned with sons from families on the Continent. Only as he neared his coming of age was James permitted to return home. He came back solidly schooled by the Jesuits, as mannerly as a Frenchman, and fearlessly confident as horseman, swordsman, and marksman.

In the succeeding seventeen years before the Forty-Five, always under the eagle eye of William, James learned how to manage the Barony of Kirkconnell, always with his own eye looking out for methods of improvement, hinted at by such episodes as his search with William Craik of Arbigland in 1736 for veins of coal. His rewards were to be infeft in 1734 and to receive a Crown Charter under the Great Seal of George II in 1738. At least as gratifying were those succeeding rewards for another kind of service which commenced, in earnest, when he heard that the Young Chevalier with seven men had landed at Moidart.

James lost no time. Undoubtedly it was his father's experience in the Fifteen that warned him to make over a commission of factory to his mother Janet as a means of circumventing confiscation; after goodbyes — the farewell to his father was a last farewell — he rode northwards with his servant William Carruthers and other Kirkconnell retainers to offer his sword in the Stuart cause. As precaution, he could have travelled in the company of William Maxwell of Carruchan, his eldest son William, James Maxwell of Barncleugh, and their men. This war party's coming up to Charles Edward would have been, surmisedly, between the time of the raising of the Prince's standard at Glenfinnan, 19 August, and the advance upon Perth, 3 September.[11]

Abroad adherents to Jacobitism numbered a majority of Catholics; but in Great Britain, almost certainly, they numbered a majority of Protestants. Religious differences, nevertheless, were made subordinate to the common aim of restoring the Stuart line. Every follower caught something of the Prince's chivalry and gallantry, talked something of justice and honor, and heard something like this Gaelic song of Alexander MacDonald:

O God above, forbid
> That might prevail for e'er o'er right!
Ochone! One God in Three,
Thou seest everything!
Relieve us of our swinish yoke,
> And send the speckled, mangy brood
Of snouted hogs o'erseas;
And clean fore'er Whitehall,
> For that royal family, who of old,
Had there their dwelling-place.[12]

Before Perth James Maxwell was among his own. Drawn to the royal cause like him were the Menzies: Chieftain Gilbert and five of his sons, including Captain John, who like his eldest brother Gilbert had served as an officer in the French army ever since the Fifteen. Unlike the Kirkconnell and Pitfodels heirs, Thomas Riddell of Swinburne Castle was too young to fight. He continued as cadet-scholar at Douay; but his father, who had distinguished himself in the Fifteen, staunchly supported the Jacobite forces, much as William of Kirkconnell did.

Throughout the Forty-Five, James Maxwell of Kirkconnell, reputed the best swordsman in Scotland, served in the Prince's Life Guards and as major of Lord Elcho's cavalry. He was at the taking of Perth and helped to secure a hesitant Edinburgh on 17 September. Four days later he rode into battle at Prestonpans against the English under Sir John Cope, as the six Menzies of Pitfodels, dressed in plaid waistcoat, Highland sash, and white cockade, officered the front line of Prince Charles's army with some three hundred of their clan at the very center. News of the Jacobites' complete victory sparked their recruiting, many Lowland gentlemen joining up after the Earl of Nithsdale and his wife Lady Katherine went to Edinburgh in order to wait upon the Prince.

Six weeks of triumph for the Young Chevalier at Holyroodhouse came after the routing of Cope at Prestonpans. If one allows the romance of such a ball as Sir Walter describes in *Waverley*, one might allow the possibility that it was at such a ball that Captain John Menzies of Pitfodels first danced opposite his bride-to-be, Marion Maxwell of Kirkconnell, and that Major James Maxwell of Kirkconnell, Marion's eldest brother, first touched hands with his own bride-to-be, Mary Riddell of Swinburne Castle. Whatever: the sound of revelry by night *was* heard, and lamps *did* shine over brave men and brave women, and soft eyes *did* look love to eyes that spoke again.

On 31 October the Prince's army left Edinburgh and, in three columns by three separate routes, moved out of Dalkeith to converge at Carlisle. Within two weeks that city was subdued, its castle secured so that Charles could enter on a white horse preceded by a hundred pipers. From Carlisle the Jacobites advanced into England as far as Derby before what they had begun in full optimism developed well nigh into desperation. Turning back on 'Black Friday', retreating before the harassment of the Duke of Cumberland, they grimly re-entered Carlisle on 19 December, staying not much longer than it took the Prince to receive a united petition 'praying that he would be pleased to discharge all Roman Catholics from his council'. His crossing of the Esk, the next day, is recalled by James Johnstone in his memoir:

> Our cavalry formed in the river, to break the force of the current, about twenty-five paces above that part of the ford where our infantry were to pass: the Highlanders formed themselves into ranks of ten or twelve abreast, with their arms locked in such a manner as to support one another against the rapidity of the river, leaving sufficient intervals between their ranks for the passage of the water. Cavalry were likewise stationed in the river, below the ford, to pick up and save those who might be carried away by the violence of the current. The interval between the cavalry appeared like a paved street through the river, the heads of the Highlanders being generally all that was seen above the water. By means of this contrivance, our army passed the Esk in an hour's time, without losing a single man . . . a few girls, determined to share the fortune of their lovers, were the only persons who were carried away by the rapidity of the stream.[13]

Once over the Esk, these forces marched through Gretna into Scotland and then westward to Dumfries, which they entered by way of St Michael's on 20 December. For the twenty-second the Reverend Mr George Duncan of Lochrutton entered in his journal, 'A melancholy day — the rebels in Dumfries — about 4000 — with the Pretender's son at their head — in great rage at the town.'[14] Duncan's jaundiced view extends to shops pillaged, shoes pulled off gentlemen's feet in the road, and stables robbed. If Prince Charles was, indeed, in rage at Dumfries, he may have chosen that moment to ride across the Nith into Kirkcudbrightshire to spend a night at Kirkconnell. On Christmas Day, he and his men marched to Glasgow, there to be refreshed by a halt of a week. Hogmanay of that week was particularly joyful for James Maxwell because it was then that his friend and neighbor William Maxwell of

Carruchan, the Prince's chief engineer at the siege of Carlisle Castle, rode into camp on a horse lent by Sir William Maxwell of Springkell. Carruchan had been taken prisoner on the retreat out of England; now he had escaped over the castle walls at Carlisle and ridden hard to rejoin his leader.[15]

James Maxwell started the new year of 1746 as he had ended the old: in loyal service to Prince Charles. In January he participated in the successful action at the Moor of Falkirk; in February, that at the Barracks of Ruthven; in March, that at the Castle of Inverness. In April, these successes stopped short with the bitter, full defeat at Culloden. James may not have shared the sentiment of the alleged last words of Lord Elcho to Prince Charles after Culloden, 'There you go for a damned, cowardly Italian'; but when he made good his own escape from a battlefield where the dragoons of Cumberland and Hawley were already at their pleasure of putting testicles in the hands of their dead owners, he escaped with Lord Elcho and Elcho's servant.[16] For almost three weeks, the three men fled westward, now sheltering in the house of Macdonald, now eluding redcoats, now hiding in heather, now helping to bury six casks of money which had arrived in a French ship too late to supply the Jacobites, now watching through a spyglass a naval encounter, and finally going out to the French man-of-war *Mars* in the Sound of Arisaig and sailing for France. On this unhappy voyage, the Duke of Perth died at sea; but Elcho and Maxwell arrived safely at Nantes on 6 June.

James Maxwell lived out the years of his exile attached to the Court of Louis XV at Saint Germain, where he could look down upon the windings of the Seine and away to Paris on the eastern horizon. For the first year and longer, the news was as black as black can be: word of his father's death; word that the Menzies had been outlawed and their estates confiscated; word of the executions at Carlisle; word that the chaplain to the High Sheriff of Yorkshire had preached to several of those judging the Jacobites on the text, 'And Moses said unto the judges of Israel, Slay ye every one his men that were joined unto Baalpeor'; and word that his own whereabouts were 'unknown'. Plunder and pillage continued in Scotland as prisoners died in hulks off Tilbury before they could be executed, banished, or transported. Horace Walpole, still in his twenties, passed on to friends accounts he had received of some of the London executions. Lords Kilmarnock and Balmerino — Walpole wrote Horace Mann — were taken from the Tower at 10 a.m.[17] The executioner in white apron chopped at Kilmarnock's head first. After the head and torso had been rejoined in a coffin and fresh sawdust had been strewn about the block, Balmerino came on, treading 'with the air of a general'. The old man looked out to the ships in the Thames and then to the spectators, commenting, 'Look, look, how they are all piled up like rotten oranges.' He then pulled out his spectacles, read a treasonable speech, took the axe and felt it, gave the executioner three guineas, put on a nightcap of Scotch plaid, and placed his head on the block, while being heard to observe, 'If I had a thousand lives, I would lay them all down here in the same cause.' No news for Maxwell was much brighter than the indirect report that his mother had not only charged a troop of English dragoons quartered at Kirkconnell for forage but had managed to make the charge stick.

As solace and 'while things were fresh in mind', James sat down early in his exile to give his own account of the Forty-Five. The manuscript is partly in his hand, partly in the hand of his secretary. The dedication reads, 'In Memory of William Maxwell, Esquire, of Kirkconnell, Kelton, and Carnsalloch, who died at Kirkconnell, 13th April, 1746.' Maxwell's narrative is straightforward, impersonal, soldierly, correct, and all but free from bias. Thus, while lamenting the verbosity, divisiveness, and great warmth of the contention between Lord George Murray (Protestant) and the Duke of Perth (Catholic) for command under the Prince, James reports honestly:

> They [the supporters of Lord George] said that in England Roman Catholics were excluded from all employments, civil and military, by laws anterior to the revolution: that these laws, whether reasonable or not, ought to subsist, until they were repealed; that a contrary conduct, without a visible necessity for it, would confirm all that had been spread of old, from the pulpit, and from the press, of the Prince's designs to over-turn the Constitution both of Church and State; that indeed the Prince in his present circumstances, would not be blamed for allowing a Roman Catholic the command of a regiment he had raised, or even a more exten-sive command, if a superiority of genius and military experience entitled him to it; but these reasons could not be alleged for the Duke of Perth.[18]

Only rarely does the author intrude. On the elopement of English prisoners taken in the Battle of Prestonpans, Maxwell says, 'It is true, the decay of virtue and honor in our Island since the Accession is very remarkable, and the progress and barefacedness of vice is astonishing . . . hitherto a gentleman's word of honor has been looked upon as sacred.'[19] And of his intention to give an account of the Duke of

Cumberland after Culloden, he explains, 'I find myself unable for such a task; it is not in my power to dwell upon a continued series of massacres.'[20] The narrative begins with the Young Chevalier and concludes with him: 'I leave the reader to judge if I had reason to say in the beginning of this work, that whatever may hereafter be the fate of the Prince, he has early been trained up in the school of adversity, and knows, by his own experience, the greatest vicissitudes of fortune.'[21] On his own vicissitudes, Maxwell is silent.

In addition to the solace he found while writing his history as well as that of being near a younger brother, now Father George, S.J., James Maxwell took solace from planning ahead much as Charles II had planned ahead, when he had imagined as exile at Paris what it would be like to live once more in the sun. Maxwell's projects included a new Kirkconnell built of such bricks as he had learned to make in France and a large garden walled after the French fashion.

Knowing that more than eleven hundred Jacobites had been banished or transported after the Forty-Five and that another seven hundred had been listed 'fate unknown', one can be positive that James Maxwell did not live his years in the environs of Paris without the company of such close friends as Captain John Menzies and William Maxwell of Carruchan. The precise time when these men, now middle-aged, were allowed to return to Scotland cannot, perhaps, be known; assuredly, they were not among the first because of their names and deeds. No more likely time could be advanced than 1750, when the enlightened, public-spirited William Grant of Prestongrange, Lord Advocate for Scotland under George II, had his greatest influence at Whitehall. Pardon for Maxwell and Menzies, moreover, seems to have been prior to release of their lands. A flurry of legal papers suggests that in 1750 James, through the influence of such Protestant families as the Craiks of Arbigland, won personal if not legal rights to his lands by a conveyance in favor of George Guthrie, merchant, Dumfries, and that after a further cooling-off period, Guthrie was able to convey them back to Maxwell on 12 April 1753.[22] Two years later James's name appears as witness on the marriage contract of his sister and John Menzies; one year later still, 15 August 1756, Marion was delivered of a son John, the last Menzies of Pitfodels.

The Maxwells, the Menzies, and the Riddells all knew economic distress during the early '50s as one more penalty of their having 'gone out'. By the end of that decade, however, they had all but recouped their losses. James Maxwell's beginning had a double thrust: to consolidate family lands and to make some of his dreams come true. Thus he sold the estates of Carnsalloch, to which his mother had fallen heiress, in order to purchase the estates of Mabie which abutted those of Kirkconnell and Carruchan.[23] All the while, such transactions went on during his building the modern part of Kirkconnell House from bricks made in the front field. First the house itself (today the oldest brick house in Scotland): four levels from kitchen to drawing room to bedrooms to quarters at the top for some of the twelve servants. A chapel with entrances from within the house on the two main floors and a sacristy with its altar pieces, vestments, cords, and linens. A library with telescope and barometer, charter chest and map cases, books of hours and volumes of Anacreon and Cicero, Boccaccio and Grotius, Corneille and Bossuet. Then the outbuildings like coal-house, stables, carriage-house, tool-sheds.

Likely James prided himself on his extensive plantings of trees, lawns, and gardens, especially on the main garden which he surrounded with a double wall of brick from his own kiln. Between the walls was a hollow through which warm air could be forced from coal fires in furnace rooms at each corner. On the southside corners, these rooms were built into two garden houses, two floors high. This was the first heated garden in all Scotland. In it James could raise exotic figs and almonds, as well as damsons, pears, and apples, black and red currants, green gooseberries, and raspberries in such quantities as to be able to market them with his cabbages and onions from the vegetable gardens and his honey from hives out in the flower gardens.

New growth was slower at Pitfodels and Swinburne Castle. Menzies' affairs still rested in the hands of the patriarch Gilbert, born in the year of the Glorious Revolution. Menzies had ordered his family 'out' in 1715 and again in 1745 when their wounds had been cut deeply and Cumberland's salt had kept them open. Forgetting and forgiving on both sides, therefore, had been painful and reluctant. At Swinburne the young Thomas Riddell, Mary's eldest brother, had succeeded after his father's death in 1754 and just before his mother's in 1757. The father Thomas had added a new wing to his seventeenth-century manor house after his marriage to Mary Widdrington; the son Thomas tore down and started all over again with a great mansion of pale biscuit stone as well as refinements like an orangerie after his marriage in 1760 to an even wealthier Widdrington heiress, Elizabeth Margaret.

The Riddell community in which Mary and her three older brothers and four sisters were nurtured was all but self-sufficient with its gatehouse and manor, chapel, hermitage, tenants' homes, brewhouse, smithy, cornmill, and sawmill.[24] As children, their playground was acres upon acres of fields, woods with streams, and meadows brushed with wildflowers. About them was history antedating the tesselation of Great Swinburne Castle: a tall menhir, primitive terraces, and three barrows yielding Bronze Age jet necklaces. Everywhere were views tempting them to mount and ride away. Whether because of her father's direction or her brothers' companionship, Mary was as accomplished in horsemanship as in domesticity. She knew and loved horses.

Daughters born to the first eighteenth-century Maxwells, Menzies, and Riddells appear to reveal, consistently and unanimously, the same virtues in their lives. Mary Riddell was honorable, affectionate, resolute, and unswervingly loyal to her family. Physically, morally, spiritually, she was exceedingly strong. She not only learned by heart but practised by habit the wisdom of St Paul's first epistle to the Corinthians: 'And now abideth faith, hope, and charity, these three; but the greatest of these is charity.' Mary knew that charity, the bond of perfection, is kind; she was to learn through marriage and motherhood that it 'suffereth long'.

James Maxwell of Kirkconnell married Mary Riddell, next to youngest daughter of Thomas Riddell of Swinburne Castle, in August 1758. Four witnesses signed the marriage contract on the twenty-first.[25] Shortly thereafter the two wedding ceremonies took place. In the settlement approved by Mary's two eldest brothers, Mary was to have a free life-rent annuity of £200 if she bore no children, £160 if she did; £1,000 for each of the first three children; and, if James predeceased her, possession of the mansion house during the minority of the heir. What Mary herself was to bring to the marriage is unspecified; nevertheless, one can assume that her dowry was more than handsome, consisting of a one-fifth share of and years of accumulated interest on, first, the money her father had designated for either the marriage or the coming of age of his five daughters and, second, the more substantial inheritance from her mother's fortune.[26] In the eyes of the Roman Catholic Church, James and Mary became husband and wife when they were joined in holy matrimony in the chapel at Swinburne. In the eyes of the Establishment, they became married legally only when a Protestant minister published their banns and read the marriage service. Any man of property such as James Maxwell accepted the second ceremony, whether Anglican or Presbyterian, as imperative.

Kirkconnell had but a brief time to live after returning to Scotland with his English bride: less than four years. Yet this was long enough to assure continuance of his line. Mary bore three sons in three years: an heir called James after his father and paternal great-grandfather, a son called William after his paternal grandfather buried before the high altar of Sweetheart Abbey, and a son called Thomas after his maternal uncle and grandfather of Swinburne Castle.[27]

FROM ROBERT BURNS —

The tide-swoln Firth, with sullen-sounding roar,
Through the still night dash'd hoarse along the shore;
All else was hush'd as Nature closèd e'e;
The silent moon shone high o'er tower and tree;
The chilly frost, beneath the silver beam,
Crept, gently-crusting, o'er the glittering stream.

                           — 'The Brigs of Ayr'

        My talents they were not the worst;
        nor yet my education.

        — First Commonplace Book

I learned to look unconcernedly on a large tavern bill.

                       — To Dr J. Moore

        And then a' doctor's saws and whittles,
        Of a' dimensions, shapes, an' mettles,
        A' kinds o' boxes, mugs an' bottles,
                   He's sure to hae;
        Their Latin names as fast he rattles
                  As A B C.

        — 'Death and Doctor Hornbook'

—FROM ROBERT BURNS

God knows, I'm not the thing I shou'd be,
Not am I even the thing I cou'd be,
But twenty times I rather wou'd be
                                An atheist clean,
Than under gospel colors hid be
                                Just for a screen.

— 'To Rev. J. M'Math'

Edin^r news. — . . . everything going on as usual — houses building, bucks strutting, ladies flaring, blackguards skulking, whores leering, &c in the old way.
                                — To John Richmond

. . . my brother wanted my hare-brained imagination as well as my social and amorous madness, but in good sense and every sober qualification he was far my superior.
                                — To Dr J. Moore

Farewell, auld birkie! Lord be near ye,
And then the Deil he daur na steer ye:
Your friends ay love, your foes ay fear ye,
                                For me, shame fa' me,
If neist my heart I dinna wear ye
                                While BURNS they ca' me.

— 'To Terraughty, On His Birth-day'

CHAPTER TWO

Fair Seedtime

. . . the essence of the eighteenth century is the creation of the 'Romantic' and, in a variety of ways, the modern.

— Walter Jackson Bate

From five yards of 'worsted quality' and five yards of 'Norwich crape', servants at Kirkconnell cut children's mournings to be worn by the three young sons of James Maxwell on his burial day.[1] More or less secretly, prayers were spoken by the deceased laird's brother Fr George and the family chaplain before the funeral party escorted the corpse to Sweetheart Abbey; after interment, friends remained with the widow long enough to consume twenty-two pounds of cheese, to drink off eighty-two pints of ale, and to break one wine glass (6d). The next day, 24 July 1762, Mary turned to new responsibility so as to merit such admiration as Dunbar's 'Now of wemen this say for me,/Off erthly thingis nane may better be.'[2]

The husband had anticipated such responsibility during the year preceding his death when Dr Ebenezer Gilchrist had been unable to arrest his failing health.[3] In an execution dated 14 January 1761, James Maxwell had nominated Esquires John Maxwell of Terraughty and Adam Craik, the Younger, of Arbigland as his sons' 'Tutors and Cura-tors' and had stipulated further that Mary was to have £20 a year for each of their three children until age ten to provide them with whatever was necessary for their aliment, clothing, and education.[4] Wisely for the times, both trustees were Protestant; thus, they were able to advance legal matters so that the lad James could be served heir at age five and infeft with the Barony of Kirkconnell under the seal of George III before age six. Catholic supervision rested in the hands of chaplain,

23

schoolmaster, and mother.

Mary's account-books show that her duties did not extend to supervision of the Barony itself.[5] An overseer or factor, recommended by some such friend as Maxwell of Carruchan and served by the elder John Syme, W.S., and other solicitors, collected rents from tenants at Mabie, Airds, Maxwellbank and a dozen more farmsteads, notched which trees in Shambellie woods were to be felled, directed placement of the salmon seines, and supervised the loading of coal and the unloading of lime. In the meantime, Mary managed at Kirkconnell House. There she paid 'Thammy's' nurse her £1 a year and 'Jemmy's' and William's schoolmaster his 19s/2 8/12d, the forester his £6, the cook-maid her £1 10s, the hypothecator his 2/6 for 'raising' or 'setting' potatoes. She hired James Rig as gardener; James McClackery as mower; John Fleming as molecatcher; Peggy Lewars, Jenny Chraiton, and nine other lasses as servant girls; a coachman, a herdsman, and a stable boy; William Coverly as butler and his wife Nanny as personal maid; and Robin Kirk to run errands. Nelly William and Marion McCracken received 3d a day to launder; Meran Rig and Jennet Turner, 1s to spin. For the board in the servants' hall, Mary provided oatmeal and bran, prunes and currants, lamb and fowl, salt cod and herring, milk and ale; for her own board, she added white bread, oranges, almonds, veal, quail, oysters, 'shurumps', and 'old hermitage'. An occasional entry in her household books tells of shoes for 'Jemmy' at 1/6d or stockings for William at 2/6d; a frequent entry reads 'to a poor man 2d' or 'sugar candy 3d'. Busy as she was, Mary found time to look beyond the day into the future so to arrange her worldly affairs in her lifetime 'as that every possible dispute respecting the same among my Children and Relatives after my death may be obviated'.[6]

Growing up, the three brothers wanted little, least of all something to do when they were released from their lessons. In the sun they had the walled garden where they could hide from one another; farms where they could watch the dung-spreading, drain-cutting, smithing, grinding, sawing, and fleshing; woodside where they might catch sight of old William Tweedie killing foxes; and Nithside where they could look down upon the line of haaf-net fishermen. On pony-back they might see an eagle attacking a lamb or ride over to the corn miln of Drummillan, past the spot where lightning had killed the cow; from any hillside during the season for heather burning, they could admire Criffell on fire. When it rained, they could race up the tower steps to the parapet; tease a servant girl busy in the silver or lamp room; or stretch out on the library floor to trace their father's escape on his maps of Great Britain and the Continent.[7]

Away from Kirkconnell Mary's boys shared other happiness. There were outings in the company of favored playmates like those at Carruchan. There were horses racing on Solway Sands. There were the Sanquhar, Beltan, and Penrith fairs with judging of cattle, sheep, and horses accompanied with such pride as came from the announcement that John Williamson at Gateside of Kirkconnell had won the purse as proprietor of the best stallion. And there were visits to their relatives.

At times it must have seemed to Mary that her sons ran the risk of being spoiled by these relatives. Her husband's mother Janet of Carnsalloch and three of Janet's daughters lived comfortably in Dumfries; grandmother and aunts welcomed the boys into their homes.[8] Each visit was a feast for eyes and ears: the crowd of mechanics at Bridgend; the recruiting soldier and sailor seeking stout lads; the appearance of Lords Kennet and Hailes riding circuit as judges of the High Court of Justiciary; the auction of foreign china in the Assembly Room; John Williams' laying down cloth at Bleach-field; the Scots carpets in Robert Kempe's linen factory, the Spilbury Drops on Alexander Wylie's drug counter, and the books offered by William Boyd. Gossip spoke of John Graham branded for stealing, of lectures on magnetism and electricity, of wandering swine terrifying inhabitants, of the constable's having been attacked by three men in women's clothes.[9] Yet how could these sights and sounds have compared with those remembered from a visit to Edinburgh when the family of Kirkconnell had been joined by that of Pitfodels and the three brothers had shared the excitements of the capital with their cousin John Menzies!

Mary's own family became as close to her sons. The favorite sisters Bab and Dolly as well as the favorite brothers Thomas of Swinburne Castle and Ralph of Cheeseburn Grange were generous of time and money. Often one or more of the Riddell aunts and uncles slept at Kirkconnell; and each summer one of them, probably Thomas, took one or more of his nephews off Mary's hands. William was only three years old when he first travelled to Swinburne in the custody of a Kirkconnell retainer for a full August of holiday.[10]

Mary seems never to have found a right diminutive for her second son as she did for both the first and last son. William always appears in his mother's daybooks as 'William Kirkconnell'. Still there is no room to doubt that the ties between him and his mother were as deep and

C

strong as those between her and his brothers or those between him and James and Thomas. The father's early death had made such bonds remarkably sure. Stern, strict though the mother could be, she seems never to have been without a treat for her sons; and provoking, difficult though these sons could be, they delighted in pooling their pocket money to please their mother with a new cap or a new Skye terrier.[11]

The measure of just how near to each other the three brothers were as children may be taken from the all but complete impossibility of seeing them as three individuals, not one. Of the three, William appears to have been the only boy to have suffered 'long and severe' attacks of sickness.[12] Anxiety which surely accompanied such grave illness may have given rise to his defect of stuttering which in turn fed his stubborn rebelliousness while denying any wish he might have held in secret to follow his uncles into the Society of Jesus. Secluded, moreover, by the series of attacks and recuperations, William was forced to turn from hard play to such quieter diversions as those of the library and garden. He more than his brothers was fascinated by flowers and birds. In the library he discovered his father's books on gardening and the plans for what had been built at Kirkconnell; about the Barony he could all but endlessly record species of birds from the whooper swan, the puffin, and the greenfinch to the oyster catcher, the goshawk, and the pipit. Convalescences gave him, too, more than his share of hours to listen to the stories of his grandmother Janet. She could tell about Latimer's Grave, about the Kirkconnell ghost who announced himself with four knocks, and about the appearance of Bonnie Prince Charlie. She knew which of the pistols, swords, and daggers had been worn by his grandfather and which by his father. She could say just where to look for his father's tartan bonnet that he had worn at Culloden and just where he could find the manuscript of his father's narrative. Honor and loyalty, idealism and rebellion, cause and principle became the stuff of his huge cloudy symbols of high romance belying his outward character of shyness, reserve, and quiet. When Mary at last found a name other than 'William Kirkconnell' for her second son, it was with good reasons 'don Quixote'.[13]

At age ten, as their father had directed, the boys were to go abroad for their 'better education and Improvement'.[14] A law still on the books forbade that Catholic youths be sent out of the country for instruction by priests; but as it was not enforced with great rigor, Mary could not have had keen fears for her eldest son when he departed Kirkconnell for the Jesuit College at Dinant, 15 September 1770, just after his turning eleven. Before leaving, James empowered his mother to act in his behalf at Kirkconnell, much as his father had empowered his own mother when he had 'gone out' in '45.[15] A year later, 5 August 1771, Mary saw William and Thomas follow their brother.[16] Even though Thomas would be going at the beginning rather than at the end of his tenth year, as in the cases of James and William, the trustees had decided that it would be more manly to enter him at Dinant together with William than to have him remain the lone boy at Kirkconnell.

Choice of Dinant for the three brothers instead of their grandfather's and father's Scots College at Douay can be attributed directly to actions against the Jesuits in France and to the advancement of their uncle Fr George by Jesuit authorities. George Maxwell had entered the Society in 1732; since 1744 he had served and risen in the Scotch Mission so that by the time his nephews were ready for formal education, he could offer the prospect of their matriculating at the College of Dinant.[17] Maxwell and other Scottish Jesuits of Douay had been permitted to go to Dinant in 1765 after the expulsion of the Jesuits from France; lately he had been installed as the rector or principal. Thomas' age as well as the unsettled times must have argued pointedly in favor of Dinant as Mary and the trustees spoke of alternatives. Finally, selection of Dinant seems to have promised the opportunity of the three boys having a temporary home with one of their aunts; for Mary Maxwell's sister-in-law Marion Menzies had enrolled her only son and heir John in that college and had gone to Dinant to provide something more than the boarding-houses could. This was not at all unusual and, in the case of Marion and John Menzies, must have been most easily arranged because Marion's brother was the rector.

Because in his years as a Jesuit Fr George had returned regularly to Kirkconnell, his birthplace, it is possible that he rode with William and Thomas when these brothers left home for school in early August 1771.[18] What is more, the boys' mother may have accompanied the party as far as Swinburne Castle to share the hospitality of her brother Thomas. Before the travellers went on to Newcastle for passage to Ostend, their number was increased by other prospective students, one of whom was Widdrington Riddell, their cousin. Once having landed at Ostend, then the chief seaport for the Austrian Netherlands, the boys and their escorts would have again rested at such an inn as the Hotel de Angleterre.[19] Their next stage was by way of barge to Bruges, where, at least, the uncle pointed out the Cathedral de St Donat treasuring the silver- and gold-thread vestments of Thomas à Becket.

Then on by horse-drawn barges to Ghent and by daily coach to Brussels, past the unforgettable spot where Flanders exposed the bodies of her malefactors on racks, wheels, and gibbet. Upon entering Brussels, they found themselves at the seat of the Governors-General of the Austrian Netherlands, administered under Empress Maria Theresa by her brother-in-law Charles of Lorraine. For the British residential representative, the capital of Brabant may have been 'the fag end of the diplomatic ladder',[20] but for the Maxwell brothers and their cousin Widdrington it must have been a beautiful city of elegant buildings, melodious carillons, lighted shops, soaring fountains, fashionable theatres in which nobles took dessert and wine in their boxes between acts of French comedy, and such alien events as the nightly closing of the gates. All too soon their last leg started, the south-easterly coach trip to Namur and the Meuse flowing across from Liége; here the party once again boarded a barge for the seventeen miles to Dinant. From a rail, the boys could look back at Namur's castle atop an escarpment with the red marble columns of the Jesuits' church down below; and they could look ahead to the next lock, the next chateau with its geometries of tree and shrub, and the next bankside angler unhooking his carp, trout, or salmon. It was on 3 September, all but a month since leavetaking at Kirkconnell, that William and Thomas with their maternal cousin Widdrington Riddell stepped ashore to be greeted by their brother James, their Aunt Marion, and their paternal cousin John Menzies.[21] Education now united the new generation of Maxwells, Riddells, and Menzies as the Jacobite causes had united the preceding generations; Catholicism remained the constant connection.

What Dinant could boast of today is very much what it boasted of in the eighteenth century. Its natural setting is still admitted to be most lovely, to be *séduisant* with the gentle Meuse quietly flowing under profound perspectives, high horizons, and massive rock formations shaping mountain passes. The grotto 'La Merveilleuse' is still hung with stalactites; 'La Roche-à-Bayard' still attests to fairies. Swallows still nest in the *clochetons;* buyers from all over Europe still covet the hand-beaten brass pieces known as 'dinanderie'; visitors still gorge on *saucisse Ardennois* and *jambon d'Ardennes. Pax et Salus* still can be read on the town hall, and the two famous chasubles of the great, ancient church La Collégiale Notre-Dame still can be touched, although the three reliquaries with bones of St Perpète have been long lost to the French Revolution. From the bridge house at midstream, one can still see the cross of the Collégiale directing upwards from its onion-shaped dome to the long fortifications of Das Schloss on the rocky ridge high above.

Today and yesterday the civic pride of Dinant's inhabitants reflects their sturdy independence.[22] Today nothing is more grim than to round a bend in an ascending woodland path only to come upon a marker remembering those citizens QUI N'EN REVENRENT JAMAIS from their forced exile into Germany on 4 December 1916 or a tablet vowing N'OUBLIONS JAMAIS after naming those from Dinant who had been killed, executed or led to death in captivity by the Germans of World War II. Yesterday, at the time of William's arrival, similar independence was making the citizenry restless with a falling economy, heavy taxation, and token representation to the point of their becoming ripe for revolutionary tendencies.

William's first impression of the town must have been that it belonged wholly to the Prince-Évêque. If the Collégiale commanded the Right Bank, it was not without troops to command. William would be in Dinant some time before he would be able to distinguish St Martin's from St Peter's, and St Jacob's or the chapel of the Hôpital Saint-Jean-Baptiste from the chapels of the Cordeliers, Capuchins, Ursulines, Carmelites, and Sœurs Grises. Churches and religious communities crowded the narrow strip between river and cliff; not without rivalry and rancor among themselves, ecclesiasticals helped to crowd each passageway. And not without grievance. The Pastor of St Michael's, yet another church, complained to the burgomasters that his home and tiny garden abutting the cliffs were not worth the rental of eleven florins. What was the value of a vegetable marrow as compared with the danger of falling rocks? Who in his right mind would dare live where boulders landed so close as to smash one's pots of flowers?[23]

Destination of the three brothers that September day was the Jesuit foundation which they approached by way of the Rue du Collège. Henri de Sommalle of Dinant, who had been taken into the Society by Loyola himself, had started this college in 1563.[24] Before 1600 he and the other fathers had been asked to leave town, and they had; then asked to return, and they had. From that time on, the way had been smoother, chiefly because of important financial assistance from the citizens. The Chapel of St Vincent's ceded to the College early in the seventeenth century was incorporated with a new church, one of the most beautiful ever built by the Jesuits, before the end of the century; in the same period scholars admitted to the three classes of Grammar, Syntax, and Poetry so increased in number that the fathers were able to raise a new college and to enlarge their curriculum with classes in Arithmetic and Rhetoric.

In William's day the Jesuit holdings and curriculum were even more impressive.[25] Outside the town the fathers owned farms, vineyards, forests and granaries from which they derived handsome profits, even after having deducted for their ample menage. In town their buildings, on the Rue Grande facing the top of the Rue du Collège, included acquisitions of a late councillor's home, a late lord's vast estate, and a late canon's dwelling as well as the college and its church. Somewhere among these buildings was Fr George's residence; somewhere near at hand William was to live as a pensioner under the after-school care of his aunt Marion Menzies.

Eighteen fathers and four coadjutors conducted the day-school of 250 students at Dinant. Excellent teachers in a learned society, the Jesuits aimed by means of their *Ratio Studiorum* to educate their scholars as good Catholics and useful citizens according to their rank in the world outside.[26] They sought to make discipline agreeable and obedience pleasant; but always their primary end was salvation of souls. The school year commenced with the reading out of class lists and the singing of the Mass of the Holy Ghost followed by the hymn 'Veni Creator'. The schoolboys in their distinctive caps, waistcoats, breeches, stockings, and shoes were known as 'Humanists'; for the backbone of their studies remained religion, ethics, and belles lettres. They conjugated and declined Latin and Greek, and translated to and from these languages as well as French, English, and German. They memorized and declaimed; they presented plays. After all this, they studied geography, mathematics, experimental physics and, especially, astronomy, the Jesuits' best-loved science. Twice a week two pensioners were invited to reply to precepts and authors explicated in the classes of the day. Rewards for excellence came on 'good days', such as the 'Choir Good Day' on the Feast of St Cecilia, 22 November. For additional fees, the boys could take lessons in dancing, drawing, music, arms, and riding. Occasionally they could find a few minutes for informal play at rudimentary cricket and football. Four times a year they had a 'vacancy' or holiday when they were released from classes, but obliged to remain under college authority. The three short 'vacancies' of approximately a week came at Christmas, Easter, and Pentecost; the 'Great Vacancy' of a month was in late summer. Such education was severe, as anyone might infer who has observed just how narrow the church pews were to encourage sitting up straight and how polished from constant use.

Records show that William had all of his eleventh year and most of his twelfth at Dinant; they show, moreover, that his mother paid the College about twenty-four guineas a year, without deductions for holidays, as the cost of his education and paid Marion Menzies about the same for his room and board. The £72 which she caused her banker to send 'for the use of Mrs Menzies', 4 October 1773, was undoubtedly towards the expenses of her sister-in-law's providing a home for all three of her sons.[27]

The Jesuit system of education invited criticism because it imposed those rigidities of mind promulgated by the Council of Trent. In the eighteenth century, pressures upon the system had been mounting before 1771, although the final bursting would be delayed until the French Revolution.[28] Hostile to speculative thought, such as Protestant science with its infidelity, rationalism, and tendency towards materialism, the Jesuits had been expelled from France to the regret of at least one of their French enemies, Voltaire, whose response to the expulsion was, 'It is to be a monster not to love those who have cultivated our soul.'[29] They were being suppressed in Portugal. They suffered, too, the displeasure of Maria Theresa. Already she had deprived them of exclusive control over the University of Vienna, and she was about to release a state paper prescribing what education must be throughout her dominion.

Thus William Maxwell studied under the Jesuits at a time when Catholic education was in ferment, when the Jesuits themselves were being ever more sharply controlled and curtailed, and when many thinkers in and out of Catholicism were teething dissent. He and the other young scholars must have stood amazed to see that authority, which they knew painfully well, not only questioned openly but also put down flatly.

Even before William's matriculation, Fr George must have admitted the distinct possibility that he might be made a rector without a college; and once having admitted the possibility, he and his counterparts in various other Jesuit colleges skirting Brussels must have sat down to determine what would be left for them and their students. One would believe that they prayed for more time than they were actually given. When it came, the attack was two-pronged: Pope Clement XIV's brief of suppression 'Dominus ac Redemptor' of August 1773 and Theresa's determination to use this brief against the Jesuits as one means of implementing her new plans of study and new plans of education for all her subjects.

One by one the doors closed: at Namur, at Bruges, at Liége, and at Dinant. As they shut, what had been predetermined became known: some, at least, of the displaced students would gather in the free principality of Liége to continue their schooling at an 'Academie Anglaise', which would be the suppressed Jesuit college renamed to postpone future intervention. When suppression caught up with the College at Dinant shortly before July 1773, the reaction of most parents was to sound immediate recall of their sons. Jesuits could no longer direct Jesuit schools; they could no longer teach as they had taught, even though they left the Society for the priesthood. News of the day, moreover, made parents uneasy for their children, particularly those whose sons were out of the country. The Maxwell brothers and their cousins, all a special case through Fr George, were to pick up their studies in Liége at the beginning of the new school year. William may have left down the Meuse before his uncle, because the Jesuit did not receive his allowance for travel and clothing until early October, after he had helped arrange compensations for the Society's properties in Dinant.[30]

Travellers to eighteenth-century Liége generally agreed as to what was characteristic.[31] This prosperous city was the inferno of women because they worked harder than anywhere else; the purgatory of husbands because wives dominated them; and the paradise of priests because 'the whole country almost belongs to the clergy.' Women dragged barges and carried heavy burdens; men thronged taverns to choose from an unusually diverse offering of wine. As replete with vice as it was with inhabitants, Liége was reported as unequalled in France and Germany for churches, convents, and other religious foundations. That traveller is exceptional who does not have a word for the Jesuit College, 'well situated on the top of a hill, with a handsome garden in which there is a variety of dialling'.[32]

The three years in Liége differed sharply from the two years in Dinant. In the first place, William was more a young man than a little boy, he was no longer a beginner. He resided, moreover, in an important city, not a scenic town: a city as close to what is now Germany as Dinant was close to France. And he lived at the school, not in a town house. At Liége his uncle was his prefect, not his rector; William now had two dozen fellow pupils, whereas he had had more than two hundred. His teachers now conducted classes not as Jesuits who could honor their feasts and devotions, but as priests still uncertain of new directions. Liége's greater wealth was reflected in the long, narrow library of its Jesuit college holding books valued at more than 60,000 guineas in 1794; in the size and quality of its observatory built in the second of a three-level garden; and in the magnificent garden itself with such curious effects as the hours marked by a fountain.

It could have been that the Maxwells of Kirkconnell and their cousins — a Riddell, a Menzies, and, presumably, a Maxwell of Munches — accounted for a fourth of those students who began the English Academy at Liége.[33] If the 'George Maxwell student' whose name appears in Dinant and Liége cashbooks was truly son to William and Agnes Maxwell of Munches, Fr George was uncle to five of these six youths and teacher to all six.

The cost of a year's tuition was thirty-two guineas paid in semi-annual instalments. For another eighteen guineas a year, the school pension included board, lodging, table and bed linen, fires, and light. Other expenses for all parents were £6 for the school greatcoat; £2. 10s for book rental; tuition fee for some such extracurricular activity as voice, flute, violin, fencing, drawing; charges for excursions and jaunts; and the ubiquitous 'to his pocket'. Other expenses for some parents were the costs of watches, globes, quadrants, guns, pistols, foils, kits of salmon, 'gloster' cheeses, and lottery tickets. Other expenses for a single parent were the price of 'a pair of spectacles for Thorpe' and the price of a funeral for 'Mas.ʳ Howard Meynell', £10 after allowing for 'to his pocket' change discovered in his pocket. For the period between departure from Dinant to arrival back at Kirkconnell, Mary Maxwell expended £181. 1. 9 2/12 for her son William's tuition, pension, clothes, travel, and allowance. She expended about the same on Thomas, more on James; her brother Thomas spent considerably more on his son.[34] Ultimately Mary's expenses for the education of William and Thomas would be deducted from interest upon the £1,000 contracted by the father for 'younger sons'.

A portion of Mary's expenditure went for the return of William and Thomas to Scotland after their completing the traditional five classes of the Jesuit training. September 1776 marked the end of their fifth year; so October brought them home.[35] A year earlier their brother James had gone back; a year later Fr George would leave for Edinburgh, semi-retirement, and eventual death (1805).[36]

For all intents and purposes, the last classes at Liége were regarded by mother and trustees as terminating the formal education of the

Maxwell brothers; thus, Mary could submit her final accounting for what had been spent on William and Thomas from birth to age sixteen and just beyond: £689. 7. 3 8/12.[37] Another kind of calculation must have filled her mind as she arrived at this figure. What difference had the years abroad made in her sons? How, for instance, had William Kirkconnell changed?

He was now a young gentleman, well mannered, conscious of posture, equally at ease in English and French, having familiarity with Greek and Latin and German. Polished, yes; and generous, but rather too careless with money. Just as obviously, he was gaining full growth fast and furiously; even now it was not too early to see that heavy frame, big bones would give him the height and size of the Riddells. Clear, also, was the deepened affection of brother for brothers, of brother for cousins at Swinburne Castle and Pitfodels. Studies with the Jesuits had left other marks: William had had to practise enough letter-writing to become adept, he had been encouraged in his love for books and gardens, he had gained algebra and geometry to quicken his interest in science, and he had been captivated by drama and the theatre.

Pleasure from science had been manifested in the boyhood at Kirkconnell through the observation and identification of birds. At Dinant and Liége William had begun to collect specimens; later he was to mount these birds and show them in glass cases side by side with displays of shells and crabs.[38] At first his zeal for cartography had been, perhaps, not unlike that of his companion Lord Stourton who was docked 4/1d by the Jesuit fathers for 'Chocolate & Maps';[39] but, sooner or later, he had had his own theodolite for mensuration as he had had his own 'glass' for zoology and biology. He had been given, too, the experience of gazing long hours through school telescopes.

At first thought, it would seem far-fetched to attribute delight in drama to training under the Jesuits. But school presentations of plays during the *ludus literarius* or other festivals was an integral part of their education from almost the time of their founding. The play was to be in Latin and it had to be 'decent', not to contain female roles or to be given in church. Participation was thought to cultivate understanding and to develop character and sentiment, poise and voice, ease and grace. Even before William's day, it had become possible for the students to select or write a play on a subject out of profane history; for example, the Fall of Dinant. By his day it had become traditional for the teacher of rhetoric to make up a Latin tragedy in verse to be presented by the boys either in a classroom or out in one of the gardens; other annual events featured comedies and interludes full of song and dance. When a play was given before the public, it was customarily offered the first night to women only, the second night to men only. Rules under which James Joyce shared this experience at Clongowes in 1890 were somewhat less strict; and those under which students of Stonyhurst wrote, staged, and acted their *Frank Ass/The Francis of Assisi Musical* in 1973 were indubitably less so. Speech defect would have limited William's participation as actor or singer, but not his participation in some of those hundred-and-one other businesses that an all-school play generates. These activities were to make it true of his later life that one of the surest places to catch up with him of an evening was at the theatre. By the same token, his active support in mature life of garden clubs, of assemblies, and of shooting associations reflects, at least in part, proficiencies acquired from his years under the Jesuits. One cannot be certain as to whether life in Dinant and Liége introduced him to the girls being instructed by the Ursulines, most probably it was not through the dance; but one can be assured that before William left Liége, he knew how to handle the foil, the gun, and the pistol.[40] Entries state that he had been provided such weapons as a true son of James Maxwell.

Challenges to authority both within the private life of the school and the public life of the world-at-large could not have settled William's innate tendency to rebel. That rejection of authority which had brought down the Jesuit regime in Dinant and Liége before his very eyes was to continue with him to his dying days. Meanwhile constitutional authorities were being more and more questioned and attacked, even successfully abolished. Shortly after William left Dinant, citizens of Massachusetts had enjoyed the Boston Tea Party. Shortly after his arrival at Liége, American patriots had convened at Philadelphia to protest at such measures of the British government as the Quartering Act; midway through William's studies at Liége, Edmund Burke had pleaded conciliation in London and opposing militias had exchanged shots at Lexington. With the beginning of the last year of William's study abroad, Thomas Paine had fired thought with his *Common Sense;* in July of that year, the Americans had declared their independence of Great Britain; and in that October, even as William was sailing back to Scotland, Benjamin Franklin was sailing to Nantes aboard the *Reprisal* as an American commissioner to France dining on salt beef, 'the fowls being too hard for my teeth'.[41]

William's years of coming of age were spent at Kirkconnell with his mother and brothers; they included what had to be the darkest years of his life. From the time of his nineteenth birthday in August 1779 to the ninth month of his twenty-second year, April 1782, William was deathly ill. Again one cannot specify what ailed him, but whatever it was it induced high fevers. Several years after his recovery his elder brother had occasion to remind him of this illness and of the anxiety and fatigue their mother had known as she sought 'night and day' to afford her son 'the least relieve'.[42] Evidence of just how sick he was is to be read, moreover, from entries in Mary's cashbooks. All was well in 1777 and 1778 when William lived freely, £30 above the annual £77 of interest from his estate. Such spending becomes a slight trickle for the period of the sickness: only £3 for 1780 and £15 for 1781. The single persistent entry throughout his being bedridden is the deadly 'Dr Gilchrist £1. 1. 0'.[43] Being so ill, William had not only to defer plans for the future but also to wonder if he would have a future. First thoughts of entering the medical profession may have come with returning health and a clear head which made it possible for him to consider what he had been through and what Dr Ebenezer Gilchrist had been able to do for him.

James came of age in August 1780; William in August 1781; and Thomas in December 1782. Zealously and meticulously the trustees had prepared for the days. Three years before James received full authority over Kirkconnell, Mary, John Maxwell of Terraughty, and Adam Craik of Arbigland had appealed to the Court of Session to determine what would be a fair way of calculating interest on monies left by the father.[44] Final decisions on how principal and interest on the £1,000 willed William and Thomas were to be invested had been postponed until William had full recovery of his sickness and Thomas had his twenty-first birthday. In August 1783 James gave his younger brothers satisfactory security on their estates so that by means of bonds of provision he could invest their inheritance in making Kirkconnell prosper.[45]

James was well cast in the role of family head. He was never to be other than exceptionally honest and generous with each of his brothers. What is more, he gave a place at Kirkconnell to his mother, his brothers, and his mother's sister Dorothy.[46] Like his father he came to marriage late, so that he found no immediate need to exercise his right of sole occupancy; more important to him during this period were the presence and experience of Mary and the companionship and helping hands of William and Thomas. Mary, nevertheless, anticipated the day of her having to leave and having to establish a home elsewhere for herself and, possibly, either or both of her younger sons by looking to her properties in Troqueer parish opposite Dumfries at the Nith.[47] The £300 which she borrowed from William, 27 November 1782, may have been put to such purpose.

Unlike James, William and Thomas were not bound to Kirkconnell, but could live rather much as they pleased. Happy for both brothers was the prospect of another visit to Swinburne Castle or to their cousin and schoolmate at Pitfodels, where John Menzies had succeeded as laird in 1780. William seems to have got away to Pitfodels often and to other places as well. So he had a holiday in the north-west of Scotland during July 1778 and four months with his mother of sojourning in Edinburgh at the height of the winter season, January-April 1779. After his illness, he allowed himself a month at Cambridge.[48] While Mary had used some of her time in Edinburgh to talk with Fr George about the chance of his making a loan to James, William had been spending freely, so freely, indeed, that by the time of his Cambridge visit Mary had cause to note, 27 April 1782, 'This day I have taken from him & have his receipts for all paiments to him pressing this date.'[49] Spend though he did, William had enough left over to open his first bank account.[50]

Travel for William and Thomas remained an exception, not a rule. Most of the time they were at home helping their brother as they could in the management of Kirkconnell lands and sharing with him the headaches. Now it would be announcing that Butterside was to be let or reading the proposals of those who wished to let Burnside; then it would be the felling of fir trees or the purchasing of herring on sale by the West Highland Fishery. Now it would be alarm because of great numbers of salmon dying of disease; then it would be anger because of promiscuous shooting of Kirkconnell game by poachers. James did not have to tell his brothers that money for improvements was tight or that hard as times were becoming there always remained the usual Dumfries bridge-custom on everything: for each horse and cow 2s if sold in the local market, 8s if not; 4s for a sheep, 2s for butter, 6d for four pecks of pears.[51] So it went; and at fairs the charges doubled. Even after these expenses, the fleshmarket, William Hyslop's wheat mill, and numerous other services exacted their own customs and fees.

Kirkconnell aside, Dumfries was the center of the brothers' civic and social life as well as business. They supported the efforts of paving, cleaning, lighting, watching the town; they attended the races, they curled; they browsed in Boyd's and Mitchell's bookstores; they subscribed to the new Assembly Room; and they helped pay for the new Infirmary. In the *Dumfries Weekly Journal,* they took note of who had been named bailie, became aware that gingerbread makers were using colored glass for frosting, and chuckled over the plight of the Reverend Mr Babington who posted a two-guinea reward for return of a melon on which he set 'a very high value'. This melon, lifted from a hotbed in his garden, could be easily distinguished by its largeness and 'a singular nob at the smaller end'.[52]

Of serious news there was more than enough to go round. Burgoyne had surrendered to Gates at Saratoga, France followed by Spain came into the war on the side of America. A letter to the printer of the *Dumfries Weekly* points up 'the disgraceful situation' in which Great Britain stood in terms of heavy taxes, insults from the French, condemnation by all powers, ruined empire, and 'fatal moment'.[53] In 1777 Dumfries hoped that 'the rebellious game of the provincials' was nearly over.[54] A year later one of those rebels dared come ashore from the *Ranger* at Whitehaven and on the same day make off with Lord Selkirk's plate from St Mary's Isle in the Solway. What hurt most for those in and around Dumfries was that John Paul Jones was a local boy, having been born at Kirkbean not far from Kirkconnell. Naming Jones 'the greatest miscreant under the canopy of heaven' may have let off steam; but subscribing to the recruitment for the old regiments and the navy was more constructive.[55] Doctor John Gilchrist gave £10. 10s, Robert Maxwell of Largen the same.[56] Nobody at Kirkconnell appears to have contributed. A year later (1778) Captain Jones commanded the *Bon Homme Richard* standing off Leith below Edinburgh; his presence gave reason for the Orkney antiquary George Low to write his fellow antiquary George Paton at work in the customhouse of Edinburgh, 'I am not positive but I shall see you in April or beginning of May, if it was not for that B-----d Paul Jones.'[57] As 'the trans-atlantic insurgents' were making their case, loud Irish voices were exhorting countrymen to make the same case for Ireland. Lord North was listening to these cries by the time the combined French and Spanish fleets lay off Plymouth. The American states won the war at Yorktown in 1781, the Irish parliament received its independence in 1782, and Great Britain ratified the peace treaties in 1783.

Such events uncovered fundamental differences between the sympathies of James and those of William. James stood for King and

Country as tall as he could in the coincidence of war and his succession as laird. William, on the other hand, was the second son born with a mind of his own and a silver spoon in his mouth, although like Gulliver without the advantages of primogeniture. Politically their paths would diverge more and more widely; yet no matter how widely, the bonds between them never broke, mainly because James had balance for two.

Disorder from serious and prolonged disease, disorder from rebellion and open war: religion became the third major source of disorder for William during these years. The fact that the Maxwells of Kirkconnell did not, apparently, subscribe for local recruitment was not so much because they were out of sympathy with that end as because they were in sympathy with at least one end of the Irish Catholics: toleration. Through laws of the day, Scottish Catholics still could suffer what Burke called 'deprivation of all the rights of human nature'.[58] Legally William and his family could not meet 'where there is altar, mass-book, vestments, Popish images, or other Popish trinkets'. They could not serve in the army which they were expected to support by voluntary contribution; they could not buy Catholic books; they could not acquire real property; they could not hold public office. William could not become a schoolmaster; as for that, he could not become a servant to a Protestant either. Many of these laws were no longer enforced, but they *could be*.

Since the Forty-Five, Scotland had had a greatly diminished number of Catholics. William Robertson, Moderator of the General Assembly, estimated in 1779 that there were no more than twenty thousand, and of these not more than twenty who possessed a hundred a year and not one of any eminence in the commercial world.[59] But changes were in the wind. In 1777 and '78 a Catholic Relief Bill was slowly moving in parliament against popular opposition such as was apparent in Dumfries. At a general meeting the parish of Tinwald unanimously voted to oppose to the utmost of its power, 'in a legal and constitutional way, any alteration in the penal laws against Papists'.[60] Each day the Dumfries bookstores were able to offer some such anti-Catholic pamphlet as the *Protestant Catechism*, which argued that the Church of Rome had no claim to antiquity and that its doctrines were 'a gross corruption of Christianity'.[61] The day of this diatribe might never wane, but a new spirit of enlightenment was stirring to be felt and expressed. For example, the *Dumfries Weekly Journal* for 20 October [?]1778 carried a letter to the printer which included the following:

The Popish act abounding with just and humane sentiments is everywhere approved, [notwithstanding a few zealots]. What would have irritated this kingdom to rage and madness about thirty years ago, is at this moment received by a people grown wiser from experience with the most hearty congratulations. The disposition of Roman Catholics is kind and obliging; their peaceable conduct has been tried, and stood the test; and why should not such useful citizens and undissembling friends of our excellent constitution meet due encouragement.   /s/ IMPARTIAL

Mounting opposition to the Catholic Relief Bill, which had finally passed both houses, turned to open riot when an attempt was made to apply the act to Scotland. By 29 January 1779 Edinburgh was alive with unbridled anti-Catholic feeling. A handbill, which was 'to be read carefully, kept clean, and dropped somewhere else', urged the city's Protestants 'to meet at Leith Wynd . . . in the evening to pull down that pillar of Popery lately built there'.[62] William Robertson had foreseen such agitation and had tendered his resignation to the General Assembly in 1780 when he had recognized the dilemma it put him in: either he was to abandon the principle of toleration or defy the majority of the assembly over which he moderated. Early in June Lord George Gordon led his swelling ranks of protesters up to the Houses of Parliament, where he presented a petition signed by more or less than forty thousand men pledged to the blue cockade. Dickens allows Lord George in *Barnaby Rudge* a raven 'Grip' able to shriek the battle-cry, 'A devil, a kettle, a Grip, a Polly, a Protestant, No Popery.' Richard Gough, in a series of letters to George Paton, describes what it was like to have witnessed those events which became known after Lord George and high food prices got the London mob into the streets.[63] Gough saw Catholic chapels gutted and all their furniture and ornaments burnt in the open. Not satisfied, the mob set fire to Newgate, the King's Bench, and the Fleet after releasing their convicts. This mob went on to ravage the home of Lord Mansfield, strip furniture from the home of Sir George Savile, who was the first mover of the bill in favor of Catholics, bear Lord George in triumph through London, and put torches to distilleries as it drank their vitriol and alcohol and as soldiers pushed many fellow rioters into the flames. 'Raw spirits ran down the streets like burning lava.' Looking back on these days, Gough commended parliament for 'The wisdom & Headiness [it] has shown itself in not repealing the Bill', expressed satisfaction that the hanging of some twenty-five looters was carried out with 'much solemnity and regularity', and prayed, 'God send these Convulsions both at home and abroad may give final vent to the Spirit of Discontent, & overwhelm it for ever in its own ruin.'

Events like the Gordon Riots left William poles apart from James, Fr George, and John Menzies on the question of religion. For them the Catholic Relief Bill was but a first step on what would have to be a long road of challenge leading ultimately to where each Roman Catholic citizen might enjoy every civil right of any other citizen. Along this way they would need to remain relentless, painstaking, strong, and very patient even as they were given more reason to be hopeful and confident. For what they had to do, they must curry favor at Whitehall while exercising extreme caution not to give Whitehall any cause to turn its back. Without exception the reforms which they sought were secular, not religious; they were perfectly content with their church as they had been brought up in it. William was not. He now began to regard James and their cousin John Menzies as stopping short in their concept of toleration. Why did the Roman Catholic church overlook its own intolerance within as it strove to be tolerated by those without? If the Government advocated civil reform to the advantage of Roman Catholicism, why did Roman Catholicism remain so impervious to ecclesiastical reform of and by itself? Already for William an even more ideal goal was becoming defined: the challenge of all authority to permit freedom of the individual conscience.

Fundamental differences on matters religious and political did not stand alone as reasons for William's decision in 1784 to change his way of life. He had been given time for restoration of good health, years that had taken him up to his twenty-fourth birthday, past the age when most of his friends had entered their careers; James had established himself competently as laird; and Thomas had begun planning for his future. What was finally agreed upon for both William and Thomas had the full support of the entire family. For Thomas there would be the opportunity to enter the rapidly expanding commercial world. To this end, Mary would loan her youngest son enough of her own money whereby he might purchase a full partnership in a Manchester fustian manufactory that specialized in printing and dyeing that thick, twilled, cotton. Thomas remained, indeed, the 'Maxwell' of 'Taylor & Maxwell, Brown Street, Manchester' until his premature death in 1792.[64] For William there would be the chance of becoming a physician.

Medicine was a most appropriate choice for one with a natural bent for science. Edinburgh University offered the best M.D. degree in all

D

Europe, as Dr Ebenezer Gilbert and his son Dr John, who had earned that degree in 1767, vouched. Over in Dumfriesshire, James Currie had just completed the same course of study during which time he had proposed Ebenezer as an Honorary Member of the Royal Medical Society; closer by, John Ewart, son of the minister to the Kirkcudbrightshire parish of Troqueer and brother-in-law to John Gilchrist, had also graduated as doctor from Edinburgh.[65] Trouble was, all of these gentlemen worshipped in the Church of Scotland. Would it be possible for a Scottish Roman Catholic to be admitted? Dr John Gilchrist gave answer: before 1762 candidates for the degree of Doctor of Medicine had had to swear to oaths or *sponsiones* that they were true, pure Christians cleansed of all errors of Roman Catholicism ('*Spondeo, me in veritate et puritate Religionis Christianae ab omnibus Pontificiorum erroribus repurgatae*'); but this religious qualification had been removed from the oath in 1762 just as soon as William Robertson, king's historiographer, royal chaplain, Moderator of the General Assembly, and champion of the Scottish Enlightenment, had been appointed principal of Edinburgh University.[66] Relatives like Mary and Fr George, John Menzies and Thomas Riddell could have known qualms that William would study where Robertson led; but William himself would have felt none.

Because it is so simple to document William's pursuit of medicine at Edinburgh University, one is left to wonder how the myth of his having taken his M.D. in France got its start. Who is to say? Perhaps that first somebody syllogized badly, as follows: 'William Maxwell was a doctor, William Maxwell was a French sympathizer; therefore, William Maxwell was a French M.D.' Everybody else has merely played follow the leader.

The years of William Maxwell's advanced study at Edinburgh University, 1784-1787, were a lull after the war with America. In London Prime Minister William Pitt, with solid support from Henry Dundas, who held the wide world of Scotland in his hands, was transforming politics and administration. The ease with which Dundas could deliver each and every Scots vote to Pitt was remarked scornfully by Fox: 'When we look to the Kingdom of Scotland, we see a state of representation so monstrous and absurd, so ridiculous and so revolting, that it is good for nothing except perhaps to be placed by the side of the English in order to set off our defective system by comparison of one still more defective.'[67] Politically, such was the unfortunate case. But physically, Edinburgh was dressing herself in the beauty of the

New Town; and, intellectually, she was bearing the pride of being synonymous with 'the Scottish Enlightenment'. Now in its third and final phase, this enterprise of mind and spirit continued virile enough to foster Hutton's *Theory of the Earth*, Playfair's *Elements of Geometry*, Reid's *Essay on the Intellectual Powers of Man*, and, by stretching the point, Boswell's *Life of Johnson*, with strength left over for a Scott, a Lockhart, and a Jeffrey. Taking its blood from liberalism, democracy of the intellect, deistic bias, and scepticism, this enlightenment welcomed debate and forbore controversy in order to win others to its purposes of benevolence, toleration, equality, utility, truth, and literary fame.

The center of the Scottish Enlightenment within the nation was Edinburgh, its center within Edinburgh was the University, and its center within the University was the College of Medicine. Edinburgh's medical faculty included such pathfinders as the chemist Joseph Black, the nosologist William Cullen, and the surgeon John Hunter. It was their colleague James Gregory who lectured the medical students on what their education was to mean beyond conferment of the degree: 'Men whose minds have been enlarged by knowledge, who have been accustomed to think, and to reason upon all subjects with a generous freedom, are not apt to become bigots to any particular sect or system. They can be steady to their own principles, without thinking ill of those who differ from them; but they are impatient of the authority and control of men, who would lord it over their consciences, and dictate to them what they are to believe.'[68] This essence of the Scottish Enlightenment would lie at the heart of everything memorable that William Maxwell of Kirkconnell would ever accomplish. Romantic idealism had drawn his father to Edinburgh in the cause of Charles Edward; a generation later, the strong light of ethical idealism, not that of the Jesuit fathers, but that of Professor Gregory, helped to attract his son there. When William at last found his own causes, he would fight to advance them under the combined spell of his father's romance and Edinburgh University's ethics.

The first order of business upon arrival in Edinburgh sometime in fall 1784 was to take lodgings. Even if Fr George did offer to share his space with his nephew, it is doubtful that William would have accepted. Such accommodation would have been too much like a retreat to Dinant, particularly if Fr George lived in or near those lodgings maintained by the Roman Catholic Church on Blackfriars Street chiefly for priests serving the new St Margaret's. Blackfriars was just north of the University, two blocks away from South Bridge; Nicolson Street, where William found what he was looking for, was the extension of South Bridge just south of the University.[69] William had independence of money to go with independence of mind; but the debts he piled high during these years signify that where and how he lived in Nicolson Street indulged dear tastes. Not that he had come to play, not that he was unready to study intently. He was eager to learn; moreover, he was being driven with some of that quiet desperation which comes from looking about the classroom to discover that one's fellow students are too young to shave. For all that, he was an ardent spectator of horse races and far from a reluctant better; he was fond of oysters and of the goings-on in oyster cellars. Being a Maxwell, he enjoyed a drop or two or three.

Advertisements in the *London Chronicle* announced the classes of the College of Medicine at Edinburgh.[70] Six of the eight began in late October: Anatomy & Surgery, Chemistry and Chemical Pharmacy, Dietetics & Materia Medica, Theory of Physic, Practice of Physic, and Theory and Practice of Midwifery. Mid-November brought the first class in Botany; the next May, the first Clinical Lecture. Most of the classes were held at the University; several took students to places like the Royal Infirmary and the Botanic Gardens. Cost of admission was the library fee of 2/6d. Tuition beyond this modest sum was paid directly to the individual professor. That treasure of a book, the *Matriculation Album*, proves that William went through each hoop of the three-year curriculum under the training of the illustrious Alexander Monro, William Cullen, Joseph Hope, Joseph Black, Francis Home, James Gregory, and Alexander Hamilton.[71]

Three months before graduation, a candidate for the M.D. degree had to pass an examination testing not only his knowledge of medicine but also his knowledge of Latin and the extent of his general knowledge. Once over this hurdle, he still had to submit a satisfactory thesis.[72] Precision and taste in the style of William's thesis match his father's. Unsurprisingly, William chose to write about birds. Unsurprisingly, his thesis represents original research, not the conventional essay. What fascinated him was variety in the flight of birds which became apparent and capable of definition only after careful, informed observation. Very surprising, for one seeing through Fr George's spectacles, are both the source and the context of the motto which William selected. These words are from Scaliger, a Roman Catholic convert to Protestantism, a professor in Calvin's college at

Geneva, a devotee of Scottish ballads.[73] The words themselves? 'True understanding of these things is from these things.' Custom required that a thesis be dedicated to a professor, one's father, or one's uncle. William dedicated his not to Fr George but to his elder brother James. Was it William or James who commissioned that it be bound handsomely in full red Morocco with tooling and edges in gold leaf, with rich endpapers? Was it James's pride in William's achievement? Or William's love and gratitude for James? This tossed coin would land on edge. The volume belongs at Kirkconnell; today it is there in the library.

William seems to have spent less time with his classmates than one would expect because he had so many relatives and old friends in and not far from Edinburgh. He seems, also, to have joined fewer clubs than was customary, indubitably because their chief exercise was debate, an activity that would have exposed, all too painfully for a shy man, any speech handicap. This is not to deny, however, that he belonged to the Royal Medical Society (original signatures for the period are lost) or that he relished hearing public debates. Easily he could have found arguments for such questions as 'Are Religious Establishments usefull or pernicious?' and 'Are the Laws of Right & Wrong, which are binding on Individuals, applicable to nations?'

No, William Maxwell did not find Edinburgh University as Robert Southey was about to find Oxford University: 'The truth is . . . institutions of men grow old like men themselves, and like women are always the last to see their own decay.'[74] No, Mary could not have complained to William at Edinburgh University as Thomas Phillipps, sr, was complaining to Thomas, jr, at Oxford University: '. . . you say you "find there are lectures upon law, but they are given at the beginning of the long vacation *or near it*." So you have been three years at the university to Study and prepare yourself for a Lawyer, before you were certain there were lectures at all, perhaps in three years more you will find out the *precise time* they are delivered, and after three further years it is to be hoped you can inform me you have attended one of them — this will be making wonderful proficiency in the Study of the Law.'[75]

That the Edinburgh years were not all work and no play may be inferred from William's frequent and successful demands for money. Two, three, four times a week, he would cross the city to the New Town where he would knock at the door of Hugh Corrie of Culloch, W.S., on George Street, to be given what money he requested.[76] Corrie

had property in the same general area of Kirkcudbrightshire as Kirkconnell. If he did not know William well before 1784, he certainly did
before 1787. William would arrive in Edinburgh each October for
opening of college with a draft from James for £90; nevertheless,
October was not too early for the first trip of the new academic year to
Corrie. Now, more than a little careless with money, William went
through more than £200 a year and anticipated graduation time as the
likeliest moment to ask James for another hundred to clear his debts; it
was as though horses ran on Leith Sands every day of the college year
— sleet, snow, or shine. To soften such blows, the extravagant one
tendered blackmail of something like 'a Long leged [sic] Terrier'.[77]

Out of class, William did not hesitate to act in Edinburgh, even in
Glasgow, on behalf of his brother. Pheasants might be needed at Kirkconnell, a copy of a new book not stocked in Dumfries, 'Gravie' spoons
to be supplied by the Edinburgh silver merchant William Robertson.
During the long holiday of August-September, the brothers were
reunited at Kirkconnell with some such advance notice from William
as, 'I shall probably see you soon tho not I think till about the end of
the month, I have so much English blood as to please myself with the
thoughts of seeing good horses at the races.'[78] Once home William
conducted some of the experimentation for his thesis; paid the new
year's Game Duty alongside James, Wellwood Maxwell of Barncleugh,
and John McMurdo, Chamberlain to His Grace the Duke of
Queensberry; renewed his membership for £5 5s in the Dumfriesshire
and Galloway Hunt which afforded him the pleasures of riding to the
hounds in the company of James, their cousin George Maxwell of
Munches, and Robert Riddell of Glenriddell; and shared James's pride
of election as burgess of Dumfries.[79] Evenings James and Mary would
bring William abreast of the lastest news about town: some matter-of-
fact, some unpleasant, some comical. His Dumfries aunts were leaving
some of their money to the three brothers and John Menzies;[80] Maxwell
of Carruchan and John Syme, son of the writer, were promoting a new
wing to the Dumfries Infirmary as an asylum for lunatics;[81] the
'Catholic Congregation at Munches' had subscribed £2; tradesmen in
the parish of Kirkmahoe, almost £8.[82] More seriously, Alexander
Gordon, Sheriff for the Stewartry of Kirkcudbrightshire, had protested
that James had allowed his name to be used as 'Informer and
Prosecutor of the shooters' who had lately invaded Kirkconnell. Never
mind — Gordon advised — that the shooters had been poaching; the
only important point was that the times were particularly unlucky for a

Roman Catholic gentleman to have his name arise in any penal prosecution. Further Acts against the Catholics were soon to be repealed so that it was of much consequence for each Roman Catholic 'to be very quiet'. Gordon then continued, 'I find Mr Syme is the person who uses Kirkconnell's name and when I sounded him this day [30 April 1787], I found it was best to say little to him. Several country people have spoken to me as much irritated at Mr. Maxwell's having raised such prosecution.'[83] More amusingly, the *Dumfries Weekly* had reported the death of Mr Harry Prentice, 'who first introduced the culture of potatoes into this country'.[84] Prentice had bought his coffin for two guineas in 1703, the year of his birth, and, for the nine years preceding his death, had hung it in his house. Under written obligation, the undertaker had had 'to screw him down with his own hands gratis'.

By early September 1787, William had completed all requirements for the degree of Doctor of Medicine at Edinburgh University. Elation upon being able to add 'Dr' before his name and upon thoughts of what lay immediately ahead had him walking on air. Sweating over packing boxes for carriage to Kirkconnell as he crammed lecture notes tightly against his Rousseau and Voltaire, he sat down for a few minutes of 'a very warm day' to cool off and to keep his mother posted:

> I am really surprised you make so much ceremony in desiring me to accompany you to Northumberland, I would do it *immediately* with the greatest pleasure were I not engaged to be at Pitfodles on Friday next but if you find it convenient to wait till the end of this month, I promise I shall be your *Valet* before the first of October; I am very sorry to be so much hampered at present.[85]

William fulfilled at Pitfodels every prospect he had fashioned for his first days of new freedom. Lazily or strenuously as he was inclined, he angled for salmon in the Dee, rode, inspected John Menzies' improvements, sat before the fire with his Aunt Marion playing that game of memory, 'Do you remember at Dinant when . . .?' Reluctantly, as always, he mounted for the long trip back to Queensferry, over the Forth to Edinburgh, and down to Kirkconnell. A day or two of catching up on sleep was all he required before escorting his mother to Swinburne Castle for another holiday: the pleasures of a full season of hunting and shooting with his cousin Thomas. Then it was the carriage trip back home for a few days with James before heading for Edinburgh to participate in the winter social season. Late February brought John Menzies and his mother to Edinburgh for the same reason; so William postponed his departure for Kirkconnell while writing James 'affectionately' for 'about twenty pounds more' so that he would not have to deny himself the happiness of their company; the blackmail this time was 'six pounds of Baked Tea . . . greatly better than you can procure at Dumfries'.[86]

All this travel, all this relaxation, all this indulgence led to the climax of March 1788. On the raw, cold day that was the twenty-fifth, William left Kirkconnell for Dumfries to take a seat in the Glasgow-London stage. The £60 in one pocket, double that amount in drafts comfortable at the bottom of an inner pocket, and James's promise that Sir Robert Herries & Co. would see that he didn't fall short could have brought a whistle to his lips.[87] 'Setting out for London & Paris' *did* mark the initiation of his very own quest, although William was unaware that it did when his stage rolled over the Esk and out of Scotland.

FROM ROBERT BURNS —

A fig for those by law protected!
  Liberty's a glorious feast,
Courts for cowards were erected,
  Churches built to please the priest!

— 'The Jolly Beggars'

Is it not remarkable, odiously remarkable, that tho' manners are more civilized, & the rights of mankind better understood, by an Augustan Century's improvement, yet in this very reign of heavenly Hanoverianism, & almost in this very year, an empire beyond the Atlantic has had its REVOLUTION too, & for the very same maladministration & legislative misdemeanors in the illustrious & sapientipotent Family of H----- as was complained of in the 'tyrannical & bloody house of Stuart.'

— To Mrs Dunlop

Now, as to these inquisitorial informers, Spies, Persecutors, &c., may the devil & his angels be let loose to ———

— To Mrs Dunlop

God Save the King's a cuckoo sang
That's unco easy said ay

— 'A Dream'

—FROM ROBERT BURNS

King Louis thought to cut it down,
     When it was unco sma', man;
For this the watchman crack'd his crown,
     Cut aff his head and a', man.

— 'The Tree of Liberty'

I am a BRITON, & must be interested in the cause of LIBERTY: I am a MAN, and the RIGHTS OF HUMAN NATURE cannot be indifferent to me.

— To Editors . . . the *Morning Chronicle*

. . . those happy days when my heart was yet honest and my tongue was sincere.

— First Commonplace Book

What is Right, and what is Wrang,
     By the law, by the law?
What is Right, and what is Wrang,
     By the law?

— 'Ye Jacobites by Name'

CHAPTER THREE

Track of the Storm

It was the best of times, it was the worst of times, it was the age of
wisdom, it was the age of foolishness, it was the epoch of belief, it
was the epoch of incredulity, it was the season of Light, it was the
season of Darkness, it was the spring of hope, it was the winter of
despair, we had everything before us, we had nothing before us, we
were all going direct to heaven, we were all going direct the other
way.

—Charles Dickens

'No young man,' Hazlitt wrote, 'believes he shall ever die. There is a
feeling of Eternity in youth, which makes us amends for everything . . .
Like a clown at a fair, we are all full of amazement and rapture, and
have no thoughts of going home, or that it will soon be night.'[1] This
very abandon must have pounded at William Maxwell's temples as his
coach left Scotland in the spring of 1788.

William was only twenty-seven, a young doctor without one patient,
with no bounds to his inclinations. The three days to London during
which his coach horses were changed some forty times to maintain the
pace of ten miles an hour (a speed believed to cause damage to the
brain) would have given him time to mull things over. James had
accounted for the money now burning his pockets with the note, 'By
Cash paid my Brother William before his setting out for London
paris &c &c'; but both brothers knew that if the Grand Tour was to be
the object, it would lie hazard to the times.[2]

One doubts that William ever got beyond Paris and her environs or
that, once in Paris, he could have found anything but a passing fancy
to leave. If the French capital was too inspirational to be separated
from and if he did, therefore, remain in it for the duration of this trip

abroad, one must be able to recall, no matter how sketchily, what the sources of his inspiration unquestionably were.

In Holland, a late assault upon the House of Orange, as a revolutionary upheaval to bring down all aristocratic privileges, had failed when the Prussian army had entered the Netherlands to occupy Amsterdam. In Belgium, new edicts of Joseph II, successor to Maria Theresa, had roused another revolution. Neither of these countries, however, had become more ready for its run at justice than France. There absolutism had already started to disintegrate because of antagonism between the Crown and the privileged orders; more recently and more rapidly, it had been continuing because of antagonism between the privileged orders and the Third Estate. One financial crisis after another was the catalyst. So Thomas Paine, Carlyle's 'rebellious Needleman', sailed for France with high hopes of re-enacting what had just brought down the curtain in America. Thanks in great measure to his *Common Sense*, the colonies had won their revolution and written their constitution to fulfil the promises of their 'Declaration of Independence'.

To see the way in which students and young citizens of Brittany and Provence in March 1788 went about lighting the Ancien Régime to its end must have warmed the cockles of Paine's heart, just as the Paris Parlement's April remonstrances against Louis XVI's edict covering loans, its May list of fundamental laws, and the provincial parlements' joining battle. Riots, disorders, revolts, and arrests moved the King in July to issue a royal edict announcing his intent to summon the Estates General for the first time since 1614, in August to fix the date at 1 May 1789, and in September to advance it to January. The patriots of Nantes forced registration of their famous petition in November. Before December 1788, the fundamental issue had been drawn: would the form of the Estates General remain as it had always been or would it be modified so as to give due weight to the new importance of the middle class by increasing the number of representatives from all three orders to vote collectively, not separately? The National Assembly, born at the January 1789 meetings of the Estates General, was to give France a constitution, to ordain a new set of laws and institutions, to abolish feudalism, and to break the power of the old privileged orders and of the Parlements before 1791.

News from France would have encouraged William not to tarry in London where citizens had little more on their minds than Pitt's latest tax. Via Dover and Calais, in coaches and aboard pacquet, he travelled to Paris, probably by April and certainly more than £20 lighter. Along the way William remarked in village after village what Arthur Young was calling 'excrementitious lanes'; everywhere he observed evidence of a shortage of raw materials, hunger, even scarcity of wine; and he caught sight of such uneasiness as is illustrated by the following anecdote attributed in the travel books of the age to Mme de Genlis:

> It happened in the country; an officer of high rank ordered a farmer to carry out some work which he had no right to demand; the farmer refused, and the officer said to him: 'You have to do what I wish, or I will give you twenty strokes with my cane.'
> 'Monsieur,' replied the farmer in a calm voice, 'I advise you not to, for you could not have the time to count them.'[3]

Possible evidence as well as probable surmise leads to the conclusion that once in Paris William appears not to have moved far or very long from it; every draft of this period (three, each for £100) was docketed 'from Paris' by James.[4] Chaises may have splashed greasy black slime up on the young doctor, and gutterless roofs may have poured cold water down upon him; but living in the heart and center of France at such a time as when the rich listened to the exquisite airs of Rameau while the poor at the Pont Neuf compelled passers-by to take off their hats to the statue of Henry IV of Navarre, their one king who had cared for them, made him oblivious of personal discomfort. As he found friends among those Frenchmen being swayed to the ideals of Liberty, Fraternity, and Equality, as he talked far into the night with fellow Britons about the spectre of national bankruptcy, the mutinous provinces, the failure to gather taxes, the calls for *cahiers*, and the helpless king, he could agree with his companions that a day of reckoning was not far off. Increasingly, week by week, a deluge of pamphlets carried him along. Today it was one titled 'Creed of the Third Estate'; tomorrow, 'When the Cock crows, look out for the old Hens.' Twenty-five hundred or more political exhortations like these have been collected.

Not yet Don Quixote, William could still listen to his mother's and elder brother's appeal that he be doctor in action as well as in designation; thus, he recrossed the Channel bound once again for Kirkconnell. By letter and draft from the period, spring 1789 to fall 1790, one is able to recover his attempts, ever more half-hearted, to set himself up in practice. London was the obvious choice, as any young doctor liked to deduce from the examples of Lettsom, Pringle, and John Moore. So William went down from home to try his luck. Before an honest effort, he and everybody else in the capital received the intelligence from France of the flight of Louis and the royal family to Varennes and of their forced return to Paris. Less than a month later, 14 July 1789, came the far more violent jolt of the fall of the Bastille as an end to absolute monarchy. Months immediately thereafter brought correspondence between British liberals and leaders of the democratic faction in France. Living the shock of such events, William could not have felt different from Samuel Romilly who was writing a friend in Paris, '. . . how much I have rejoiced at the French Revolution which has taken place. I think of nothing else.'[5] Tumblings of mind and heart show in William's announcement to his family that he would abandon thoughts of a London practice. 'There is scarcely anything,' he confided in his letter to James, 10 January 1790, 'that can bring a person into immediate practice in London, it is generally by the deaths of others that a person succeeds, the hopes of immediate success would be highly pre-sumptious.'[6] But the tenor of this letter, back to back with William's revelations after returning to Kirkconnell from Paris, so much carried expressions of contempt for Lord Selkirk's political blunders as well as support of 'political schemes of happiness' that James and Mary recog-nized the moment as one for removing William from London by urging him to look about in Scotland for professional opportunity. In spring 1790, therefore, he was searching Glasgow and living by means of money drafted on Hugh Corrie.[7]

James's alarm at his brother's restlessness is apparent in his deter-mination to bring their financial affairs up-to-date. On 12 May 1790, between William's giving up in Glasgow and his beginning to explore possibilities in Edinburgh, the brothers agreed at Kirkconnell that William had spent all of the interest entrusted to James as well as most of the principal 'received at sundry times'.[8] By October 1790, the day that Corrie informed the laird that he owed £288 9s 8d 'for Tact of Teinds of Troqueer and cash advanced to your brother',[9] James kept but a thin hope of checking William's enthusiasm for the French Revolution because he had talked himself out with his brother; so, also, had Mary; and so, also, had John Menzies who had invited William to Aberdeen just to enter his own pleas. All to no avail. Dr William Maxwell had removed himself to London for the purpose of seeing how far £129 from James would take him in openly and unqualifiedly defending the French Revolution.[10] Ready for the perilous joust with visor lowered, breastplate shining, and lance poised, he was spurring down upon his first windmill.

William was ever too magnanimous to become callous and indifferent to his family. Honor-bound, commanded by his conscience to run counter to their wishes, he could not have taken French republicanism to his heart without making it heavy. That not a single Roman Catholic champion in Britain could have seen from such allegiance anything but harm to his cause of changing the governmental and public views of Roman Catholicism might have been answered by William with a shrug and a 'Never mind'; that he was hurting Mary, James, and John Menzies was never to leave his moral sense.

Escapes back to Kirkconnell had only confirmed William's assurance that those whom he most dearly loved had more than enough troubles of their own. James seemed never without a full day at Kirkconnell, yet others like John Maxwell of Terraughty and George Maxwell of Carruchan expected him to make time for such business as calling a meeting of the parish trustees to determine what they would grant for a new road opening communication 'thro' Cargen to the road leading to New abbay at Gillfoot'.[11] What is more, affairs of the Riddells drew in James frequently. When Mary had lost her eldest brother in 1789, James had had to witness legacies left his mother and her sisters; a year later he attended the marriage of the heir Thomas Horsley Widdrington Riddell, the 'Widdrington' cousin of schooldays; soon thereafter he allowed himself to be named one of Thomas's executors.[12] As laird, James placed his brothers as well as his mother before himself. Still unmarried, he would get off a letter of encouragement to Tom, only to remain in candlelight to straighten William's account and then indulge himself by ordering 'a double Magnifier' for his doctor-brother before seeking bed.[13] It might be remembered that James's deep anxiety for William after their farewells of October 1790 never permitted him to trouble his brother on account of his own worries introduced through the chaos in France. Each year money became tighter and tighter so that James stood almost at wit's end in borrowing: £100 from the wife of a deceased exciseman, £300 from Hugh Corrie and Thomas Goldie, and, with George Maxwell of Carruchan, £800 from 'Mrs Margaret Edgars, Dumfries' in a loan witnessed by John Maxwell of Terraughty and John Coverly, 'serv! to J. Maxwell'. As much as James could, wherever he could, he borrowed: altogether £4,100 between 27 May 1790 and 1799.[14]

Otherwise, William's riding out on quest couldn't have come at a

worse time for James. In the winter of 1789-1790, Mary had taken ill so
as to draw the solicitude of William in London. 'I am sorry to hear,'
William wrote his elder brother, 'of my mother's indisposition but the
truth is, the inclemency of the weather will almost invariably affect her
health.'[15] Thomas, too, had fallen sick, so sick that he had been sent
abroad, presumably to find a milder climate. William had heard from
Thomas in Paris (25 December 1789) that he, Thomas, had not
observed any alteration in his health.[16] This sickness of mother and
younger brother sounds suspiciously like consumption; if it was truly
so, one has an explanation for William's prolonged sieges and 'goat's
whey' convalescences.

Even a glimpse of relief from perturbation is rare. Such as was given
was usually provided by John Menzies. A shrewd, cool, practical
realist, this cousin was making a fortune in Aberdeen. His swift rise in
the world paralleled his rise to the position of first Catholic layman and
bishop-maker in Scotland. Menzies well knew the little chapel-house
where Bishop Hay lived in retreat; and Menzies' visits to Edinburgh
often purposed consultations with Hay's coadjutor for the Lowlands,
John Geddes. Because the Laird of Pitfodels only recently had not been
above taking advantage of Aberdeen's westward expansion by selling
the grounds of his ancestral home, he was left with the need to build a
new dwelling just south of the Dee on two thousand acres of high land
overlooking that river. This mansion with its own garden after that at
Kirkconnell and its own winding approach shaded by trees and
bordered with lawn became known as Blairs. Its construction did not
abate with John's decision to raise a collusive action against his sole
surviving uncle, the heptagenarian Alexander, to settle who was heir of
tailzie; rather it hastened with John's decision to take a wife.[17]
Thoughts of their cousin marrying brought smiles to the countenances
of the Maxwell brothers; word of whom he had selected as his bride
broadened these smiles to grins. Just after Hogmanay 1790, William
gleefully and bawdily answered James's notice that the marriage had
been celebrated:

> As our friend at Pitfoddles has in addition to his wife, taken a hand maid,
> he may according to *his feelings* pass the winter with tolerable *Comfort*,
> he is the *only* man of my acquaintance, with whom Virgin flesh rises in
> estimation in the exact ratio of its age. Tho difficulties [of] the asses bridge
> are Vexatious, They may perhaps in a little go over it backwards which is
> a property peculiar to some animals.[18]

Once having buckled on the high kilt, William wore it a while longer in order to comment upon Betty Gracie, daughter of the banker James who had been born at New Abbey. Betty, unmarried but pregnant, had managed to abort herself with a sharp instrument, but not before dangerously tearing her innards. She had not reflected, William tells James, 'that when she shall have been pricked by it, she cannot dispose of it at pleasure'.

By winter 1790-91, William had located suitable London accommodation at No. 73, Great Portland Street, in the Parish of Saint Mary le Bow.[19] Here, between Oxford and Marylebone Streets, he was close to Hyde Park and its neighboring hospitals, should there happen to be calls for his professional services. The books which he unpacked and the pamphlets which he bought and rushed home to consume reveal the Janus-like station he held. On one side of his den, his Boerhaave, Cullen, and Pringle; his Fyfe's *Anatomy*, Hamilton's *Female Complaints*, and Adam's *Morbid Poisons*; his Burns on midwifery, Beddoes on consumption, and Bell on gonorrhea and *lues venerea* (syphilis). On the other side, his Montesquieu, Voltaire, and Rousseau; his *L'État de la France*, *Junius' Letters*, and Mackintosh's *Defence of the French Revolution*; his copy of Burke's *Reflections on the Revolution in France* next to his copy of Paine's answer, *The Rights of Man*; his Fox's *Letter to the Electors of Westminster* and his *New Constitution of the United States of America*.[20]

Knowledge of what William did accomplish in the last half of 1792 assures us of what he had to accomplish in the year before. First days erased much of that disquietude which remained after his departure from Scotland. More than one of those about Dumfries had begun to regard him 'as daft as a yett on a windy day', and surely one of his elders had reproved him with 'Ne'er break oot o' kind to gar your friends ferlie at you.' But William was bursting too much with individual energy, too filled with that eagerness which hurries one to a sad extreme to pay heed. An incurable optimist, he responded to the challenges blown from the embers of the Bastille, much as poets like Wordsworth, Coleridge, and Southey were responding; and like them he could have had too little patience for such sober reckoning as

> Perhaps there's too much order in the world;
> The poets love to haul disorder in,
> Braiding their wrists with her long mistress hair,
> And when the house is tossed about their ears,
> The governors must set it right again.
> How wise was he who bann'd them from his state.[21]

E

The question was not whether William would haul disorder in, but when and how. Finding the means, as he had already discovered the determination, took more than a year of his life.

For William Maxwell had very little to build upon: mastery of the French tongue, familiarity with such scenes of action as Paris, Calais, Ostend, Brussels, and Liége; and more or less random acquaintance with some of those he had known at school or had met in France two years before who sided with the Revolution. To become recognized, to become trusted where plans were being made and executed were the slow, hard assignments that William wrote out in his mind. Day by day, however, he made his way, now in London, then in Paris, until he finally had a place at councils in both capitals. Given the very nature of his efforts, it should come as no surprise that his advancement to prominence can be documented only ever so barely. Did Thomas aid his brother on the Paris end? Or in Manchester and Birmingham? Just when did William and Horne Tooke fall in? Or William and Tom Paine? To what extent was William responsible for the formation of the London Corresponding Society in early 1792? Who can say? What one can say, nevertheless, is that William Maxwell, sooner or later, had friends among the leaders of the French Legislative Assembly instituted in 1791 and had access to the most influential Jacobins of 1792, access which helped gain him his place among British sympathizers as it resulted in ever more responsible instructions and missions.

From the first, William must have been made to realize that he could best serve the French revolutionists by working for them in Great Britain. When his presence was required across the Channel, it was all too easy for him to lose himself among fellow Britons flocking to France for the grandstand view. Once he had new directions, he would return to London. Contacts at Dover and Harwich, Calais and Nantes became as familiar to him as the routes he had by heart. Nobody shared more of his confidences at this time than Dr George Edwards.[22] He, too, had studied medicine at Edinburgh; but, unlike William, he had a practice in London to neglect as he made time to address British citizens on the regeneration of their country and French citizens on their new constitution and unfolding promises of prosperity and good fortune. Such writings, however, were attracting not much more attention than it takes to conjecture that an author's sanity is imperfect. Now openly with Edwards or now secretly and alone, William was shuttling between London and Paris by the time of the second anniversary of the fall of the Bastille.

On the day of that anniversary, whatever the stability in Great Britain to meet increasingly strident cries for reform, it was not of the throne; for this was the day of George the Third's getting out of his carriage in Windsor Great Park and greeting an oak tree as the King of Prussia. Looking behind the throne, that 'Immortal Boy' William Pitt, his Secretary of State for the Home Department Henry Dundas, and his Foreign Secretary William Grenville saw nothing to bolster confidence: only six princesses a-row all dressed alike and six princes a-row over-shadowed by their brother George, heir apparent. Amoral, the Prince of Wales lived insolvent despite the fact that he would do anything for money, short of marrying.

Prime Minister Pitt had graver trials than the King's insanity and the Prince of Wales's £400,000 indebtedness. He faced squarely Roman Catholic appeals for extended relief by getting behind the English Act, which was tantamount to the law's permission for Catholics to exist; and he met each wave of emigration from France without losing his balance. Pitt's sorest tests by far came from that democratic ferment which was working over the shires where Paine's doctrines had become passwords not only of the worker at the loom but even of the soldier in the barracks. Popular reform organizations were mushrooming. M.P.s like Horne Tooke and William Wilberforce were moving bills that radically opposed tradition as many an enthusiast such as Helen Maria Williams left for Paris 'with hot unutterabilities' in the heart like 'a pilgrim towards a miraculous shrine' and came back convinced that the new French federation was 'perhaps the finest spectacle the world had ever witnessed'.[23] As ominous as such extravagance was the rising incidence of political incitement to violence: to demolish a house or set it on fire; to bury persons in ruins, their legs burnt off and their pockets loaded with liquor; to interrogate fellow Methodists with 'Query VII: Does not both reason and revelation teach us that in order to lay the axe to the *root* of the tree of wickedness we must begin with Kings and Princes, and Bishops and Priests?'[24]

Outside London as well as inside, Pitt saw what he could fear. At Birmingham ninety gentlemen met on 14 July 1791 to commemorate the French Revolution, while a mob in the streets cried, 'Church and King.'[25] The same mob burned down Priestley's home because he had propounded theories of parliamentary reform; and the intelligence report from Birmingham to Pitt for 17 July boasted, 'D.͏ʳ Priestley, a wicked fellow with no Religion at all, is decamped, he must come here no more, he would be torn to pieces — he was talking a long while to

Chew the Church up, but Swift Destruction came upon his House and Meetings.'[26] On the day that he learned some Birmingham houses bore in chalk 'damn old Priestley', Pitt turned from ordering dragoons for Dumfries and Edinburgh Castle to requesting 'a survey of quarters of Troops at Birmingham'.

Friends of Priestley in Liverpool were quick to decry his persecution. William Roscoe held that such action was part of 'a conspiracy against Liberty' at a time 'When the welfare of Millions is hung in the scale'.[27] Dr James Currie, another Merseyside 'fraterniser with French republicans' and 'strong democrat', reminded Priestley that because 'truth has nothing to fear from the severest discussion, [you should] go on then in your career of exertions fearless of consequences'.[28] In Manchester Thomas Cooper and James Watt associated with the cotton merchant Thomas Walker to advance the Constitutional Society; in Sheffield a similar society started by 'five or six mechanicks' enrolled new members who would number 2,500. Inland informers reported to Pitt incidents of rioters' burning barns and breaking into jails to liberate prisoners; at seaports like Ipswich and Newcastle other persons noted a rebelliousness of sailors that could induce mutiny.[29]

Dundas was unable to give the Prime Minister more encouraging word about North Britain; for, as Dr Currie was writing to a son of Dr John Moore, 'I hear there is a wonderful change in Scotland.'[30] Currie might have cited the trees of liberty planted at Dundee, Stirling, Glasgow, and Edinburgh; the *Vindiciae Gallicae* of James Mackintosh; Captain Wilson's offer of 'a seven-barrelled gun' to the French Jacobins or Professor John Anderson's offer of 'a cannon the recoil of which was stopped by the condensation of common air within the body of the carriage'; the rapture of Thomas Christie of Montrose with the Revolution; or the attendance by Bishop Geddes at a meeting of the National Assembly.[31] William Pitt knew every bit of this and more: that Dr Robert Watson, ex-secretary to Lord George Gordon, was active in forming new corresponding societies; that the brothers John and Benjamin Sword were at the periphery of a solid core of Glasgow radicals; that the burgesses of Lochmaben near Dumfries had protested their exclusion from the burgh council through force and violence, bribery and corruption, by unanimously electing to parliament John McMurdo as 'a Man fearing God, of the true Protestant Religion'.[32] And Pitt was wide awake to the fact that Scottish nobles were diverting themselves with such pettiness as the Duke of Buccleuch's fuming lest he be not at Dumfries as 'Steward of the Races there', while other Scotsmen like

William Maxwell of Kirkconnell were in London boding no good for the Government.[33]

If William Pitt required further evidence of King George's failure to retain sanity, he was offered it at the opening of parliament in January 1792. The state of the nation was very bright, George told both houses; the era was one of 'tranquillity'. Anybody else knew better; for, as the king spoke, a whirlwind was blowing all over Europe; this wild storm would gather in intensity throughout the year and not wear itself out until after Britain had declared war on France. The clouds billowed in March when France declared war upon Francis II, King of Bohemia and Hungary, at his succession after Leopold II. Other European monarchies seized this moment as auspicious for stamping out French republicanism lest it topple one throne after another; thus, they formed behind Charles-William-Ferdinand, the Duke of Brunswick and Lünebourgh, who would lead into battle their forces as well as his own Prussian army. In July, at Coblentz, Brunswick published his famous manifesto that he would march by way of Lorraine to Paris, where he would bring that capital to its knees through famine. Britain would aid the royalist army with money, supplies, and some troops because, as Burke pointed out, 'The Duke of Brunswick is as much fighting the Battle of the Crown of England as the Duke of Cumberland did at Culloden.'[34]

Threatened invasion carried France into the extreme phase of the Revolution. Jacobins put themselves into power on 10 August with the Legislative Assembly's metamorphosis into the Convention that would abolish the monarchy and proclaim the republic. Jacobin seizure of control was lit by frenzied burnings. Incredibly, the new government raised an army of citizens under Dumouriez to march against Brunswick; even more incredibly, this hodgepodge of tricolor sashes won victory at Valmy and put Brunswick into full retreat even as mobs erected guillotines of oak and iron for the September Massacres, 'fulginous as Lapland witch-midnight'. The same guillotines filled tumbrils with stripped corpses of aristocrats and priests. Stunningly, Brunswick suffered further defeat at Jemappes in November and General Dumouriez captured Brussels.

In fact, George the Third's year of tranquillity mirrored the tumult of France. Early months of 1792 saw the strengthening of political reform associations from London and Manchester to Hawick and Dumfries. February gave these radical groups their bible, Paine's *Rights of Man*; April began the Society of Friends of the People; May brought bread and meal riots, a dock strike in Liverpool, a collier strike in Wigan, and Pitt's rolling up his sleeves.

The Prime Minister directed that funds be appropriated to speed up building of new barracks (£5,000 for Birmingham, £7,900 for Manchester); he added troops to garrison such stations; he advised the Throne to proclaim suppression of seditious writings that excited discontent, tumult, and disorder; and he advised parliament to indict Tom Paine. Still, rioting continued. Leicester had three days of meat riots driving butchers from their stalls, and Leeds in apprehension of riots demanded troops.[35] In June a second gagging bill, this time for libel, passed the House of Lords. On 15 July the King commended Henry Dundas for 'yesterday's perfect tranquillity . . . the conduct of both the landed property and the bulk of the nation shews that solid good sense on the present occasion that makes one proud of one's countrymen as well as of our Glorious Constitution.'[36] A day later the Government ordered additional troops to Birmingham. The last day of July lengthened the list of disaffected and seditious persons with the names of 'Koppe, a Shoemaker', several Methodist preachers in Wales, and 'Dr Beddoes, near Derby'.[37] During August George III seems to have been more concerned for the safety of the French royal family and Horace Walpole more concerned for 'the French Queen's women . . . butchered in the Tuileries'[38] than either of those gentlemen was concerned for the Glasgow resolution 'That the Sovereignty of every nation ought to be vested in the People' or the Manchester flyer 'To the Affrighted Nobles of the Land' which harangued, 'The laws, instead of protecting the weak against the oppression of the strong, are become so perverted that they are the scourge of both rich and poor'; or the Perth Society member's affirmation, 'It is a maxim of mine . . . that a King should be sacrificed to the nation, once in a hundred years.'[39]

Doubts that Pitt could control threats of 'diabolical phrenzy, contagion, fatal conspiracy, preachers of regicide, and seditious doctrines' entered the minds of many Britons throughout the month of September 1792.[40] The fearful spoke of daggers and incendiary torches which threatened whoever dared avow himself attached to lawful authority. The *Sun* wrote of Scots Jacobins 'endeavouring to execute a spirit of sedition';[41] the Government gathered transports at Leith to carry troops to Holland and exported four hundred thousand bushels of wheat for use of the combined armies; and the Earl of Westmorland wrote King George, 'Your Majesty may be assured that I shall pay the strictest attention to your commands, shall watch with the greatest vigilance the machinations of every description of person, who have designs inimical to the peace and happy constitution of your Majesty's Kingdom.'[42]

Rumors of Pitt's resignation ran rampant during the months of October and November. At Covent Garden Jacobins hissed 'God Save the King', and at Whitehall the Attorney General preferred seven bills of indictment for libel against publishers as the Army cashiered Lord Edward Fitzgerald for having attended a Paris dinner at which he participated in a toast to the abolition of hereditary titles. In Dundee Henry Dundas was burned in effigy. In Dumfriesshire Sir William Maxwell of Springkell wrote of how he had tried to quiet Scots peasants roused by 'emissaries of sedition': 'I have . . . desired it to be imprest on their minds that the French who were formerly Papists are now absolute Infidels, Ruffians, and Marauders and have no other object in view than to render all the rest of the World as wicked as themselves by abolishing Christianity and every other Religion.' Thomas Milbank of Dundee had just such a person as Sir William in mind when he addressed Dundas ironically: 'I am delighted when the Lords and Lairds come forward *to recommend the Scriptures*. This is indeed a *Revolution*. Nine-tenths of them are infidels.'[43]

Having weathered the storms of October and November, Pitt turned in December to Dundas's warning that the poisonous rage for ideal liberty could not be crushed 'without coercive measures'.[44] Quickly, orders went out to stop and search all mail coaches and other vehicles for traitors, to place the Bank under heavy guard, to strike from the Army List the name of Colonel Dalrymple, President of the Glasgow Association, to arrest Frost, to prepare the Tower 'for the defence of this country', and to augment the army. These measures notwithstanding, Lord Daer, as 'Citizen President', conducted at Edinburgh a meeting of the Scottish reform societies; citizens of Manchester rioted and so did those in Cambridge. Such government declarations as a state of emergency, 15 December, and martial law, 18 December, were interpreted by dissenters as having that ulterior motive of the *Iolanthe*-like poem 'National Alarm':

> There can be no harm in giving alarm,
> And scaring the people with strange apprehensions;
> By brewing this storm, we avoid a Reform,
> And securely enjoy all our places and pensions.[45]

But the Government was not feinting, rather it was preparing to receive the blow of war. On 19 December Lord Grenville introduced his 'Alien Act' that would require strict surveillance of immigrants, 'safe' areas, and passports. The House of Lords voted this act on the twenty-eighth as the House of Commons sat rapt by Edmund Burke's 'Dagger Speech' which pointed at William Maxwell of Kirkconnell. By then, however, William had fled London under warrant for arrest.

'*Dagger*' *Maxwell, warrant, flight* are episodes in William Maxwell's history for August through November 1792, but not the only wild ones for that period of escapade. The complete fiasco of Thionville, which opened Brunswick's campaign in France, signalled William's most daring deeds in the cause of the Revolution. His ultimate object was to guarantee Liberty, Fraternity, and Equality for every Frenchman by making it possible for him to defend both himself and those rights as a soldier under Dumouriez. To fight meant to arm. But where were the arms? And where the money to pay for them? And where the time? One must understand that in advancing the immediate object of furnishing the French citizens with arms as well as actually procuring the weapons themselves, William steadfastly believed himself an honorable British subject. No law forbade such activities; therefore, as a free Scotsman, he was restricted only by the bounds of his conscience. Of course, William was not so naive as to think that a statutory declaration of war would not wash out the ground from under his feet. A risk and a gamble? Yes. Treason? No. Sedition? Yes and no.

Looking back, one is led to surmise that William's determination to carry through his purpose of aiding the French people never came more close to being shaken than in June 1792. For it was then that his younger brother prematurely died. Whether William arrived at Kirkconnell to be with Tom before death is uncertain; but he did attend the funeral and was present to see his brother's body lowered into a grave dug close to that of their grandfather William at Sweetheart Abbey.[46] Such a time would have left William weak to the dissuasion of Mary and James, to the cautions of other relatives and close friends of the family; nevertheless, his convictions held firm. What appears to be true is that Tom's death doubled and redoubled the mother's and the elder brother's love for and patience with William, whereas it prompted William to get away from Kirkconnell just as soon as was meet, lest his own love prove stronger than his pledge.

A rush of events tended to dull grief. Brunswick's July manifesto set in motion those loose French plans made for such emergency; so

William went back to London and then over to France. By late August he was closeted with Joseph Servan, who, only days before, had received the portfolio of war from the National Assembly.[47] Out of the meeting came the decision that William would return to Britain, where he would set about immediately ordering carbines to be used against the invaders of France. At best, Servan was vague as to how these weapons were to be paid for; what seems probable is that William was left with the understanding that he would have to solicit sympathizers for funds as well as place orders and oversee delivery.

Even though laws did not prohibit such designs, William was entering perilous fields. Already foreign riffraff infested London seeking to line pockets at every opportunity. The Italian Rotondo, who had been whipped, branded, and turned out of Paris, was about Westminster propagating maxims of a revolted people; so were Pialas of sunken eyes and pocketed cheeks and Cervantes 'large and lusty', 'with striped stockings'; 'A very fair Child of eight years old always is with him.'[48] The Government had had these men closely shadowed from the minute they had disembarked at Dover; for Pitt's spy system was both extensive and effective. Throughout England such non-professional agents as the vicars of the Anglican Church reported whatever appeared suspicious, while professional agents remained spotted at strategic places, even among the troops and tars. Other informers patrolled the countryside on a per diem salary of 5s and an allowance for two saddle horses at 10s.[49] Intelligence reports from the field came to the desk of Under-Secretary Evan Nepean at the Home Office. Nepean served fearlessly, not hesitating to send sheriffs against even such an august personage as the Earl of Glencairn; his right-hand, his troubleshooter, was 'Col. DeLancey'. William Maxwell was soon aware of his coming under the surveillance of those directly under DeLancey.

Following Servan's request, the doctor had hastened back to London with tocsins ringing in his ears. The French Assembly had decreed that every citizen who should refuse to deliver up his arms or to march would be declared 'infamous and a traitor to his country'. Hordes of volunteers waited for arms despite the day-in, day-out effort of casting them from the metal of church bells, coffins, and other objects that had been seized and melted down. Indeed, so overwhelming was the citizen response that Servan had to warn the people not to quit their habitations in order to join the armies, but to remain where they were until they could be armed, either by his care or their own. 'I hope,' Servan addressed them, 'the moment is not far distant, when I shall have it in my power to put you in a condition to join your brethren in arms, to attack and vanquish the enemies of Liberty and Equality!'[50]

But the French citizens would not wait. Some arrived at Dumouriez' outposts with nothing more than the corn, forage, straw, cattle, or horses they could confiscate; others had a musket; and if not a musket, then a pike; and if not a pike, then a hatchet or a dagger. Knowing these urgencies, William went into action.

First things being first, William wrote an announcement for publication by London newspapers on Friday, 7 September, in which he requested that friends of France meet at his house in Great Portland Street at 2 p.m., 12 September, to consider ways by which they might better serve the cause of liberty.[51] The one way most clearly fixed in William's mind was subscription of money for purchase of arms. On the day that this advertisement appeared, he was at his writing desk again to inform his brother James fairly of the die cast:

> You shall hear my name frequently mentioned from the part I have taken in French Affairs. You have frequently heard me express my intention that if the cause of Liberty should come to the decision of the sword I should think myself obliged to take part looking upon Justice to be inseparable from Liberty, and being fully convinced that the happiness of Mankind depends upon the fate of this [?war]; I think myself as much obliged to take a part in it, as to procure Justice to the oppressed in the most flagrant case. I wish much to see you that we may arrange money matters, I will meet you either at York, Derby, or Manchester.[52]

For such news, William's father would have been able to summon more understanding than the brother James. But James had clear understanding of what lay behind William's request for their meeting: his younger brother was determined to put his money where his mouth was, to contribute every shilling he could command by way of advancing the subscription he had publicly proposed.

William had left himself all but too little time for his next step: inquiries about arms procurement. In his deposition given at the Hotel Vauban, Paris, 9 November 1792, he stated that at his interview with Servan he had undertaken to arm some men with carbines, but that when he had travelled to Birmingham he had, instead, contracted for two to three thousand daggers [*dards*] at a price of a guinea a dozen, seven hundred of which were to be furnished with scabbards.[53] His introduction of daggers into the scheme appears to have been made independently upon realization of just what a number of carbines would cost and after listening to Americans in Paris boasting of just what damage could be inflicted by a long knife in the hands of an expert. By September 1792, in fact, the dagger had become an all too familiar sight and symbol. Combatants at Culloden having proved the bayonet to be the queen of weapons and the American woodsman having demonstrated the deadliness of the sheath knife, others had been quick to learn. The Home Office was hearing almost daily reports such as the passing from Harwich to London of large posses of Frenchmen 'armed with daggers' or of 'Twenty five Marseillois sent over to this Country armed with daggers for the purpose of assassinating and cutting off any obnoxious characters.' 'Naples Bravoes' could be seen in London streets, 'each with a dirk in his right-hand, a muff on his left'.[54] Lyons Jacobins were being harangued by a mayor-aspirant with a drawn dagger in his hand, and the Girondin 'Megaeras' were about to exchange distaff for dagger. This was the day of Walpole's writing Hannah Moore, '. . . the black and bloody year 1792 has plunged its murderous dagger still deeper.'[55]

On the Saturday or Sunday following the *London Chronicle's* carrying his advertisement, William travelled to Birmingham so as to begin negotiating for daggers and carbines bright and early Monday morning, 10 September.[56] His approach was perversely by way of his brother James to David Blair, a Scotsman well known about Dumfries as 'a violent Leveler' who had given his name to the gunmaking firm of Blair & Lea, Navigation Street, Birmingham. Blair took William round to James Woolley, manufacturer of all kinds of swords, sword-hilts, bayonets, ramrods, matchets, and daggers. Woolley recalls their meeting in his confession to the Home Office dated 16 January 1793. Maxwell had described a pattern for a dagger of which he wished to treat for a quantity of not less than '20,000'. They were to be delivered weekly and paid for as they were delivered. The weapon was to be about twelve inches in the blade with a common wood handle for cheapness. Woolley later swore that he had told the doctor that he could not furnish such a quantity and that the doctor had then taken his leave after promising to return that afternoon at two o'clock.

Knowing that Maxwell would be obliged to call upon Samuel Dawes and Thomas Gill, the only other Birmingham manufacturers who could make these daggers, Woolley anticipated those visits by getting in touch with Dawes, agreeing with him on the price they should ask, and urging him to contact Gill so as to have his concurrence. Maxwell discovered their price-fixing on his afternoon rounds. It was then, too, that he took time to answer questions that had arisen in Woolley's mind. Did the pattern hurriedly fashioned by Woolley's people represent what he had in mind? Yes, it did. Would two thousand a week meet his needs? No, they would not. Why must the daggers be so sharp? They were intended to face and resist a body of horse. At this point, Woolley contended that he had grown so suspicious, that the purpose now appeared so absurd and improbable, he had cooled off and decided not to make these weapons and not to wait upon Maxwell again. William, the meanwhile, had gone on to Gill and Dawes, then back to Gill in the late afternoon, to place an order that was 'to be gone on with as fast as possible'. He then returned feverishly to London.

On Tuesday morning Woolley awakened so befuddled that he sought out Blair, from whom he learned that Blair himself had been a stranger to Doctor Maxwell, but that 'he well knew a brother of his', that William had been well recommended, and that he had wanted Blair to sell him '50 rifle Barrel' and to suggest those persons who might make the daggers.

Gill's self-defense, published in *Aris's Birmingham Gazette* for 29 October 1792, differs from Woolley's substantially.[57] The terms that the three manufacturers agreed upon were 22s per dozen for the daggers, 12s per dozen for the boarding spikes, a 5% discount for cash on the barrel, and no alteration without mutual consultation. Gill would have it that William had been unhappy with both Woolley and Dawes so that he had elected to give Gill all his business. Before returning to London on the evening of the tenth, William had placed an order for four thousand daggers with Gill and had promised that when he came back to Birmingham in a week, he would have an order for twenty thousand more.

The day of Birmingham vexation, trouble, and disillusionment was only the beginning of William's distress. Tuesday in London sharpened it as he became aware that the city was buzzing with words about the next day's meeting. Since Friday's announcement, an opposition had had time to make its displeasure apparent. William's subscription for the new France would be colliding head-on with another subscription endorsed by the British Government to benefit an element of the old France.[58] Since 10 August, fugitives who had been ruthlessly rooted out by the very ones whom William sought to aid had been arriving thick and fast all along the coasts of Kent and Sussex: a baron with his money stowed away in the ballast, a duke who had concealed himself under faggots aboard a deckless ship, a bishop of eighty years off a fishing vessel.[59] But it was the misery and distress of particularly the French clergy that were to be alleviated by a country-wide subscription. British leaders had anticipated possible reluctance of Protestants asked to succor Roman Catholics with such notices as the following: 'It is constantly hoped that a difference in religious persuasion, or political opinion, will not shut the hearts of the English nation against their suffering brethren, their fellow-creatures, and their fellow Christians.'[60] British Catholics were helping to allay fears by tracing to the ground any wild rumor insinuating invidious intent. Those in Wexford thus advertised in their local paper, 'The Roman Catholics of the Town of Wexford being informed, from unquestionable authority, that a man passed through the streets of the aforesaid town . . . warning and foretelling that "Protestant throats would be cut from ear to ear." If the before mentioned man is not insane, they offer a reward of twenty guineas to any person who shall prosecute him to conviction for the said heinous offence against the statute 5 Eliz. c. 15.'[61]

Edmund Burke, whose mother was a Roman Catholic, was not without reservations of his own with respect to the subscription; he saw inherent dangers to food supply and employment as well as larger issues like religion and the Revolution. Henry Dundas offered his reassurance by pointing out that the Government was 'not indisposed to the plan of Subscription' and that the King had promised his house at Winchester for the French clergy;[62] so Burke accepted membership on the Committee for the Relief of the French Clergy, arguing in a reply to Dundas that such acceptance was politic as well as charitable.[63] These priests had escaped 'from the most barbarous system of assassination ever known', they had been 'forcibly expelled from their Country by the unjust decree of an usurped power', to help them would be to counteract 'the wicked industry of the Jacobin Papers who attempt to excite the common people here to imitate those in France'. 'But perhaps,' Burke continued to Dundas, 'the temper of the common people may be best seen in the event of the late advertisement by Dr Maxwell for the support of the Jacobins, and the maintaining of a war against the allies of this country, the Emperor and the King of Prussia; whom he had at the same time the insolence to revile in the coarsest language [? a reference to William's *the present impudent combination of Despots against the Rights of Human Nature*].' Burke could not have been writing before the results of William Maxwell's meeting of 12 September.

The various accounts of this meeting show some agreement: before the time appointed, a 'Colonel Glover' intimidated William; and those ill-disposed persons who had infiltrated the otherwise friendly gathering of prospective subscribers made their presence known to him through insult and threat; William left; Horne Tooke arrived and, having taken in the scene at a glance, led the wavering subscribers to his own home in Soho Square, where he conducted a meeting and opened the subscription.

That is the air; its variations are as many as they are embellished. As sympathetic as most is the one sent from London to Paris for *Le Moniteur Universel* of Tuesday, 25 September:

> From London:— Doctor Maxwell had inserted in several newspapers an invitation to friends of the French Revolution to meet on the twelfth at 2:00 P. M. in his lodgings, rue Porstand [sic], to consult about ways of serving the cause of Liberty. A bully named Glover, in no way related to that esteemed Glover, author of the beautiful poem Leonidas, but the colonel known to have continued a lawsuit against the celebrated Duchess of Kingston, determined to break up the assembly; he went to Doctor Maxwell's home at 8:00 A. M. on the same day and so menaced the doctor that he managed to intimidate him and get his promise to absent himself and to remove his doorplate. Those many patriots who arrived became confused without this guidemark. The famous Horne-Tooke had taken it upon himself to go to Maxwell's where he saw a large, riotous assemblage. On opening the door, he saw the colonel who had been able to frighten such a revolutionary as Doctor Maxwell. The colonel, however, lost out in the end; he was obliged to save his own skin, and the crowd was dispersed. Horne-Tooke led those interested in the subscription for providing the French with arms to his own house in Soho Square. That subscription has now taken place and has resulted in a large order placed at Birmingham.

No account more sullied William's name than that presented before the National Assembly presided over by Petion, Sunday, 30 September.[64] The speaker was 'the mad Colonel Oswald', a Scotsman turned vegetarian after a tour of duty in India, a confirmed atheist who was for putting to death every suspected man in France, a commandant of pikemen to whom Paine remarked, 'Oswald, you have lived so long without tasting flesh that you now have a most voracious appetite for blood.'[65]

Oswald lost no time in swelling to his pleasure of vilifying. Glover was 'an abject servant' bent upon suing the Duchess of Kingston, celebrated pervert (*fameuse tribade*) of Marie Antoinette. Maxwell, on the other hand was an honorable patriot; but he simply did not have courage equal to the occasion. Glover, in the name of the King, his exalted master, had told Maxwell, 'You have invited a mob to your home for the purpose of arming notorious regicides, Jacobins; but I warn you that if you go ahead with your meeting, I'll burn down your house; and if you don't get the hell out of here immediately, I'll cut off your nose and your ears.' Maxwell — Oswald has to admit — did not fall for Glover's threats, but went ahead with his meeting. When, however, he saw the gang of hired thugs intent upon repeating the scene at Birmingham, he fled. Many of the informers in the crowd were rebellious priests and emigrant nobles who now infected England much as locusts once poisoned Egypt. Finally, Oswald had welcome news for the Assembly: the subscription had got off to a good start and was increasing daily, thanks chiefly to Horne Tooke, a true-blue Jacobin not to be shaken by intimidation or unmanned by sweets of the Civil List. Oswald's report, all together, seems more accurate with respect to the Revolution's capacity to inflame passion than to state fact.

William rather simply had not reckoned on a mob that promised to make his family's every fear a reality. Even as he was choosing discretion as the better part of valor, James was answering his news that he proposed taking a part in French affairs. This letter speaks of James's sorrow, of 'much hurt' given Mary 'particularly after our late loss', of fearing the worst consequences because William was throwing himself entirely out of the professional line in which he had every reasonable prospect of success. James then turns to the subject of money: Mary will not advance any nor will he, for giving William money at this time would be too much like endowing 'the Club des Jacobins whose proceedings are now reprobated by many of the warmest friends of the original French Revolution'; Tom's estate was tied up, Mr Taylor having two years to refund Mary what she had advanced her youngest son. James concluded with advice against William's plans, '. . . listen to your real Friends and sincere wellwishers, and consider maturely every point before you join a Party which seems now so much condemned for its brutality.'[66]

William's short reply to James shows that his own experience in having witnessed such brutality surface had not driven him from the field:

From some articles in newspapers you may perhaps have been a little alarmed for my safety. — I am as usual tranquil and happy in Portland

Street — Everything has been done to frustrate my intention of meeting my friends in Portland Street, and from the well grounded apprehensions that a plot was laid, I was obliged to put off the meeting of friends to liberty.[67]

That William was not quite so calm and collected as his understatement implies becomes apparent in his own account of just what had happened on the twelfth, an account published in the *Morning Post* for Monday, 17 September, between the announcement that the farce *Katharine and Petruchio* was playing at the King's and a report of the meeting in favor of French exiles held on the twelfth as William's competition. Because this letter to the editor of some two thousand words is the fullest extant statement of William Maxwell's principles as well as his view of the proceedings, it merits careful reading. William begins:

When the character of an individual has been wantonly attacked, and, when, in gross violation of every principle of justice, an attempt has been made to overawe him in the exercise of his rights as a citizen, a regard to truth, and, a decent respect to the opinions of mankind, require that he should vindicate the conduct which he has pursued.

Unfortunately for Englishmen, we live at a period, when mobs are excited by those very persons who are themselves the first to clamour against sedition, when law itself affords no protection, or, what is still worse, when it is perverted to purposes destructive of the end for which it was originally framed.

After speaking in some detail on *faction*, William turns to the subject of France: '. . . even the most hardy Defender of Despotism will not dare to deny, that during the course of one hundred and fifty years, France groaned under a rigourous and unremitting tyranny,' the Court of Versailles oppressed the liberties of all Europe, but 'the period was to arrive, which was to free France from the fetters which had been imposed upon her, and to convert a great and respectable Nation from a restless and formidable enemy into a peaceful neighbour, and, perhaps, a useful friend.' The Fourteenth of July had driven away 'a herd of vermin Courtiers fattened upon the industry of people'. The new France's affirmation that the only solid basis for government was the broad basis of popular confidence had been answered with German and Prussian tyranny and Louis' attempt to take refuge among enemies:

Such was ONCE, and such is *now* the situation of France. — It may then be demanded of me, what was the object of the Meeting which I proposed? The question is a fair one, and I will answer it with that plainness and confidence which truth inspires.

I have held it my duty as a Member of Society, (as far as lay within the circle of my abilities) to defend the rights of human nature when unjustly attacked, and to succour the victims of oppression. — I am at liberty, I suppose, equally with every other man, to hold my own opinions; and if my actions, conformable to those opinions, do not violate the laws of my country, to pursue that system of conduct which appears to me to be the best. As I never yet heard any reason which could justify the armed slaves of foreign tyrants to interfere in the interior regulations of another country, and as there exists no law which prevents the subject of this country from affording assistance to the subjects of another country, provided they are not in a state of actual war with that country, I felt myself justified in the measures which I had undertaken.

The money raised was to have been transmitted to the Executive Government of France (who, from the support which they receive, appear to possess the full confidence of the People,) to be employed by them for the national benefit, as their wisdom should direct.

It was not, as has been falsely and audaciously asserted 'to assist the ruffian mob of Paris.'

. . . .

ALL VIOLATIONS OF LAW, WHETHER MANIFESTED BY THE MASSACRE OF IMPRISONED FRENCHMEN, OR BY MINISTERIAL MORES, HIRED TO PREVENT FREE DISCUSSION AND BENEVOLENT PURPOSES, I EQUALLY REPROBATE AND DETEST.

All revolutions, William continues, have occasional outrages; but the important thing to bear in mind is the general principle behind any revolution, which in the case of France is a good one:

I now calmly ask those who blame the Meeting proposed, upon what principle they condemn it. Is it the Object? The object is to succour the distressed.

. . . .

The Laws of my Country, not the Opinions of Individuals, are to regulate my conduct; and I now dare the most corrupt hireling, either in or out of the Profession, to prove the illegality of the Meeting which I proposed.

In the past, William points out, no fuss had been made when Britons were asked to aid Corsicans or when they were asked, only a few weeks before, to help oppressed Poles:

F

By what rule of Logic, then, or principle of ethics, I would ask, is it more criminal to subscribe for a Frenchman, than for a Corsican or Pole? The duties of man are general, as well as particular, Benevolence is of no country, but embraces in the wide circle of her arms, from Lake Huron to the walls of China, the brotherhood of the human race.

Why, then, William asks, did he abandon the meeting? He had sought to promote a subscription, legally and peaceably; his object had been either misunderstood or wickedly misrepresented. So a mob had been raised about his house before the meeting was to start, and it had been given 'strong indications' that it would disturb the peace by such acts as destroying his house:

> Desirous as I was not to disturb the public tranquillity, but to preserve it, I suspended the just exercise of my rights as a Citizen, and abandoned my habitation, which the law emphatically states our CASTLE, but which now, it seems is no longer to be regarded as a Sanctuary for Englishmen. I speak from indisputable authority, that there exists persons in this Metropolis, who degrade the character of Gentlemen by assuming it, and who openly asserted, that they would lead on the mob, and involve in one undistinguishing massacre all those who should be present at the Meeting which I proposed. The Riots of Birmingham were too fresh in my memory to provoke a repetition of those horrid outrages. — I, therefore, silently withdrew, and acted upon this, as I trust I shall do upon every similar occasion, in a manner calculated to promote the good, without disturbing the Peace of Mankind.

Before concluding, William reports that the subscription is going along well. Then the end of his letter:

> I have now proved the consistency of my conduct, as I have never abandoned the object which I proposed; and I have also cleared it from the imputation of sedition, by sacrificing my own rights, in order to pre-serve the Public Peace, to the extreme disappointment of those who sought to disturb it.
>
> As an Individual my Sentiments may be of little importance, yet I enter-tain none which I should be ashamed to avow in the face of the world. — I lament the evils and condemn the excesses which invariably attend the great revolutions among mankind; but I sincerely rejoice, that twenty millions of my fellow creatures, bursting from the gloomy caverns of Despotism, have broken the bonds of Slavery asunder, have assumed their proper rank among the nations of the earth, and vindicated the Rights of Nature and Society.
>
> WM. MAXWELL
>
> No. 73, Great Portland Street

It is true that William walks a very thin line between disclosing that the subscription money is to go to the French Government and concealing that, as a representative of the same government, he had just got back from Birmingham where he had ordered arms to be paid for, apparently at least in part, with the very same money. Otherwise, his *apologia* rings true. However else the likes of Glover and Oswald would have it, William Maxwell was every bit as idealistic, as honorable, and, yes, as courageous as his father.

William himself did not press on as a leading proponent of the subscription in aid of French liberty. Others did, more or less spasmodically, so that two months later somewhat less than £800 had been collected to be returned ultimately to the various subscribers. In roughly the same time, Edmund Burke and his committee took in more than £20,000 for relief of the French clergy.[68] William remained in London to read his letter in Monday morning's *Post*. That same week saw the beginning of the bombardment of Thionville as hop-picking went on briskly in Kent and Surrey; the reviling and stoning of Tom Paine at Dover as 'his Majesty did not walk' at Weymouth, but the princesses did bathe in their machine; the inundation of the plain of Sedan to impede the invaders as a Romish Chapel in London raised £100 at eight masses for the emigrants; and the defeat of Brunswick at Valmy as Ostend published the first lists of those clergy who had been murdered in the convent of the bare-footed Carmelites in Paris.[69]

William's contentment to let others take full responsibility for the subscription seems to indicate that somebody with the authority of Horne Tooke had advised him that feelings were running too high to risk spending this fund on Birmingham arms. If he was denied such contributions, William had more reason than ever to see James in order to determine what of his own he could command. So his plan for the rest of the week was to get off another letter to James by way of explaining himself and then check Gill's progress in Birmingham before going north to meet his family at York.

FROM ROBERT BURNS —

I have much to tell you of 'hair-breadth 'scapes in th' imminent breach'

— To John Murdoch

Oft have I wonder'd that on Irish ground
No poisonous Reptile has ever been found:
Revealed stands the secret of great Nature's work:
She preserv'd her poison to create a Burke!

— 'On Edmund Burke'

I have, literally like that great Poet and great Gallant, and by consequence,
that great Fool Solomon, — 'Turned my eyes to behold Madness and Folly.'

— First Commonplace Book

O, why the deuce should I repine,
And be an ill forboder?
I'm twenty-three and five feet nine,
I'll go and be a sodger.

— 'I'll go and be a sodger'

—FROM ROBERT BURNS

And even children lisp the Rights of Man

— 'The Rights of Woman'

I imagine that the time is not far distant when a man may freely blame Billy Pitt, without being called an enemy to his Country.

— To Mrs Dunlop

The injured Stewart line is gone,
A race outlandish fills their throne:
An idiot race, to honour lost —
Who know them best despise them most.

— 'On Seeing the Royal Palace at Stirling'

The Merry are . . . the jovial lads who have too much fire & spirit to have any settled rule of action; but without much deliberation, follow the strong impulses of nature.   — First Commonplace Book

CHAPTER FOUR

Tending Fast

The licht nae man has ever seen
Till he has felt that he's been gi'en
The stars themsels instead o' een.

— Hugh MacDiarmid

Mary Maxwell, who had not heard from William since Tom's burial, had her hands full accounting to relatives for her misguided son's behavior. She tended to get the subject out of her mind or, at least, to the back of it as in the instance of replying to Alexander Maxwell's queries from London: 'I hope you will not pay the least attention to the Don Quixot [sic] appearances my Son William has made in the French Politics, I have not heard from him since he left Kirkconnell altho' I have wrote thrice.'[1] William did not expect his mother to understand, but he trusted that his brother would. Patiently, therefore, on the seventeenth of September, he laid himself open to James:

> I was not surprised to find that many of my friends have reprobated my conduct, but feel myself much hurt with the censure of those who are well acquainted with my sentiments. Nothing perhaps could militate more against my Interest than this step appears to do, but I wish you and all those to whom I am attached and whose good opinion I wish to retain would recollect that the part I have taken corresponds with the sentiments and intention I always expressed and which I thought myself bound in duty to follow, and if this be believed by my friends, they can only blame me for my erroneous Judgement.[2]

The latest word from Gill had been that he had stopped employing his entire manufactory in making daggers after word had reached him

of the London mob's action against William.[3] Once in Birmingham,
William reassured Gill by arranging that, for the time at any rate, Blair
would take full responsibility for honoring his orders. Although Gill
went on telling himself that he was 'perfectly at Liberty to make such
Daggers' and that doubtless 'every one of the Manufacturers of Swords
and Daggers of this Place would readily engage to compleat and to
supply' them, being 'not more virtuous' than himself, he had cause for
alarm beyond that of the twelfth. The rector of St Martin's, Birmingham, had taken much pains to dissuade him from proceeding, but
without effect save that Gill promised to send one of the daggers to 'the
loose-tongued placeman' Mr George Rose at the Treasury.[4] Not
satisfied, the Reverend Mr Charles Curtis wrote anonymously to the
Home Office on the Thursday of William's arrival. His warning reads:
'A friend to his Country deems it his Duty to inform his Majesty's
Ministers that D[r]. Maxwell has ordered of Mess[r]. Woolley, Gill, &
Dawes, who have each sword Manufacturies in this Town, great
Quantities of *poignards* of a particular Construction & *pikes* — & it is
difficult to say in what Country the democratic William intends them
to be used.'[5] On the next day, another friend of the Government
informed Nepean of the same orders of pikes and poignards as well as
of a considerable order of rifle barrels, all of which were to be sent to
Maxwell in London.[6] Pitt's interpretation of such news was that an
armed attempt might be made to revolutionize Great Britain and that
the daggers were intended for this kind of conspiracy; somewhat later
he is supposed to have told his ministers that soon they might not have
a hand to act with or a tongue to speak with.[7] Knowing just how
serious the Prime Minister was in regard to such reports as those
coming from Birmingham, Evan Nepean did not have to be cautioned
to maintain strict surveillance over Gill's operations and Maxwell's
every move. The wonder is that Gill dared continue manufacturing
daggers for some time to come, perhaps as many as four thousand of
what was probably a final order of ten thousand.

What the family hoped to accomplish by the York meeting was to
turn William from his engagement in French affairs by withholding
their own money and discouraging him from going into the hotbed that
was Manchester to make Taylor hand over his share of Tom's interest
in the fustian firm. Already Mary had expressed her displeasure by
refusing William £200 he had requested of her, this upon James's word
from York about the state of his brother: 'He has been misled and
hurried by designing persons farther than I think would have been the

case had he given himself time to reflect.'[8] Mary answered James that she had refused William after 'seeing in the public papers the ridiculous imprudent appearance my son William had made in the detestable Politics'; furthermore, she had begged Alexander Maxwell, as a mutual friend in London, not to advance William a farthing, 'but on condition he left London immediately for Scotland (I mean to see me here) where he would meet with every mark of reconciliation on my part, if he meant to divest himself of the worthless connections he had formed &c. You may easily imagine my concern.'[9] On Sunday, the twenty-third, Mary again wrote James as he was awaiting the arrival of William in York. She would continue steady in her resolve not to give her 'unfortunate son duped by a party' the £200:

> My conscience will not allow me to answer any demand for money he may make upon me, and I dare say you will observe the same conduct — Pray God convert his heart and give me a perfect resignation and submission to his holy will. I do not read any newspaper, nor is ever William's name mentioned to me on this occasion. Silence appears to me prudent as it is in all afflictions in God alone we must look for comfort to him.[10]

James had been in York well in advance of William to lay plans for their meeting which would exceed William's wildest imagining. To make his case as convincing as possible, the Laird of Kirkconnell had kept in almost daily contact with his mother, had (it is all but certain) obtained John Menzies' considered opinions, and had relied heavily upon the influence of those at Swinburne Castle. Thomas Riddell had provided the services of his own barrister, Sir John Lawson, and pointed out that Sir John's son, Dr John Lawson, a graduate of the University of Edinburgh medical school in 1784 and a friend of William in London, would be standing by, as would William Withers, barrister-at-law and former city councillor of York.[11] Mary was to remain at Kirkconnell, not to be called upon except as a final resort.

The meeting was not *a* meeting, but several; not only on Monday the twenty-fourth, but also on Tuesday, Wednesday, Thursday, and Friday. The first session brought the two brothers face to face, alone. William did not budge. So James took his brother to the lodgings of Sir John Lawson, where he left William with Sir John and still another supporter of the family view, an unidentified 'M.' Trafford'. Lawson reported to Withers on Wednesday what had gone on at this Monday meeting:

Agreeable to your request I send you the particulars of the meeting held at my lodgings on Monday last.

In consequence of the Violent part which Dᵣ Maxwell has lately taken in the affairs of France, Mᵣ Maxwell of Kirkconnell his elder Bᵣ requested Mᵣ Trafford & myself to speak to the Dᵣ & to represent to him the impropriety not to say folly of the step he was about to take, should he persist in his resolution of entering into the Service of the French nation.

Notwithstanding every argument on our part to prove the folly of such an act both as it regarded his own private Interest, as a professional man & its being universally reprobated by his friends, the Dᵣ was obstinately determined. He told us 'that having embraced these principles from conviction & having pledged his honor to the representatives of the French Nation to serve their cause to the utmost of his abilities, he could not secede with honor which he should always consider dear to him as life.'

The Plans which the Dᵣ had in view in France could not be accomplished without a considerable supply of money, & it was not reasonable to suppose that either Mᵣ Maxwell or any of the Dᵣˢ friends whilst they reprobated his political principles & the step he was about to take, would be very sanguine in assisting him. His Younger Brother Mᵣ Thoˢ Maxwell was lately dead at Manchester the Dᵣ was entitled to part of his effects. The Nature of his deceased Bᵣˢ Commercial engagements were such as to require a Year or more before they could be compleatly settled. To raise money upon a distant tho' certain prospect was not to be done unless at exhorbitant interest. This however the Dᵣ was determined immediately to do, & to obtain it as he expressed 'Either from Jews or Gentiles.' The Dᵣ could not risk his presence at Manchester, where political parties are excessively violent, without probability of exciting a tumult.

Under these considerations, notwithstanding Mᵣ Maxwell highly reprobated the step his Brother was determined to take, it was thought advisable to supply his Bᵣ with a certain sum of Money, both with a view to prevent him otherwise obtaining it at usorious interest & to prevent the disagreeable consequences which might attend a riot in Manchester.¹²

Nothing is more important in this letter than the first inkling we have of what must have been slowly dawning upon William. Even before the fiasco of the twelfth, he must have sorted out the various ways by which he might serve France. The dismal negotiations with the hard-nosed Birmingham arms manufacturers had brought him little satisfaction and much distaste, but it was the appearance of Colonel Glover and the London dregs that had made him see the light. If his warfare was to be against such scum, ever so much more ungentle than those English prisoners who had broken their word to his father after Prestonpans, what honor would be his? William could walk away from Glover because he had his first clear realization of what he would be walking towards: the proffer of his sword, not his pocketbook, to France. Thus he could with equanimity turn over the subscription to Horne Tooke and the arms contracts to Blair. Thus the money which he sought in York was not intended as a down payment on Birmingham daggers, rather as a means of escorting whatever he could of daggers, pikes, and rifle barrels to France, where he would exchange civilian clothes for a uniform. Only such a determination makes sense of the York ado throughout the week of 24 September.

Sir John's letter of Wednesday to Withers with enclosure of the late correspondence among Mary, James, and William was by way of preparing Withers for his Thursday talk with William so as to be able to advise Sir John and the family how to proceed. Withers sent over his recommendation on Friday:

> From the above Extracts which I have examined with the originals, it is clear that the wild enthusiastic schemes of D. Maxwell relative to French Politics have been undertaken by him and are now proceeding contrary to the advice and wishes of his best friends; and it is much to be lamented that he cannot be diverted from them.
>
> It is stated to me that the deceased Brother made no will in writing, but declared in the presence of two witnesses how he would have his personal property disposed of; which declaration was soon afterwards reduced into writing. — I think that such parole declaration, being only made in the presence of two witnesses, cannot be established as a good [*one word*] will under statute of frauds (29 cas 2.c.3.1.19). I therefore conclude that the deceased brother died intestate; on which event his Mother and two surviving Brothers become entitled to the residue of his Personal Effects in equal third parts after full payment of his debts and Funeral Expences.
>
> I apprehend that D. Maxwell could not recover from the Administratix of his late Brother his distributive share of the Effects, until after the expiration of one year from his death; and also after a settlement of the Partnership Accompts with the Surviving Partner. However as M. Maxwell has from very laudable motives, to prevent his Brother running into greater extremities, and probably interrupting the public peace of Manchester promised to advance him some money, I am of opinion he may with great propriety advance D. Maxwell what upon a fair calculation will be nearly the amount of his Third part of the clear surplus of his deceased Brother's Effects; taking a Release for such money and proper stamp.

It appears by one of M.ͬ Maxwell's Letters that he is already in advance
to D.ͬ Maxwell. — If so I should recommend it to him to deduct his own
demand out of the Doctor's distributive share, and thereby reduce the
sum now to be advanced. For I conceive it can neither be deemed true
friendship nor Brotherly Affection to increase his property by any benevolent act at this time, when he is obstinately determined to squander it
away in the most forlorn & desperate expedition.[13]

James's own efforts had proved futile; so he capitulated to William as
he called Mary down from Kirkconnell to York. Hers, the last inter-
cession, on Saturday, appears only as a letter to William enclosed in a
note to James at York and as a copy mailed to William in London,
should he have departed York already. The note to James reads:

Dear Son
I enclose a letter for the Doc[tr] the [?purpose] is requesting if possible to
disentangle himself from his political plan at all rates to wait for some
weeks, when I have little doubt he will see things with such a face as will
convince him how far persons may be mistaken in their politicks the last
papers prove it, if he has left York, read it and burn it for I have sent a
copy of it to him at London by this post. beside your own Affairs I do
think your presence here necessary on acc.ͭ of my Sister's moving. I begg[d]
William to tell you so, this moment she desires me to tell you that she is
very desirous that you were at home I am

D.ͬ Son
Your Affectionate Mother
M Maxwell

if the Doc.ͬ is gone do write to him to the same purpose that I have done.[14]

Mary's letter to William is too full of maternal love, sorrow, pride,
and duty to leave room for her sister Dorothy:

Kirkconnell Sunday 30 Sept 1792
My Dear Son
    Whilst I was with you the hopes that you would change your plan
supported me, god knows they soon fled, three different times before I got
half way home [I] was resolved to return to you. I got home but in all my
life never had such a night. You know how you found me and [I am] now
again in the same situation. You might have perceived how much my
constitution is reduced, if you can disentangle yourself, for God's sake &
mine, do it, and at any rate wait some weeks & turn over impartially all

that has past between us — whilst I breath I will do my Duty to my children — the first duty in [?human] Nature, consider well my Dr William the situation you are going to put yourself in, & the one you have in your power to be in, supported by all your friends (who I find you have given up much of late) what I have in my power you know should not be wanting, [?in] any approved situation I am

My Dear Son

Your affectionate Mother

M: Maxwell[15]

William was departing York as Mary was writing her Sunday pleading. That James had given him £500, his share of their brother Tom's estate, could not have made his journey less lonely. As his coach horses pulled south, Tom Paine was in Paris participating in the National Convention which proclaimed France a republic, the Meuse barges were loaded with ammunition destined for Namur and Dinant, Brunswick was still retreating through the unfriendly countryside of 'armed peasants' wearing rotten shoes and living off their horses. Gill was packing the day's daggers for consignment to Dr Maxwell in London, and the government agent Brook Watson was reporting to the Home Office from Birmingham of '20,000 Daggers ordered' of Dr Maxwell and of failure in appealing to the patriotism of Gill. Watson's intelligence of this last Sunday in September came to the eyes of Nepean, Dundas, Pitt, and the King himself.[16]

October 1792 swiftly brought matters to a head. On the first, William with Dr John Lawson as witness officially discharged his mother from all his claim to Tom's 'Goods and Chattels Rights and Credits' upon his having received £500.[17] On the same day James, before leaving York for Kirkconnell, wrote his brother the letter his mother had requested of him.[18] None of his letters is more personal, more affectionate. James asks his 'Dear Brother' to consider how much he owes their mother, to think of the natural duty of a child, to recall their early years when they were bereft of their father before James had scarcely attained his third year. The memory of how their mother watched over them and dedicated her whole time for many years to them should bring 'a most lively sence of Gratitude' and make William listen to her entreaties:

A tender and afflicted Mother begs by all that is sacred and entreats her son who must be sensible of all a parent's affection and of his obligations to her to Delay for a few weeks an undertaking which is contrary to the opinion of all his friends & which is reprobated by the world. Consult reason, consult the feelings of your heart, consult gratitude, consult every natural Tie a child can have to a tender and afflicted parent and your own feelings will tell you you should give up to the request of a parent putting your Design in Execution for some time. You are engaged to go to France. to whom are you engaged. to a party which is now condemned & [?execrated] by all the world who whatever their Ends may be seen to Glory in acts of cruelty which would have disgraced the most barbarous ages, to a party who trample underfoot the laws of God and Man and which with the most savage and ferocious Barbarity seems to glory in wading thro streams of Blood to the attainment of their own ends. Consider Dear Brother the advice of your friends, the feelings of your Mother. Do not [?set] your heart against your natural and gratefull feelings and Grant at least your Mother's request in Delaying for some weeks your intended plan. I remain with every kind wish to you —

On 2 October James took the step he had put off taking as long as he felt there was a chance of getting William to change his mind. As the Laird of Kirkconnell who had received his lands from King George III, as the responsible eldest son who, unlike his brother, had not come under the spell of Scotland's Enlightenment, as a devout Catholic who saw his neighbor Terregles give sanctuary to some of the emigrant French priests and had to bear the criticism of fellow Catholics for the great harm William was doing their cause, James was obliged to make his own position clear to the Government.[19] So he wrote 'The Most Honorable Henry Dundas/One of his Majesty's Privy Councillors/London':

York 2ᵈ October 1792

> Sir
> Highly Disapproving the publick part which my younger Brother Dᴿ Maxwell has lately taken in french Politicks, I have Used my utmost Endeavors to Divert him from such Line of Conduct, and as I am given to understand that he has been pointed out to the attention of the Government, I take the liberty of troubling you with the Enclosed abstracts from several Letters which have passed on the subject betwixt my Brother my Mother and myself in order to Convince you and the rest of his Majesty's ministers of my attachment to the present government of Great Britain and anxiety to preserve the publick peace.

James's postscript reads, '. . . after having pledged my word to my Brother that rather than he should go to Manchester and run the risk of

Exciting any Disturbances, I would advance him a certain sum on my late brother's count, I last night advanced him £500 on his Receipt according to the advice of Mr Withers.'

William must have spent some part of these hectic London days in looking back over his shoulder; for excitement and alarm were intensifying with each new rumor of Brunswick defeat, republican atrocity, new movement like that in Manchester to collect a subscription 'for the relief of our brethren in France', Catholic scheme to use the French priests, dubious arms delivery, and government paralysis.[20]

Nobody in Great Britain could have been more on edge from the failure of the Government to act decisively to protect the Monarchy, the Christian Religion, and the Common Law than Edmund Burke. Very early Burke had come to look upon 'the French business' as 'no light or trivial thing', but as 'the most important crisis that ever existed in the World' because 'the whole political State of Europe hinges upon it.'[21] And every action of man appeared capable of being turned political. The very charity of providing the émigrés with clothes so that they would suffer no more of the scorn and derision of the populace could be advanced as argument for opposing the plan of the Catholic Committee for new elections. Horrified and contemptuous, Burke read in the *Morning Chronicle* those resolutions to discredit the Committee: that to admit Catholics to the franchise was incompatible with the safety of the Protestant establishment, dangerous to the Hanoverian succession, hazardous with respect to the connection between Ireland and Great Britain.[22] Politics! The more magnanimously people gave for French priests, the brighter the attraction 'to all the banditti of France to chuse England for their asylum'. Politics! The more mercy, the more 'the Newspapers of Hell' stirred up the mob.[23] Again politics! With Priestley's being declared a French citizen, Burke scornfully remarked that the doctor now avowed himself 'a Citizen of that Republick of Robbers'.[24] When Brunswick ran, Burke tagged his running as 'a Stain never to be effaced from the United military glory of Europe. The Prussian and Austrian combined forces have fled before a Troop of strolling Players with a Buffoon at their head.'[25] When the guillotines rang the rights of man, Burke exploded to Lord Loughborough, 'I never will allow, that enormous aggregate of Crime and Madness, called the French System, to stand for principle in any Man.'[26]

Early September raised the yellow voice of the *Sun* in support of such convictions as Burke's. To defend Brunswick was all but impossible;

yet the *Sun* rose to this challenge by discovering the excuse that the general's retreat was to be laid to a disease caused by partaking too freely of new wine. To create admiration for the French emigrants was comparatively simple; thus, the *Sun* informed its readers that these foreigners had killed their horses and thrown them into wells before escaping; to create sympathy for the same foreigners, the *Sun* announced that 'thirty crowns are offered in France for the taking of each Priest.'[27] But the easiest duty of all which the *Sun* laid upon itself was to ignite fury against anyone or anything tainted Jacobin. Typical of its course was such a ray as appeared in the issue of 8 October: 'The *Jacobins* ought to recollect, that ENGLAND is not to be insulted or outraged with impunity. Though it is the wise system of this Country at present to leave France to reap the fruit of her folly and her crimes, yet the proposition in the *Jacobin Club* at Paris, *to murder all the Englishmen in France*, will naturally rouse the spirit and excite the vigilance of the English Nation.' Thirsting after Jacobins, the *Sun* drew up a novelty which made it glow with self-satisfaction: a series of profiles of those Jacobins at home who were Britain's enemies-number-one. Like Abou Ben Adhem, William Maxwell headed the list. Originally this spot had been reserved for Abbé Noel, general of an army of spies serving the Jacobin Club and drill-sergeant of 'such profligate and desperate Englishmen as have been bought by French gold'.[28]

Headlines for the feature article which the *Sun* ran on Monday, 8 October 1792, were

ENGLISH JACOBINS
NUMBER I.
DOCTOR MAXWELL

After recognizing that William's accomplishments so far outshone those of the Abbé as to usurp his position of pre-eminence, the writer whacks away:

> A circumstance of a very serious nature, which has just come to our knowledge, has . . . induced us to postpone the notice we intended to take of this Foreigner. Eager as we ever shall be to proclaim the worth of our fellow-subjects, so will we ever be the first to drag them forth to public notice, when their vices or their crimes require the public cognizance.
>
> No one who has heard at all of what has lately passed in this Metro-polis, can be ignorant of the audacious attempt made by a Doctor MAXWELL to disturb its tranquillity, and to induce the ignorant and

uninformed to join the seditious standard he erected. Aware of the punishment which would have attended the completion of his design, and afraid of meeting the general indignation which his impudent Advertisement had raised in every virtuous breast, he meanly stole from his house in the morning when the Meeting he had appointed was to take place; and, for a while, it was not known in what quarter of the Kingdom he had concealed himself.

It now appears, that the hours of his retirement have been passed at *Birmingham*, where he has been engaged in Negociation, for a purpose at which every honest and well-meaning man must shudder. This has been no other than the Fabrication of TWENTY THOUSAND DAGGERS, of a new and singular construction — He applied, for this purpose, to several Manufacturers in that place, and produced the money that was to pay for them. To their honour, however, be it said, they all refused to be concerned in so vile and horrid a transaction. — The indefatigable Doctor, strenuous in the execution of his commission, and not daunted by the ill success he had met with, pursued his object. All the Manufacturers of Birmingham were not so virtuous, or so considerate, as these Gentlemen had been. One among them was at length found, who, tempted by the Doctor's gold, and considering it as a thing in Trade, agreed to execute the Commission. A Contract was accordingly made, for the Fabrication of TWO THOUSAND DAGGERS weekly, to be delivered to the Doctor, No. 73, in Portland-street, till the whole number of *Twenty Thousand* shall be completed.

Such is the fact. It requires no comment from us. We leave it to the Public to determine, to what use this enormous quantity of horrid and unlawful weapons is to be applied — whether they are to be conveyed to Paris, for the purpose of being used to cut the throats of the Enemy in the field, or of the innocent and the defenceless within the walls; or whether they are to be employed at home, as sharp and cutting arguments to enforce the propagation of those doctrines of which the Doctor avows himself to be the Apostle, though he feared to be the Martyr.

The words 'Apostle' and 'Martyr' alone would have sufficed to make John Menzies rock with rage and to make James Maxwell doubly thankful that his mother had stopped reading newspapers.

On Tuesday, 9 October, William, racing against time, was in Birmingham once more. With Blair, he went on to the manufactury of Woolley, who had kept his fingers in the pie despite protestations to the contrary. Blair had asked Woolley recently to make him a dagger similar to those Gill was making, only of a better quality, which he wanted for his bedside because he slept in the country. Woolley had not hesitated to make it and charge Blair a fat price. Now Maxwell and

G

Blair came to Woolley for him to pen down under their directions an order 'for 28 fine Daggers, some of which would have to come to 2 Guineas apiece — and 2 of them to be only 6 Inches long and manifestly intended to be concealed as they were ordered to have a Button to the sheath quite flat so as to admit only a piece of Tape'. Long after the day, Woolley swore that he had refused to make them.[29]

Four days after conferring upon 'Dagger' Maxwell the degree of 'English Jacobin Number I', the *Sun* told its readers that Maxwell and other English Jacobins were already quaking 'from our exposition of them. They like not the Light of the Sun, because their deeds are evil.'[30] The newspaper then names Gill as Maxwell's Birmingham accomplice. Evan Nepean, the meanwhile, was privately instructing John Brooke, another of the agents in the Midlands, to investigate whether or not the arms being made in Birmingham and Sheffield were being sent to Ireland via Liverpool and to answer an urgent question: 'What has been done lately in consequence of the Orders of Dr. Maxwell? I am told that 500 Daggers were sent him in London.'[31]

Without more facts, it becomes possible to argue upon any one of several lines. As plausible, perhaps, as any other is that Brooke confirmed to Nepean that what Nepean had heard about daggers delivered to Maxwell was the truth and that upon this confirmation Nepean ordered judges of the quarter sessions for the borough of London in which William resided to issue a warrant for his arrest.[32] Taking these weapons to France was one thing, but the possibility of their being intended for Ireland or even Great Britain was too real in the eyes of Whitehall for any risk.

William just managed to evade the warrant of Thursday, 18 October, by diplomatically slipping away through Dover and sailing to France. One week to the day after issuance of the warrant, *Le Moniteur* carried the following satire:

> London, 18 October. —
> A patriotic bird-catcher amuses himself now by training a canary to sing *Ça ira*. Judges of the quarter sessions have learned about this person, and one who shares their point of view has issued a warrant for the arrest of Doctor Maxwell. The judges declare that if the bird-catcher does not give up his lessons, they will kill all his birds and make a funeral pyre of their cages.[33]

William left general consternation in his wake, not so much upon account of his escape as upon account of the government's failure to control the manufacture of surreptitious arms. For the life of him, Evan Nepean could not lay his fingers on the movements of these weapons. He continued to think they were traceable to Liverpool, but his agents at Merseyside like Arthur Onslow at the customhouse could not tell him whether they were for consignment to Ireland or to France. On 2 November Nepean learned from a Mr Newport, Collector of Customs at Dover, that nine cases of daggers had been shipped on the *Duchess of Cumberland* for export to Calais; and on 8 November another informer told him that 'M.ʳ Ketland of Birmingham has been employed in making arms for Ireland and is now executing an order for 5000 stand.' Thus Nepean scratched his head to ponder, while friends of the people planned conventions in strategic places like Edinburgh, Brunswick kept his record clean by losing at Jemappes, the French army posed a threat to Holland by its invasion of Belgium, and the French government proclaimed its assistance to revolutionists in all countries.[34]

Parliamentary debates of December 1792 moved Great Britain up to war against France; one of them led to Burke's 'Dagger Speech', its principal prop courtesy of Dr William Maxwell of Kirkconnell.[35] Parliament had re-convened after Christmas. On the twenty-eighth Burke rose in the House of Commons to speak to the question of the Alien Act. Atheism, Burke maintained, was rife in France.[36] Because the bill before the house would keep out of England those murderous atheists who would pull down church and state, he favored passage. Probably no more than two hundred persons in France did all the murdering; only about nineteen in Great Britain were likely to be affected by the bill. All of these individuals were known by the dagger. Warming to his thoughts, Burke mentioned the circumstance of three thousand daggers having been bespoken at Birmingham by an Englishman, of which seventy had been delivered. It had not been ascertained how many of these were intended for home consumption. Here Burke drew out a dagger which he had kept concealed and 'with much vehemence threw it on the floor':

> This, said he, pointing to the dagger, is what you are to gain by an alliance with France; wherever their principles are introduced, their practice must follow. You must guard against the principles; you must proscribe their persons. He then held the dagger up to public view, which he said never would have been intended for fair and open war, but solely for murderous purposes. It is my object, said he, to keep the French infection from this country; their principles from our minds, and their

daggers from our hearts. I vote for this bill, because I consider it the means of saving my life and all our lives, from the hands of assassins.

When the French smile, Burke concluded, 'I see blood trickling down their faces, all their cajoling is — blood!'

The dagger which Burke had hurled on to the floor of the House of Commons had been requested by him from Henry Dundas the day before the speech: 'Mr Burke presents his compliments to Mr Dundas and begs the favour of his sending him the Pattern Dagger — wrapped up in something which may not present it to Observation on the street.'[37] Gill had sent the dagger to Rose at the Treasury; Rose, to James Bland Burges, Under-Secretary of State for Foreign Affairs; Burges, to Dundas. Burke's brandishing it, the *Morning Post* reported on the twenty-ninth, 'excited quite different emotions in the House from those which so murderous a weapon ought to have inspired', and Burke was unable to continue until the House 'had resumed its wonted seriousness and dignity'. Members of the House were not the only ones to have been amused by Burke's performance. Upon reading Birmingham accounts of the speech in the Saturday morning papers, 'John Nott, Birmingham Button burnisher', a pseudonym for, perhaps, John Morfitt, barrister in Birmingham, facetiously addressed Burke by way of public letter in Sunday morning's paper. Nott is apologetic for his intrusion; nevertheless, he has to state 'a circumstance which if neglected for a single day may indeed prove fatal to our Government, and at once answer the purposes of that faction which is desirous to new model our State':

> The order for the daggers given to Mr Gill and Woolley (and which you thank God have proved the wickedness of) is not the only plan on which these desperate Jacobins have form'd their hopes. I yesterday received an order from Sheffield and Manchester immediately to put in hand and to get finished immediately three thousand Buttons of pattern like the enclosed only altering the Motto to 'Liberty and Equality,' they must be prepared before the 18th of January, our amiable Queen's birthday as they are resolved to celebrate a Bloody day and not a Birthday — they say this number is only for a Pattern as that wou'd not serve a tenth part of their Clubs — now Honourable Sir I do not mean to get up this order and hope for the Love of our Country you will immediately shew the pattern Button to the Common house of parliament. I have sent also a specimen of our Affection for our Church and King with the explanation of which I beg your Acceptance.[38]

Those Sunday papers that printed this gibe reproduced James Gillray's caricature titled 'The Dagger Scene:- or The Plot Discovered', showing Pitt and Dundas virtuously alarmed; Fox, Sheridan, and M. A. Taylor terror-stricken; Burke nervously scornful; and the Speaker disappearing in his wig.[39]

Hilarity at Burke's expense did not slacken quickly. One epigram, 'A Dangerous Bore', hailed him as being more skilled in daggers than Shakespeare; that epigram by 'Toby' read:

> BURKE from his coat the dagger drew,
> And mark what follow'd after;
> With rage quite frantic — thro' and thro',
> He *struck* them all — with laughter![40]

Behind such amusement, however, was a deeply inherent distrust of Edmund Burke. The man in the street felt that Burke looked down upon him and his neighbors as 'swinish multitude'. Others censured him for his treatment of Priestley. But most of those regarding him with disfavor could not rid themselves of their suspicion that Burke was moving Great Britain to war because of his championship of Roman Catholicism. A London report for *Le Moniteur* of Wednesday, 28 September, had spoken of Catholic intrigue in Dublin led by Burke's son who had been educated by the Jesuits at Saint Omer; and Gillray had drawn Burke furtively in Jesuit habit, chanting from the fable of 'Little Red Riding Hood'.[41]

The dagger controversy saw the old year out and the new year in. On the last day of December 1792, Burke heard from one of his supporters, a J. Overton in Birmingham who came forward because of the 'Dagger Speech' to reveal what he knew:

> In the Star Evening Paper of Saturday last, I see in the debates on the Aliens Bill, you make mention of 3,000 Daggers having been ordered at Birmingham 70 of which were executed — I beg leave to set you right on the subject — the order was given to Mr Thos Gill for 10,000 — four thousand of which were executed & paid for by Mr Blair a dissenter & Gunsmith, the whole would have been executed had not Mr Gill's friends disapproved of his conduct and dissuaded him from it. Those daggers were of a singular Construction and made to lay the point from the wrist to the elbow, by a particular movement of which it presented itself to strike a [?back] blow, on the handle or blades (of which I forgot) were stamped — Rights of Man, from which Circumstance they are distinguish^d here by the appelation of Rights of Man daggers.[42]

James Woolley's letter to Burke written on 16 January of the new year corrects Overton in its conclusion: 'With respect to any mark or writing upon the Daggers nothing was ever once mentioned respecting the finer ones, nor can I suppose it would be done upon Mr Gill's, the price would not admit of it. Mr Blair I know paid Gill for them; but his Paymaster I have not learnt.'[43]

Early January had brought Whitehall what amounted to an ultimatum from France; the twenty-first brought Burke the moral issue he had prayed for to renew strength and unity in Great Britain: the execution of Louis XVI. Little more than a week later, 1 February 1793, France declared war upon Great Britain and the Dutch Republic. The first debates on prosecution of this war led to the last mentions of the dagger incident in parliament. On 28 February, the House was inquiring into the truth of reports of seditious practices in the country.[44] Richard Brinsley Sheridan argued that these reports were much exaggerated; Burke opposed Sheridan. Their debate became personal when Sheridan charged Burke with bad taste for having introduced the trick of the dagger. Defending himself, Burke read the long letter from Woolley into the record and, thereby, named Dr Maxwell; then he stated that the only error he had committed in mentioning the business before was in affirming that three thousand had been ordered and seventy-two made, whereas in fact ten thousand had been ordered and four thousand had been made. Neither Burke nor Sheridan got the last word. It was Major Maitland's:

> Major *Maitland* said, he had no personal acquaintance with Dr Maxwell, but he knew, from undoubted information, that the daggers ordered by him were intended for no such purpose as had been insinuated, but as a weapon for horsemen, armed with rifles. The same construction might, with equal plausibility, have been put upon the daggers of a company of light horse, armed in the same manner in the American war.

In turning from Edmund Burke in the House of Commons with William Maxwell's name on his lips, it is important to bear in mind several conclusions drawn from the dagger episode which clarify those probable terms permitting William's return to his own country: everybody had his own motives; nobody in the Government was sure of William's purpose; even Nepean could not swear as to who paid for the daggers or how many were ordered or made or delivered; Gill and Woolley, out to save their own hides, contradicted themselves, over and over again; newspapers were almost as biased and unreliable as government informers or those who mailed in anonymous letters to the editor; the daggers continued to be fabricated for a longer period after William's departure from the scene than they had been fabricated before it; finally, not a single statement by William pertaining to his responsibility was disproved, not a statute was cited to show his activity as unlawful, and not a day of his interest in purchasing daggers was a day when Great Britain waged war with any country, not excepting France.

How remarkable it was that Paris remained so open to Britons during those weeks immediately preceding the 1 February declaration of war! Matter-of-factly, the French capital accepted in its midst a large community of British 'idealists, romantics, adventurers, eccentrics, heroic fools, and self-sacrificing humanitarians'.[45] Among the new tourists who came to France was Dr John Moore in attendance upon the Earl of Lauderdale.[46] Moore became one of those Britons who crowded seats in the National Assembly allotted to foreigners; on his way there, he noted how National Guardsmen insulted men on the streets; once seated, he looked down upon deputies marked by the ribbon they wore. Evenings he would visit the famous Club of the Jacobins which Lafayette blamed for all of the country's disorders and then came back to his lodgings to tell his patient how badly the citizens behaved and how loudly they beat their drums or to enter in his journal such an observation as, 'I see a great many monkeys every day, who affect to be bons patriotes.'[47]

Affectation there certainly was. But it was not of a woman like Mademoiselle Théronanne de Mirecourt, wild at the head of her pike-men, fanatic in moving women's rights: 'We shall no more be flattered in order to be enslaved.'[48] And it was not of the Culottic Girondins, the Jesuits of the Revolution, whose weapons were political philosophy, respectability, and eloquence or of the Sansculottic Mountain typified by Marat's audacity, impetuosity, and ferocity. And affectation was not of William Maxwell.

One of the two forces that were to turn William from the duty he had given himself was at work when he came to Paris in October 1792; it had been at work in September when he had sat opposite his brother James at York. William could not have been but embarrassed by the sickness and revulsion on James's countenance as he referred to the late massacres, just as he could not have been but sickened himself by what he saw and heard in France during the last months of the year. Like Romilly he must have had his moments of 'How could I ever be so deceived?' because of the quickness of the guillotines and the quickness of the axes and wrenches. Sacristies, lutrins, and altar-rails were being pulled down around him; mass-books were being turned into cartridge papers; churches were burning; patens offered mackerel; chalices, brandy; asses wore priests' cloaks and were reined with stoles; Feasts of Reason before the high altar of Notre Dame opened with a hymn to liberty. Seeing the blood, smelling the smoke, feeling the desecration, and hearing talk of pillage at Liége and the distress of his teachers there, William must have spent sleepless hours of the night wrestling with his conscience.

Keeping occupied, William permitted himself as little time as possible for reflection and recrimination. The company he kept and the narrow circle within which he moved tended to shut him off from the ugliest realities of the masses. The day of his arrival was the day of his becoming a welcome member of a group of sympathizers drawing its membership chiefly from British subjects like himself.[49] These enthusiasts assembled either at White's Hotel or the Hotel d'Angleterre, where they toasted 'the speedy abolition of hereditary titles and feudal distinctions in England' and listened to addresses expressing such senti- ments as 'Let us hope that the virtuous troops of liberty will lay down their arms only when there are no more tyrants or slaves.'[50] By November William was on what amounted to the executive committee. Members did not just talk and listen. Their names, for instance, figure prominently on the *Star's* list of contributors to a subscription opened by the London Society for Constitutional Information to assist 'the efforts of France in the cause of freedom'.[51] This list of 16 November shows that J. Horne Tooke put himself down for £50, Thomas Paine for £21, and Dr Maxwell for £100, £50 in his own name and another £50 'for a friend', possibly Dr Edwards. Later in the same month William and fifty-one of his associates, who had gathered at the Hotel d'Angleterre to draft a manifesto of common faith, signed their names to a resolution that the French citizens had taken up arms 'solely to make reason and truth triumphant'.

William Maxwell could not have been completely at ease in this company. Apparently, ill-will on the part of Tooke for his having been left to hold the bag never existed. William, however, could not have sat down in the same room with John Oswald without some such shudder as he knew whenever Colonel Glover entered his mind. Altogether his group represented a medley of misfits, including Nicholas Hickson, teacher of languages later imprisoned in the Scotch College; the

Reverend Mr William Jackson, originally clerk in a London Moravian chapel and lastly Dublin suicide by poison to evade execution for high treason; Lord Edward Fitzgerald, son of the Duchess of Leinster and husband of 'Pamela', reputed daughter of the Duke of Orleans; John Frost, companion of Tom Paine; Sir Robert Smyth, arrested 18 November 1793; Henry Redhead Yorke, so 'madly in love with ideal liberty', as he liked to put it, that he ended up in Newgate, guilty of sedition and conspiracy; and John Hurford Stone, president of the meeting, former member of Dr Price's congregation and soon to be fellow-traveller of Helen Maria Williams. Six such gentlemen over whom Stone presided met violent deaths; ten others were imprisoned in Paris to receive disillusionment and/or guillotine. Captain George Monro, the English government spy who lodged at White's the better to keep his eye on this crew, warned Nepean that some members were 'ready to put anything in execution that would injure their country, let the measure be never so desperate'.[52] It was undoubtedly this bias that convinced William Maxwell he should look elsewhere for the fulfilment which he desperately sought. So he renounced the club after November to face the more likely alternative of mid-December.

What that alternative was every reliable authority agrees upon: enlistment in the military service of France. Authorities like Captain Monro and Earl Gower, the British ambassador at Paris until August 1792, state that Maxwell had come to France to obtain a company in the French service, that an opening came in December, and that as of 17 December the doctor was 'soon to leave this [Paris] to join the army'.[53] So far nobody seems to have come across William's name in the French military tables of organization so as to be able to certify what company, if any, he obtained. Of foot or of horse? As combat officer or *chirurgien*? In what uniform? Under his own name or an alias? Question after question, but an answer for only one. Subsequent events prominently display him in the uniform of the National Guard. Dr Edwards' arrival back from London was reported to the Home Office on that 17 December as being for the purpose of paying William a visit; it may, however, have been for the purpose of joining the French army together with his friend because others of the Hotel d'Angleterre faction were signing up.[54] Colonel John Oswald, as an example, had been commissioned to organize a regiment of volunteers. One of his first acts upon assuming this command was to choose his two sons as his drummers; both lads and their commanding officer were to perish at the hands of the Vendée insurgents.[55] As testament of how few the facts, one might add that an authority could be cited as suspecting that Dr William Maxwell perished at the same hands.[56]

The January 1793 trial of Louis XVI of France would have been brought by the National Convention even if its deputies had not been in possession of Paine's assurance to them that the King ought to be tried, justly, legally, and agreeably, for having 'conspired against Liberty'. Henry Redhead Yorke, who went over from White's for the trial, remembered the galleries as having been packed 'with the vilest rabble', who, unwilling to chance losing their seats, remained where they were throughout each night, singing the 'Marseillaise' to keep awake and, as they could afford, buying wine and cakes sold by officers of the National Guard. The King, Yorke noted, was firm and erect, plainly dressed in an olive silk coat; Robespierre was in black, Orleans in blue, and Barrère scarlet in his waistcoat.[57] On the fourteenth, with twenty-eight deputies abstaining, Louis was found guilty; and on Sunday the twentieth, he was condemned to death within twenty-four hours. Knowing that William was a member of the National Guard with duties in Paris throughout the trial, one has reason to assume that he was assigned to these proceedings and still another reason to assume that his assignment was for something other than sale of wine and cake. Truth, indeed, seems to be that he had the most important assignment of all.[58]

As it had been given to the father James Maxwell of Kirkconnell at age thirty-three to guard and escort Prince Charles Edward in battle, so it was given to the second son at age thirty-two to guard and escort King Louis XVI in the days of his trial and the day of his death. Konrad Engelbert Oelsner, who bragged that he had met more Englishmen in one year of Paris than other travellers had met in three years of London, is only one of those who place William Maxwell at the scaffold with the King that Monday morning, 21 January 1793; in fact, Oelsner names Maxwell as the source for his minute account of the execution which appears in *Flucht, Verhör und Hinrichtung Ludwigs XVI Nach der Schilderung eines deutschen Beobachter (The Flight, Trial and Execution of Louis XVI from the description of a German Observer)*.[59]

Snow of the twentieth had turned to icy rain in Paris before Sanson and his assistants tried out the guillotine that night.[60] Santerre, Commander of the Temple, roused the King at five o'clock of the Monday morning for mass read by Abbé Edgeworth, an Irish Protestant turned Catholic. Then officers of the National Guard including William Maxwell escorted Louis down a long staircase and out to Clavière's carriage. Side by side, both in brown, the King and his confessor rode from the Temple to the Place de la Révolution between two rows of fusiliers and pikemen. At a signal from Santerre, drums began to sound for the King's firm ascent to the scaffold. Executioners tied his arms and positioned him on the guillotine, Edgeworth kneeling by him. So close was the priest, his face became sprinkled with the blood as he prayed, 'Fils de Saint Louis, montez au ciel.' At the four corners of the scaffold, Sanson showed the severed head while pikemen dipped their points in the royal blood and citizens rushed up to dip handkerchiefs, scarves, and scraps of paper. Devoid of sympathy for Louis as he had been, William may have found some sympathy that morning. We know, at any rate, that he was amazed at the composure with which the King entered the carriage, as if for an ordinary drive, gazed upon the objects which he passed, and helped Sanson to remove his overcoat and jacket, for which a kind of blouse, almost pinioning his arms, was substituted. No factual basis has ever been given to prove that William lowered himself to the level of dipping his handkerchief in the king's blood. The anecdote that he did rests on nothing more secure than the knowledge that some of the delirious Frenchmen did.[61]

Repercussions of the regicide took up the roll of its drums. Abroad enemies of the French people became united as they sheltered French princes. At home in Great Britain, the Prince of Wales reacted with 'je ne possède plus' ('I cannot contain myself');[62] from Rome Prince Augustus wrote his father that he had been made two days ill;[63] the Earl of Bute offered King George 'the service and expressions of zeal' of his third son Evelyn James;[64] and Pitt gave the French ambassador eight days to remove himself. Gillray drew first his 'The Blood of the Murdered Crying for Vengeance', wherein an ocean of blood mounts high with the disgust of the caricaturist. Several days later Gillray had a second drawing ready for publication titled 'View in Perspective: the Zenith of French Glory; — the Pinnacle of Liberty, Religion, Justice, Loyalty, & all the Bugbears of Unenlighten'd Minds, Farewell!'

That Monday morning may not have made William Maxwell cry, 'Enough!' But that cry was forming, nevertheless, both then and in the days immediately thereafter, when he heard those repercussions and learned of such other responses as Tuesday's singing of the 'Requiem Mass' by the scholars of the English School at Liége, where he and his brothers had worshipped together.[65]

France's declaration of war upon Great Britain of 1 February triggered cry and final resolve. Treason had ever been unthinkable; therefore, William took off his National Guard uniform and arranged for his return to England as each day made him and fellow-countrymen like him more the enemy of those they had been serving. Only one with the influence of John Menzies could have made possible the transition. Even as William was leaving Paris for the Channel, Menzies was moving heaven and earth to speak into every sympathetic ear and to direct the efforts of others like the Maxwells and the Riddells. Fortunately for William, the great desire of the Government for unity, the delicacy of the Roman Catholic question, and the pressing need not to offend Menzies and those he could persuade weighed more heavily than any of the dubious charges that might be brought into court.

Soon after 5 March 1793, Arthur Young's now rare pamphlet, 'The Example of France/A Warning to Britain', appeared on the London bookstalls. In speaking of recent grievances introduced by republican petitioners to the Government, Young denounces the petitioners for being unable to claim 'real' grievances. A footnote to his denunciation reads:

> Of which a notable instance occurred, in a formal accusation brought forward in parliamentary form, against his Majesty's ministers, for keeping the suspected domestics of Égalité — and the noted Dr. Maxwell some hours on board a packet, as contrary to law and constitution. What a panegyric upon this glorious country! that men tremblingly alive, and responsive to the faintest and almost imperceptible vibrations of discontent — of evil, could it be found; — upon the hunt — *beating* for their game, can find none — and are forced to confess, that they can find none, by pouching flies and maybugs for their quarry.[66]

Thus William had made it back safely, if not comfortably, aboard a pacquet, some time before, approximately, 5 March 1793. His discomforts of pride were only beginning with shipboard remarks and Dover inquisition. Almost certainly, weeks in London were required to keep him out of jail, and his release by authorities could have been given only after his promising to forswear participation in any movement likely to inhibit the war effort and only after Menzies accepted some measure of the responsibility for his future conduct.

Arthur Young does not stand alone in pointing to February or early March as the time of William's return. William himself becomes witness to the same in a letter which reveals that his head had not come to hang altogether low. Only the first part of this letter survives; it is addressed to 'Mr E^d Burke', it is dated 'March 6, 1793', and it bears the docket 'Birmingham Daggers':

> Sir
>
> I find that Certain Slanders which have for some time been spread against my Character, have been Countenanced by a speech of yours in the house of Commons; & particularly by a letter there read by you from Mr Wooley of Birmingham. I request that you will permit myself or a friend to peruse, and if necessary to Copy that letter, as I understand it Contains matter to which [next page or pages missing][67]

The *Morning Post* of 16 March reports that Edmund Burke gave Maxwell an interview in which his, Burke's, behavior was 'more temperate' than it had been in the House. One guesses that William sought the original of Woolley's letter to hasten the process of clearing his name, as one guesses that Burke, too, may have aided him, having found as much temperance in his guest as he commanded in himself.

That day finally arrived when William in the steady company of his cousin travelled north to Scotland. They must have stopped at Swinburne Castle and then at Kirkconnell. But it was only after they were riding alone above Edinburgh to Aberdeen and Pitfodels that William could have unburdened himself before John Menzies. Leisurely and in full detail he must have told of his encounters. He the Don Quixote, John the Don Diego:

> During all this time Don Diego de Miranda had not uttered a word but was wholly taken up with observing what Don Quixote did and listening to what he had to say. The knight impressed him as being a crazy sane man and an insane one on the verge of sanity.
>
> 'Undoubtedly, Señor Don Diego de Miranda, your Grace must take me for a fool and a madman, am I not right? And it would be small wonder if such were not the case, seeing that my deeds give evidence of nothing else. But I am neither so mad nor so lacking in wit as I must appear to you to be. The best showing of all is made by a knight-errant who goes seeking dangerous adventures with the intention of bringing them to a happy and successful conclusion. I whose lot it is to be numbered among the knights-errant cannot fail to attempt anything that appears to me to fall within the scope of my duties, just as I attacked those lions even though I knew it to be an exceedingly rash thing to do. It is better for the brave man to carry his bravery to the point of rashness than for him to sink into cowardice. And in this matter of adventures, it is better to lose by a card too many than a card too few, and "Such a knight is temerarious and overbold"

sounds better to the ear than "That knight is timid and a coward." '

'I must assure you, Señor Don Quixote', replied Don Diego, 'that everything your Grace has said and done will stand the test of reason; and it is my opinion that if the laws and ordinances of knight-errantry were to be lost, they would be found again in your Grace's bosom, which is their depository and storehouse. But it is growing late; let us hasten to my village and my home, where your Grace shall rest from your recent exertions; for if the body is not tired the spirit may be, and that sometimes results in bodily fatigue.'

'I accept your offer as a great favor and an honor, Señor Don Diego,' was the knight's reply. And by spurring their mounts they arrived at the village and came to the house that was occupied by Don Diego.[68]

FROM ROBERT BURNS—

Then that curst carmagnole, Auld Satan,
Watches, like baudrons by a rattan,
Our sinfu' saul to get a claut on
                              Wi' felon ire;
Syne, whip! his tail ye'll ne'er cast saut on —
                              He's aff like fire.

                    — 'To Colonel de Peyster'

What books are you reading, or what is the subject of your thoughts, besides
the great studie of your Profession.

                              — To Robert Ainslie

Old Father Time deputes me here before ye,
Not for to preach, but tell his simple story:
He bids you mind, amid your thoughtless rattle,
That the first blow is ever half the battle;
That tho' some by the skirt may try to snatch him,
Yet by the forelock is the hold to catch him;
That whether doing, suffering, or forbearing,
You may do miracles by persevering.

    — 'Prologue Spoken at the Theatre of Dumfries'

O HAD the malt thy strength of mind,
    Or hops the flavour of thy wit,
'Twere drink for first of human kind,
    A gift that even for Syme were fit.

— 'Compliments to John Syme of Ryedale'

—FROM ROBERT BURNS

Thou's welcome, wean! Mishanter fa' me,
If thoughts o' thee or yet thy mammie
Shall ever daunton me or awe me,
                    My sweet, wee lady.

— 'Welcome To A Bastart Wean'

And there, frae the Niddesdale border,
    The Maxwells will gather in droves,
Teugh Johnie, staunch Geordie, an' Wellwood,
    That griens for the fishes and loaves;
And there will be Logan M'Dowall,
    Sculdudd'ry an' he will be there,
And also the Wild Scot o' Galloway,
    Sogering, gunpowder Blair.

— 'Ballad Second — Election Day'

I shall promise you a piece of good old beef, a chicken, or perhaps a Nith
salmon fresh from the ware, & a glass of good punch, on the shortest notice.

— To Robert Graham of Fintry

The Nith shall run to Corsincon,
    And Criffel sink in Solway,
Ere we permit a Foreign Foe,
    On British ground to rally!

— 'Does Haughty Gaul Invasion Threat'

CHAPTER FIVE

Before Death

... it is only as present objects begin to pall upon the sense, as we have been disappointed in our favourite pursuits, cut off from our closest ties, that passion loosens its hold upon the breast, that we by degrees become weaned from the world, and allow ourselves to contemplate, as in a glass, darkly, the possibility of parting with it for good.

— William Hazlitt

Death did not claim William Maxwell of Kirkconnell until he had been given forty-one years of a new life which was born to him near Pitfodels in the spring of 1793; its visit upon him came Monday, 13 October 1834, as he lay peacefully in the Edinburgh home of John Menzies overlooking the Firth of Forth.[1] John was seventy-eight; William, seventy-four; each, the last male of his line. Many years notwithstanding, Menzies had discovered all ways and means to ensure his cousin's dying as right and proper.

In what was a gradual approach to death, William had turned for the last time to his cousin; and Menzies, cognizant of his responsibility to inform church authorities, had set in motion that cleansing by which the doctor could be brought back into the Roman Catholic Church. So to that bedroom in that spacious home at 24 York Place, the Laird of Pitfodels and Blairs had summoned Bishop Andrew Carruthers, Vicar Apostolic of the Eastern District; Father James Gillis, already marked by Menzies as Carruthers' successor although only a curate at the pro-cathedral of St Mary's around the corner; and others of the religious, such as the French Ursuline superior in her black habit with violet girdle.[2] Called, too, were three surviving kinswomen: Dorothy Maxwell at forty-seven, second wife and widow of the brother James; Dorothy Mary Maxwell at fourteen, sole child and heir of Dorothy and James; and Elizabeth Maxwell at twenty-seven, daughter of the dying, beloved and illegitimate. All that prepared for the passing continued just as it should.

Neither Carruthers nor anyone else about the bedside could have known all that entered the mind of the old man during the nights and days of his final illness. What for recollection had been given him from that new life which had begun with his riding northward out of London after his escape from France? What was the first of these memories and what the last? Nobody can say. One can, however, for unity of purpose draw from the facts of those years such truths as bear upon a particular theme, any one of which truths could have turned in the tumbling of the dying man's mind.

In the last days, William's mind had had far to range. Back from present years of King William IV and recent years of George IV to the last thirty years of George III. Back to the deaths of Pitt and Burke. Back from the Catholic Emancipation Act to the Catholic Relief Act. Back over current reform of the Poor Law, to the recent Abolition of Slavery and the Factory Act, to the Reform Bill, to the end of the Tory regime. Back through post-war years of demobilization, inflation, depression, disastrous harvest, and unrest to the victories of Trafalgar and Waterloo and the Napoleonic lessons of loans, subsidies, direct taxation, national debt, and suspensions of Habeas Corpus and payment in gold. Back to the Lancashire rise of the world's first factory system. Back to the building of his reputation as Dumfries's foremost doctor.

Like so much else, dedicated practice of medicine had had its beginning in that distant period at Blairs immediately after Menzies had plucked the brand from burning. First patients were those of Menzies' immediate household, which by then included the Maxwell aunts removed from Dumfries. Once having gained his feet, once having all but closed in London his book of republican responsibility, William had been able to pay calls in Aberdeen and as far away as the community of Aquhorties. Then, slowly, by degrees, occasional visits to Kirkconnell had become permanent residence near Dumfries; and occasional patients at Kirkconnell or emergency cases in the world about it had led to general acceptance as community physician and fellow citizen. All this in the same year as the sealing off of every dizzy rapture: 1793.

On good behavior, knuckling down at last to doctoring, William won the approbation of that Dumfries doctor he and almost everybody else most respected: John Gilchrist. Their work as physicians side by side in the same community had to be without such aids as the stethoscope, sphygmograph, and clinical thermometer; but they both had been taught at Edinburgh as well as any student of medicine could be, so that they could advance their art by enlightened approaches to such questions as smallpox and 'the fever' (typhus) and by openly supporting plans for new kinds of institutions, such as the public dispensary and the lying-in hospital. In the time that they got out of the saddle and into the gig, they had the pride of a lunatic asylum and the Dumfries and Galloway Royal Infirmary.

Dr John Gilchrist had been the one to bring William along. Well established so as to be devoid of jealousy, older and more fully experienced than his colleagues, family doctor and friend of the Kirkconnell Maxwells as his father Ebenezer had been before him, a first citizen of Dumfries, Dr John ably guided Dr William so that he could pass on his place of pre-eminence to him. Both worked in harmony with and dependence upon others. Most of their colleagues were surgeons; the best among these was Samuel Shortridge; after him, James Mundell. On excellent terms with both, William made sure that it was either of the two who went out to Kirkconnell whenever need for surgery arose.[3] His choice of druggist was first Fraser, then Inglis; the best for drawing teeth was Spence. Town fathers tended towards Gilchrist as physician and Mundell as surgeon whenever they sought an affidavit to certify that another doctor's treatment of a patient like Michael Anderson had been 'good, and not improper as ignorant persons are saying'.[4]

If William had ever doubted Mary's conviction that there was an extensive practice in and around Dumfries for his mere asking, time soon proved her right. Calls from Kirkconnell, Terregles, Carruchan, and Terraughty might have been anticipated; but, perhaps, not even Mary could have foreseen such a flood of calls as came from such families as the Lewars or the Symes or such a host of emergencies as was occasioned by the times. One all-too-constant source of trouble was dearth. Poor harvests, war, and high prices after the Corn Law introduced severe shortages, even near-famine. Some of that sickness which came to Maxwell's attention resulted from pitiful undernourishment of the poor fed by subscription on soup at a penny a quart as the best substitute for bread; and some of those injuries which he treated were directly attributable to the riots and pillage attending the same hunger. Scarcely a day broke without some violence to be mended by a doctor's skills: one day an assault upon William Hyslop's son Maxwell; the next, a knifing of John Richardson while making his rounds as sheriff-officer or the brutal mishandling of George Inglis, deserter from the Sixty-third Regiment of Foot.[5] William had his share of such cases as he had his share of forced attendance at hangings or public whippings through the streets on market day or sittings of examination committees at the Infirmary or looking over lads at the Poorhouse to determine if they were stout enough to bear apprenticeship or inspecting the cells at the House of Correction or ordering oatmeal for a sick prisoner's potage there.[6] For the execution of James M'Manes, he was expected to help take a life and then to record that the body was 'awfully convulsed for betwixt five minutes and six and exhibited symptoms of animation for nearly four minutes longer'.[7] For the dreadful scalding of Love's daughter, for the broken bones of Campbell's daughter thrown from a gig by the mad dash of her horse against a stone dyke, for the jagged wounds of the roadside traveller attacked by a party of dogs, and for the drowning of the little girl at the Nith where she had gone to wash potatoes, he was expected to save a life.[8] The *Dumfries Weekly Journal* wrote up particular successes. On one occasion a boy had gone under in the Nith between the Old Bridge and the Caul, had been brought up by his two companions, and had been bled from the jugular by the surgeon Anderson before Maxwell could be summoned. He had pronounced the lad in a fair way of recovery, though eyewitnesses claimed that the boy must have been under the water at least fifteen minutes; he was shortly after this 'restored comparatively well to his distracted parents'.[9]

Chiefly, Dr William Maxwell and Dr John Gilchrist brought Dumfries through the virulent outbreak of the yaws that closed public schools in 1799.[10] Years later, in fall 1832 with Gilchrist dead, Maxwell alone led the fight against Asiatic cholera, when nine hundred townsmen lay sick and as many as forty-four died on a single day.[11] Depended upon, he was found dependable. Highly regarded by the rich, he was known everywhere among the poor. John Gibson, cabinet-maker, kept a commonplace book for recording jobs he did in various Dumfries households. On one page he had reason to scribble:

A Genuine Medicine for the Bloody flux

2 Ounces of polan Starch (Laboratory)
1 Ounce of Double Refind Sugar
1 Egg to be well beat & a little nutmeg

Put them into a mutchkin of Sweet Milk and Boil it well and When it comes off the fire, put it in a glass of the Best Brandy you can get. This medicine is to be taken in the morning before you take any Victuals. Take half the Quantity made at a time and do not take too much Victuals untill it settles on your stomach. Take no Flesh meat, but mostly soft meat, such as whats called Sowens or any Vegetables.

if the Medicine is doing you good it may be repeated untill you get Better.

Recd. by John Gibson, Cabinet maker, from William Millar, Joiner, in the year 1809 Likewise approved by Dr. Maxwell.[12]

William Maxwell, as well as his professors and colleagues, was never to practise save at the threshold of modern medicine; yet he could take to Edinburgh for his death the high esteem of a humble John Gibson together with the love and pride of a Dumfries which he had tended faithfully for more than forty years, the same love and pride which any community still reserves today for honoring its senior practitioner.

Only Doctors Gilchrist, Mundell, and Shortridge appear to have come out of William's professional life to enter his social life as well. Even they were infrequently in his after-work hours. More likely, he was to be seen with his cousin down from Blairs or with his brother near Kirkconnell; at other times, he appeared escorting his mother to such an event as 'the German Concert' or conversing with his sister-in-law at the Assembly Rooms to which the Maxwells subscribed generously.[13] He shot with Syme or Glenriddell, rode with John Maxwell of Munches or Wellwood Maxwell of Barncleugh, employed Syme as his surveyor, and attended the theatre with Carruchan, Craik, and Terregles. Every September he was on the fringe of that 'mobbing perplexity', the Annual Fair.[14] Each October he was with gentlemen like Robert Maxwell of Cargen and Walter Riddell of Woodley Park wagering at Tinwald Downs on his favorite to win the purse of £50 for the best of three four-mile heats.

Like James, William was keen on any lottery; like him, he never could take his fill of out-of-doors with horses, guns, and pointers. Both belonged to the Coursing Club and the Dumfries and Galloway Hunt. Both were among the first to purchase the new year's game certificate.[15] Both all but forgot the time of day whenever a friend like Patrick Miller, David Newall, Charles Sharpe, or David Staig was willing to linger at the Dumfries Club to discuss the weight of the best salmon or a bagging of black and red woodcocks.[16]

As the love of both brothers for books was reflected in their steady patronage of the Dumfries Society Library, so their love for gardening after their father's is reflected in their glad activities as members of the Dumfries and Galloway Horticultural Society.[17] William, especially, was as avid a planter and cultivator as John Syme. For years he sat on the society's Committee in Management, together with Syme and the Reverend Mr Thomas Duncan, cousin of Dr James Currie. Meetings and projects planned by these three 'Extraordinary Members' attracted new 'Ordinary Members' like Provost Staig, Colonel de Peyster, Justices of the Peace Thomas Goldie and Alexander Fergusson of Craig-darroch, the laird Patrick Miller, the writer William Thomson, and the schoolteacher Thomas White.[18]

Nothing could be more erroneous than to infer from the facts of William's sharing the social life of Dumfries that he could not be content without a calendar heavy with such entertainment. His participation seems not to have extended beyond what was considered correct for a young doctor, a Maxwell of Kirkconnell. William was far too retiring for his ever becoming a gadabout. What is more, to keep bottled up effectively his continuing belief in the principles of French republicanism demanded that he pick and choose his companions carefully. At the first of his new life, he was still being plagued with details of his having made truce with the Government. This aftermath requiring his presence in London from time to time kept public something of what he had just lately taught himself to keep private. That French issues could still throw off sparks from him even as he was being pressed with the cares of opening his practice is apparent in a letter he wrote from London to James, mid-July 1793. Rankled by having had to talk daggers all over again, doubly tired by having had to tend commissions of both James and Mary while concluding his own business, uncomfortable by having been led on a string by John Menzies before his cousin had left Tilbury for a five-day passage to Aberdeen, William let his brother know what he was trying to conceal from everybody else. He cheekily dated his letter 'London 17th of the fourth year of the Liberty of France.' He concluded as he had begun: 'This being the anniversary of the french revolution, many friends to liberty and justice, dine in parties, there will not be any general meeting, that Ministry may not [have] any opp[or]tunity to excite mobs.'[19]

Capitulation to the Government, to Mary, to James, and to Menzies there had been; but it had not been written with weak regret, broken spirit, or abandoned principle. It had bound the arms, but it was never to restrain the inner thought. Altogether, William managed to contain himself rather well without loss of integrity and self-respect; yet he could not have so managed without hours of privacy, a confidant like James, and one or two trusted friends who shared his views and his pride and chafed with his submission and his unwelcome circumspection. In the old life, William had had to argue before the eyes of London that a man's home is his castle; in the new life, he was always to insist that his home was just that: the one place, if there could be no other, where a Briton could be himself, where he could speak independently as he chose, where he could entertain whom he wished. It may not have been mere chance that the key which William's servant turned to lock the front door the day the doctor left Dumfries to die in Edinburgh was the key to a home in Castle Street; in choosing that this, his last Dumfries home, be built where it was, William Maxwell, better than anybody else, may have been responsible for giving the new street its present name.

The impending first marriage of James had forced Mary to think about finding another home just at the time William himself was wondering in 1793 where he would settle in Dumfries. Ever increasing obligation for James to represent not only his mother but also her sister Dorothy still living at Kirkconnell had taken the laird to Swinburne Castle more often than he found convenient.[20] There he had suffered cousins bent upon matchmaking. More willing to trust the Riddells in such affairs than John Menzies, James had settled upon Clementine Elizabeth Frances Scrope of Danby Castle. Like the Riddells, the Scropes were English Catholics with a similar proud history of Jacobitism; their home was east of Swinburne, on the moors of the North Riding away from Whitby.

Plans for James's wedding waited upon termination of Dorothy Riddell's final illness. William tended his aunt at Kirkconnell as she lay dying and stood by to help his brother arrange for the funeral 'as private as possible' and to wind up her business. The will which Dorothy left in the hands of Mary, her executrix, remembered the Maxwell nephews in pounds sterling; it gave Mary, moreover, all of the silks and satins and James 'the green chairs and worked bottoms in my Drawing Room along with the Green Carpet therein'. Lines ruled out in this instrument suggest that William, too, would have been left something more personal than money if he had not proved such a disappointment to his mother. But his inheritance from Dorothy, together with similar inheritances from other aunts and uncles at Blairs and Swinburne, might have reminded him that he did not have to earn a living from the practice of medicine.[21]

Mary in her sixties remained well-to-do in her own right, the annuity from her deceased husband's estate being but a small part of her personal wealth. She had had years of investing her own money wisely; she now had generous bequests from the estates of two lately deceased brothers and the lion's share of Dorothy's estate to profit by. Thus even though she had made it her duty to ease the strain upon James by loaning him money whenever a crisis arose, this time £1,000 and the next £300, and by permitting herself to become infeft with parts of the Barony of Kirkconnell, she still had more than enough funds to add to her lands on both sides of the Nith at Dumfries over which she kept sharp watch and to control tenements in the town itself on which she paid the sizable annual tax of almost £90.

Mary's most attractive property was that of Troqueer Holm, a mansionhouse standing amid its parklands not far from the Nith.[22] From this site, one looked east across the river to the Royal Infirmary on the Dumfriesshire side; north, over Ryedale, the home of John Syme, and the Troqueer Road to Bridge-end; west, to Terraughtie and Woodley Park; and south, to Mavis Grove and the road leading to Cargen, Carruchan, and Kirkconnell. Some thirty-two acres of a piece of land separated Troqueer Holm from Syme's southern boundary. In anticipation of her moving from Kirkconnell, Mary successfully entered negotiations through her attorney John Glover to purchase this strip from its owners, the Anglican minister in London Erasmus Middleton and his spouse Margaret Grierson.[23]

From the marriage of her eldest son and Clementine Scrope to her death, 23 December 1805, Mary maintained the home of Troqueer Holm for William as she had maintained the home of Kirkconnell for James. No arrangement could have been happier, more convenient for the doctor. His practice was on every side immediately about him, never many minutes away. So were his closest friends, John Syme being but a few steps across the park. And so, too, were his brother and sister-in-law. Straightway Clementine won the affection of William and Mary, so that the two houses seemed one. Mary's advancing age gave William the additional responsibilities of managing most of his mother's business but, at the same time, allowed him the privacy and the freedom that he cherished. Each year Mary was more content to remain before the fire in her drawing room while William went off of an evening to Kirkconnell as one at a dinner party for those like the Laird of Terregles and his wife or to stay behind when he travelled to Edinburgh for a few days of shopping with an aunt down from Blairs or of enjoying the company of his cousin John. An accident reported by William to James, 20 February 1805, made the brothers apprehensive that Mary was failing and positive that she had become too senile to be left unwatched:

> My Mother was very near being Burnt on mondays evening by overturning Her Chair. Her Head struck on the Andiron [?Tho] fortunately the fire had been recently made on & she has only suffered by a slight bruise on the head which is now nearly well.
>
> Mrs McMurdo at Cargan has been very ill from a swelling of the mouth tongue & face. She is a little better this morning. With every kind wish to my sister
>
> Your B[24]

Finally, William attended his mother to her death as he had Dorothy. When Mary died at age seventy-seven in December, James arranged the Kirkconnell-Sweetheart Abbey funeral, which expressed the deep loss felt by himself and William through such outward display as arms for the hearse, a new mantua for the laird's wife, new gowns for his servants and his brother's, James Shortridge's breads, and more than £20 of meat and drink supplied by other local provisioners.[25]

Having been able to return Mary something of the care and attention she had shown him and having won her forgiveness through expressions of his love helped allay William's sorrow. Mary's renewal of faith in him and her gratitude for his having restrained himself so as to re-enter the family circle stand out in every sentence of her long will.[26] The doctor was the sole executor and the principal beneficiary. As the father had looked after the eldest son, so the mother looked after her next eldest. Out of Mary's 'sincere regard and maternal affection', William had full and immediate power 'to intromit with, possess, occupy, and enjoy the whole of my personal and moveable property generally and particularly above conveyed as freely in all respects as if the same were his own absolute property or as I could have done myself before granting thereof'. To William 'and his assignees whomsoever' went all the lands in the Parish of Troqueer, the 'large tenement' in Dumfries, and 'the offices' there. To William 'and his assignees whomsoever' went 'all and sundry the Goods, Gear, Debts, Sum & Sums of Money, Household Furniture of every description, Stock of

Black-Cattle, Horses, Cows, Sheep, Hogs and Poultry, Farming Utensils and Crops of all kinds, Carriages and Carriage-Horses, Heirship Moveables and paraphernal Goods, Silver plate, Jewels, Gold & Silver coined and uncoined, and every other Thing of whatsoever denomination that shall pertain and belong to me or that shall be owing or indebted to me by whatever person or persons at my death by Bonds heritable or personal, Bills, Decreets, Accompts, Bank Books, Bank-Receipts or Promissory-Notes, or by any Wills — Mortgages or other Securitys, together with the — vouchers or Instructions of such debts and sums of money'. Beyond all this, two examples may suffice to illustrate what Mary's death signified to William materially. First, he received more than £1,200 within a year from just one of the bonds his mother had with James; second, he began to take interest biennially on the principals of various sums as large as £1,000 which Dorothy had willed his mother.

The juxtaposition of the mother's death and the pockets jingling with new riches caused William to kick over the traces just about as soon as James dreaded and John Menzies predicted. Always a gambler, William now had the means to substitute the dazzle of wartime speculation in commodities for the larks of a wager at the ·Dumfries Races or a handful of tickets on a local lottery. Dreams of winning concealed realities of risk. He tied down his money as quickly as it came in and sometimes more quickly; thus, he still could know moments of financial embarrassment for James to relieve at the snap of the fingers: 'Being importuned by a needy rascal, altho an acquaintance of ours J Wood! I would be obliged to you if you would send me two guineas by the Bearer, who is a Carefull little B-----d.'[27]

It was, however, in quite another respect of abandon — spiritual, ethical, psychological, or all three — that Mary's death may be seen to have changed dramatically the life of William. He lived on after his mother's burial honor-bound not to engage in political activity. Being denied this release, he was doubly susceptible to others. Of course, he had continued, during the last years with his mother, to gamble as had been his custom and to allow himself to be attracted by the opposite sex like any other bachelor. But as long as he and Mary had lived at Troqueer Holm, he had contrived to behave rather reasonably and respectfully under her moral influence; it was only after her death that he gave himself his head completely. At about the age when his father and elder brother had turned to marriage for an heir, fate presented William with a questionable heir without marriage. Whether or not the partner was one whom he could respect, one whom he intended to marry, cannot be determined. Whether or not the event was no more than a toss in the hay with a buxom bitch cannot be unravelled.

For no episode of William's long life has been more successfully hidden than that of his fathering Elizabeth. If, as seems most likely, the identity of Elizabeth's mother is ever to be made known, it will most probably be made known through the Menzies Papers, always providing that they can be 'found' in the apostolic offices of Edinburgh, where they are presently spoken of as having been 'mislaid' or else through the several Kirkconnell letters at the Catholic Archives in Edinburgh, always providing that the seeker can gain admission. Unadmitted, one can only surmise. Perhaps, romantically, the mother was an Elizabeth, too. Probably the love was as fleeting as fruitful. Because the daughter Elizabeth lived her early years under William's roof, one might imagine either that the mother died in childbirth or that she was too unfortunate to be able to provide a home herself. But that there was an illegitimate girl Elizabeth who was never but a joy to William, that he as father cared for his daughter as though she were his by laws of church and state, that he could not wait to make a new home for the two of them as soon as she was born, and that Elizabeth was the first of those who stood close to him at his death are all inescapable facts of incontrovertible documentation.[28]

The birth of Elizabeth (?1807) and William's insistence that she be raised in his home hurried the search for a new residence that had to be away from uplifted eyebrow, yet not so far away from the scene of the doctor's practice as to make it insurmountably difficult. By late 1808 William Thomson informed the doctor that he had found just the place to translate his castle in the air to actuality: the Estate of Netherwood, which 'in beauty of scenery, fertility of soil, exposure, and situation' was 'not to be surpassed in the South of Scotland'.[29]

The 150 acres, well enclosed and subdivided, were all excellent wheatland except for nine acres of merse pasture and some woodland; most of this acreage was the richest of salt merse. Exports and imports could be made from facilities along the lower side of the farmland at the east bank of the Nith looking across to Kirkconnell. There was a large dairy, there were extensive and commodious offices in good repair and fitted out for the purposes of tillage, and there was a 'Genteel Cottage', large enough to accommodate 'a considerable family'. About this dwelling, sheltered by 'fine old wood', were a walled fruit and flower garden, a 'fruitful' orchard, a kitchen garden, shrubbery, and lawns, 'the whole laid out with taste and neatness'. The lands of Netherwood lay only two miles from the center of Dumfries with the Royal Infirmary on the way into town. Six years after William signed papers on the property, the estate was offered at sale for seventeen thousand guineas.[30]

Literally feverish, William ordered Thomson as writer to negotiate the transfer of Netherwood in his name.[31] The conditions, the terms of ownership are unknown; but they did force William to scrape the bottom of the barrel and then ask James to be his cautioner. James politely declined:

Kirkconnell 27th Febr[y] 1809

Dear Brother
    I have considered what you mentioned to me yesterday, wishing that my name should be inserted as your Cautioner in the contract betwixt you and Mr [?Taite] from whom you have purchased Netherwood. A[n]d I must say I cannot by any means agree to your proposal. I remain

[?your affectionate] Brother

James[32]

James thoroughly disapproved of William's unbounded recklessness that was now drawing him into depths far over his head. Believing that Netherwood would prove ruinous, the eldest son had every reason to protect Kirkconnell whereby, incidentally, he might once more come to the rescue after clouds had broken. William would have to learn the hard way. Where he had not been taught by such comparatively inconsequential incidents as that of the decree ordered by the magistrate Robert Jackson after the plea of 'Geo. Martin Merch[t] in Dumfries' for payment of money owed him by 'W[m] Maxwell physician in Df[s],' he might be taught unforgettably by his present rashness.[33] James, furthermore, was continuing to have more than enough trouble of his own in keeping his head above water. His borrowing on Kirkconnell and those lands at Swinburne Castle willed him by his uncles and cousins mounted. He obtained £300 from Thomas White, £700 from Professor John Robison at Edinburgh University, £1,500 from Cosmo Gordon who was a Baron of the Exchequer, £1,000 from Dr John Gilchrist, £300 from Miss Jane Currie, and £1,300 from his mother just before her death.[34] Other borrowing made a total of more than £15,000. The loan from Miss Currie brought forward John McMurdo and Dr James Currie as uncles of young William Dick

McMurdo to whom Miss Currie had bequeathed both principal and interest.[35] These times almost trebled the cost of a quartern loaf, every three of these years doubled the number of bankruptcies, each of these years closed a greater number of banks. At the end of a typical year for the period, James showed a profit of no more than £63. He simply could not take upon himself the burden of caution, no matter how his refusal might pique his younger brother. And pique him it did!

DUMFRIES 1 March 1809

Dear Brother

I am sorry that absence yesterday prevented me from removing the anxiety that my proposal of Sunday seemed to occasion; I settled my transaction much to my mind & with great facility on Monday; without being obligated to any of my relations. I think it would be well for your Credit as well as mine that the subject do not get into their mouths, altho I am glad it was proposed, as in some future time, it may be of [?service] to know what dependence I may have on my nearest relatives.

The assembly seems to go on briskly no annoyance from the number of carriages. I am confined this morning by a slight attack of fever.

Miss Brown complaining more than usual yesterday.

With best wishes to My Sister

I remain your affectionate Brother

W^m. Maxwell[36]

The sequence of Mary's death, Elizabeth's birth, and William's purchase of Netherwood caused James to protect Kirkconnell otherwise. Heirless himself, he realized that the time had come to name heirs of taillie. So in July 1809 he nominated and appointed 'Doctor William Maxwell Physician my brother German and the heirs male of his Body to be procreated after marriage duly solemnized . . . exclusive of such as have been or may be born before marriage so solemnized altho' [?legitimated] by . . . subsequent marriage . . . to possess and Enjoy my said Lands and barony of Kirkconnell and others. . . .'[37] Plainly, no female bastard was to inherit. But what if William never had a son through marriage in the Catholic Church? Then the heirs of taillie would be 'John Menzies of Pitfoddles and the heirs of his body', apparently whether male or female. This instrument further chilled the relationship of the two brothers, but could not crack it.

Possessing Netherwood gave neither satisfaction nor happiness. Nurses could feed Elizabeth, tenants could dig up potatoes, John Rogerson could wait upon the master; nevertheless, having to wage a steadily losing battle against insolvency and living at odds with James robbed William of peace of mind. By 1814 the owner of Netherwood was learning the truth of 'Hair and hair makes the carle's head bare.' In May he desperately and foolishly borrowed £2,000 from the Dumfries Widows Fund Society through his friends William Thomson, the fund's treasurer and legal representative, and the Reverend Mr Thomas Duncan, one of its directors. The terms specified that William would have to repay the loan on 11 November or else suffer an initial penalty of £400 and subsequent penalties for each term negligent. The security was Netherwood disponed to Thomson. Upon six months' notice, Thomson could have repayment of the £2,000; if William defaulted, Thomson could dispose of the lands by public roup or private sale or through advertisements in the *Dumfries Weekly Journal* and one Edinburgh newspaper; Thomson was to represent Maxwell, but was not to be held liable.[38]

In late June 1814 William paid his brother £671 due on a debt.[39] James's reward for immediately returning the full amount as a present was William's spitefully mad 'Salmon War' against James in October.[40] The doctor had hired workmen to extend his salmon weirs as though he intended to encroach upon the fishing rights of Kirkconnell. James had gone off to Buxton hoping that the waters there would relieve his rheumatism, but he had left word with his solicitor Robert Gordon that Gordon was to enter a formal protest against William whenever actual encroachment could be proved. Gordon proceeded with a warning entrusted to Robert Threshie, William's cautioner for the loan from the Widows Fund. The doctor refused to comply and kept on carting in birchwood from Mabie, 'which must have cost him no small expence', in order to extend his weirs farther and farther into the Nith; he urged his engineer, moreover, to carry on despite the laborers' having been set adrift as far as Kelton by 'a very large water from the early rains'. Before the rivalry could be resolved by the commissioners, James and William had been so thoroughly at loggerheads that they were at the breaking point.

William Thomson wrote out an advertisement on 22 November for the sale of Netherwood because William was ruined stoop and droop. The Maxwell brothers certainly could not have put up such a solid front for the ensuing bankruptcy as they did and might never have found a way back to each other had it not been for the death of Clementine Maxwell, 10 March 1815, three days after the Lords of Council and Session wrote an Act of Conformation favoring Threshie.

The occasional verses publicly lamenting Clementine's death are as bad as early nineteenth-century imitations of the manner of Alexander Pope can be.[41] In or out of poetry, however, it is apparent that James lost a wife whom he loved greatly, a gracious, gentle woman widely respected for her charity. During the mourning William represented the family of Kirkconnell. It was he who wrote the letters to close friends and passed on to James condolences such as those of the Arbigland household: 'Mrs Craik and myself have indeed felt severely the heavy calamity that has befallen your Brother in the loss he has sustained in the death of good & amiable M:rs Maxwell — it is however a great satisfaction to us to hear from you that he bears up with so much fortitude.'[42] William's attendance upon his sister-in-law as the family physician, his arranging the funeral and handling the correspondence, his obvious sense of personal loss, when he himself was being sequestrated, redeemed whatever affection of James he had wasted.

The rush of economic shock in spring 1815 preceding the Battle of Waterloo in June did not permit the Maxwells to mourn a decent period. Unfeeling souls like the widow Sweetman, who held self-interest above propriety, rudely broke in on James with April letters pertaining to his brother's doom as 'Grocer-Physician':

> Sir
>   I am sorry to take the liberty of intruding upon your present retirement, This is a matter respecting your Brother, whose small Estate is likely to be sold at a very unfavourable time, while stock is at 57 there is no chance for land bringing its value. I told D:r M that I would with pleasure sacrifice my stock at present, and, as nearly as I could, accommodate him with £2000 provided it was covered by your security which I have little doubt will meet with approbation. Your having the goodness to favor me with an immediate reply will oblige me much, as a part of the above sum has laid idle for these ten days.
>   PS I am well satisfied your Brother will give you full security on the farm, as I have heard him offer it — this letter is quite an idea of my own, but having a numerous young family can own no wishes.[43]

James's icy reply was based upon earlier consultations with John Menzies by which they had agreed that there could be no way of aiding William until his present distress had run its full course:

Kirkconnell wednesday
19th April 1815

Madam

I am only this moment favored with your Letter, I am under the necessity of declining to Interfere in any Manner whatever with my Brother's affairs.

I remain Madam your Most

obedt hble Sert

J. M [44]

As mail-coaches were spreading the news of Wellington's victory over Buonaparte, writers, trustees, solicitors, justices, directors, and widows were preparing to move against Dr Maxwell. Summer ships from Liverpool continued to arrive in the Nith to unload such goods as had brought Maxwell's ruin; lists of new sequestrations lengthened; stocks moved downwards in a dull market of sugar, ashes, oils, and cottons; notices required that creditors of men like David Newall appear; auctions offered the personal belongings of the bankrupts; and requests to borrow money 'at whatever price' became commonplace.[45] Grinding slowly, justice gathered itself throughout the fall months; not until December was Robert Threshie fully empowered and ready to act through William Thomson in the case of the doctor, every alternative having been exhausted.

On Christmas Day, William Thomson requested that the creditors of Dr William Maxwell 'meet at Nairn's Coffee-House, on Saturday, the 6th of January next, at 12 o'clock noon, for the purpose of deciding upon the measure of acceding to a Deed of Trust proposed at last meeting, and unanimously approved by those who attended. In the meantime, the Creditors are desired to lodge notes of their claims in the hands of William Thomson, writer, Dumfries.'[46] Whether reluctant or otherwise, some of William's creditors identified themselves slowly as others met weekly in January and February to refine their action. James Maxwell, at the same time, through the kind offices of John Syme and Robert Gordon, acted to make it possible for his brother to pick himself up off the ground. William would need a new home large enough for at least himself and Elizabeth, for his man-servant Rogerson and Elizabeth's governess Miss Rennie. So James took out a four-year lease at £70 annually on a Dumfries dwelling owned by William Hyslop. Because he was not about to see his mother's furniture put up at public auction, James quietly made known to those writing the inventory that he wished to be informed whenever it was ready to be announced.[47] Distracted by what his brother was suffering, the laird became careless of himself so that he fell from his horse in an accident that was particularly serious for such a heavy man.[48] As James lay crippled, William had to take to bed at Netherwood with high fevers that his neighbor Dr Shortridge pronounced sufficiently grave to threaten life.[49]

These days John Menzies had become such a will-o'-the-wisp businessman and needler of those like Lord Aberdeen, whose support he sought to protect the Roman Catholics in Inverness, that James could keep him informed of William's misadventures only through James Dundas, W.S., in Edinburgh, whom James Maxwell had engaged to represent his brother before the Court of Session. Letters between James and Menzies forwarded by Dundas show that the Aberdeen cousin had tried to keep William afloat rather early in his speculations, but that finally he like the elder brother had come to realize just how fruitless it was to throw good money after bad. Early in May 1816, Menzies was confined at Blairs 'a good deal indisposed', with time to write James:

> You will readily suppose, that, besides my own very heavy loss by the D^r, I feel much regret at his situation, on his account; tho, from what I learned when last in that Country, added to some former circumstances, I was not much surprised at matters turning out as they have done. What astonishing want of all *practical* sense, in one who certainly is abundantly capable of judging well, if he would do so. It is not however the first time, by many, that I have seen persons far from deficient in judgement, *put it*, as I call it, *into their pockets*, instead of using it for the guidance of their conduct.
>
> I am glad that you have sold a lot of your wood; as to the price, a fair one, according to the times.
>
> Yours very affectionately
J Menzies[50]

As Menzies dwelt upon the 'in pockets' of life, James was alarmed that his brother might not hold on to life. Those upon whom James relied to keep abreast reported morning, noon, and night. A typical report from his footman William Reid reveals something of James's involvement:

> I have not seen the D^r but his Ser^t says he is not better — rather lighter in the meantime but the pulse is fuller and he is apprehensive the blooding must be repeated in a short time. — I have only told Miss Rennie that you

J

will be in Dumfries tomorrow and that I will meet you in town and come down with you to see your Brother. I am now going to order a post chaise for you — [51]

James had his agents poised for the 22 May announcement of the commissioners appointed on behalf of William's creditors that they had fixed a date for sale of the household furniture and other personal belongings; intervention by these agents, however, did not become necessary, because Robert Threshie, undoubtedly hesitant to offend any powerful landowner, sat down privately with the laird to decide that James would buy everything on the inventory which John Greggan and Charles Gillies, as duly named appraisers, valued at £651. 16. 8. On the twenty-ninth Threshie wrote up the agreement with James before preparing the final deed of sequestration for entry in the *Books of Council and Session:*

> Against the fifteenth day of August next Pay me on my Order in Coffee house here the sum of Six hundred and fifty one Pounds Sixteen shillings and Eight pence Sterling value received on Dr Maxwell's Furniture etc. sold you[52]

More imposingly and correctly, Threshie began the instrument of sequestration, 'Know all Men by these presents I Robert Threshie Writer in Dumfries Trustee upon the Sequestrate Estate of William Maxwell Physician and Grocer in Dumfries conform to act of Conformation.'[53]

By his agreement with Threshie, James Maxwell assured his brother that he had not been forgotten by his own. When William recovered, when he and Elizabeth moved into Dumfries, a surprise would be awaiting them in their new home rented from Hyslop.[54] Elizabeth would discover her tent bed and mahogany desk in her bedroom; Miss Rennie would find her mahogany wardrobe and chest of drawers. Mary's china and silver, her mahogany sideboard, dining-table, elbow chairs, and tea chests would be in place; her chimney glass, her Pembroke, her tea and card tables, her Brussels carpet, and her ten black and yellow chairs with cushions would furnish the drawing-room. The cheese toaster would still be found in the kitchen, the bird cage in the hall, the old books in the study, the same carriage horses in the stables. If James lingered at all in his final inspection of what his servants had accomplished, it was upstairs in William's room where he made sure that the gold, silver, and copper coins and medals were in the chest, that the 'Boys Military Antiquities' had been suitably hung on the walls, and that his brother's 'Persian slippers' were at the foot of his feather bed.[55] Satisfied, James crossed the Nith to Kirkconnell, where he opened another letter from Menzies:

Our last letters had, I find, crossed on the Road; I am much obliged to you . . . for your information of the D^r's recovery; nor shall I, as you mention, expect further intelligence about his health, considering the fever as over; unless, which I hope will not be the case, some relapse should occur. On the unpleasant subject of his affairs, I need not say much; I am glad that his furniture &c, or as much of it as is proper, will be preserved; it had been proposed to me to make the purchase which you have done, but the terms with respect to the time of payment, on which I, at first, proposed to do so, could not, it seems, be brought to bear, and the last proposal, which I made, in consequence of Mr Threshie's informing me of the peremptory measures resolved on by the Creditors, fell to the ground, by your having come forward, before he received my letter, in a more speedy manner than I could have done, having from a concurrence of many circumstances, much more call for, than command of money at present, or for a considerable time past. I hope William will now adopt such prudent and proper plans as may suit his situation; in which case being free from the Millstone, which his wrongheaded speculations had so long hung about his neck, his business, such as I have always understood it to be, ought, I think, to place him in a better situation than has ever, I suppose, been the case since his purchase of Netherwood. What you mention, as to the Girl, I strongly advised, when last at Dumfries; and tho I was then satisfied, that no improper intimacy subsisted between him and Miss R: I think, with you, that the establishment should cease; which will, of course, be the case, when the Girl is sent to school.[56]

Other letters of Menzies to James for the same period of June-July 1816 speak of regrets for 'the direct and indirect effects' of James's fall, for 'Poor William's affairs', for the doctor's having lain 'seriously ill of a Scarlet Fever', and, as follows, for the irregularity of his ways:

I need say little about his family arrangement. Even setting aside the ideas which may be entertained in the view of morality, a governess for a child of 7 years of age, or thereabouts I believe, were she even legitimate, is not at all suitable to his situation, in any view; and I hope he will, as he surely ought, be sensible of this. As to the still more important consideration of public opinion, in another view, however unfounded the suspicions may be in fact, yet as the situation & all circumstances certainly afford ground for animadversion, a change ought, in that light also, to take place; and, in so far, I agree with you & the Public most decidedly.[57]

William was forced to pay plack and bawbee to the end of 1816. On 6 September his wheat, oat, and potato crops were sold by public roup; on 15 October his 'commodious Dwelling House opposite the New Assembly-rooms, with the Stable, Coach-house, and back Court, presently possessed by Mr Glen, writer', was exposed to public sale; and on 21 November at one o'clock, the lands of Netherwood were publicly auctioned at 'Upset Price'.[58] It seems that William lost a half-interest in certain Dumfries 'Warehouses' or 'Wine Cellars' as well. In December Threshie registered an Instrument of Protest against James upon his having failed to make good on the £651 and more which he owed for William's furniture.[59] On 3 January 1817 messengers-at-arms went out from Dumfries to Kirkconnell with Horn and Poind allowing James six days to find the money or thereafter be denounced rebel.[60] On 6 January the laird paid his bill and the £12. 17s interest thereon and donated £10. 10s to the poor of Maxwelltown; a few months later he was more or less back on an even keel, now receiving £16. 15s from William as half a year's interest on the advance for the furniture and then paying William £52. 10s for his professional services at Kirkconnell and John Syme £62. 10s as half a year's interest on the bond with him.[61]

A degree of equilibrium made it possible for James to remarry. Some years previously the Riddells had recommended the services of John and William Witham, solicitors, Gray's Inn, London. These brothers and a third, the priest Thomas, came from a family in Cliffe, Yorkshire. Their part of the country was the same as that of the Riddells and the Scropes; their English lineage showed the same Roman Catholic and Jacobite backgrounds. With each new death at Swinburne Castle, such as that of Mary's brother Edward in 1813, James Maxwell had been moving farther from the Riddells; but with each new legal squabble, he had been moving closer to the Withams. At Cliffe, William Witham had introduced his client to his spinster daughter Dorothy; and it was at Cliffe on 27 August 1817 that James, twice the age of his bride, and Dorothy's brothers signed the marriage contract by which Dorothy was to receive £500 yearly upon decease of her husband.[62] Before and after his marriage, James had proof that William was so successfully mending his ways that he could be trusted with income beyond that of his profession. He therefore returned to his brother the lands in Troqueer Parish which somehow he had managed to save from William's sequestration; and he later signed a Bond of Annuity which would pay William £100 each year if William survived him. Cautiously, after experience, James stipulated that William would not have power to assign or convey this annuity and that it could not be attached 'for any debts or deeds'.[63]

Life for all the Maxwells of Kirkconnell settled down during the year 1818. Dr William applied himself to his practice as never before and prospered from it as never before. Miss Rennie remained in his home with the responsibilities of rearing Elizabeth. At Kirkconnell James gave his new wife £70 to pay the servants, paid Walker & Gordon £115 for wine, and supplied the household with barrels of herring, wheels of Cheshire cheese, and 'tartan'.[64]

Once life turned humdrum, James took that holiday at Blairs which he had promised himself and his cousin. John Menzies, who in 1805 had lost his wife Mary Westby, daughter of a staunch Catholic family in Lancashire, was not about to take another, even though he would have to die childless. Alert and contentious, he lived on at Blairs, a *bon vivant* of sixty-two, happy with his portraits of Mary Stuart and Charles Edward, his beautiful library, and his Sheraton furniture.[65] Menzies had sold as many as 3,700 Scots acres for as much as £50,000. An astute man of business, he could recite from memory the tables of rates and duties upon the Aberdeen trade and shipping; he had the trust of the House of Commons to audit accounts of the Trustees of the Aberdeen Harbours; he seemed always on his way to or from Edinburgh and London; he knew both Scots and English law as well as he knew the church fathers or how to read French, Spanish, and Latin. Menzies had found Friar Gordon for his own chapel; he had discovered Father Thomas Bagnall for St Mary's Chapel at Kirkconnell. Few Scots Catholics of his day could have been more sensitive to the taint of religious persecution; perhaps not one more valiantly presented the Catholic view to Lords Aberdeen, Melville, and Liverpool. Pitfodels was a stickler for protocol, a tyrannic moralist. One of his pet schemes was to advance the seminary at Aquhorties. There he could name all thirty seminarians and already had plans for the most recent arrival, James Gillis. Upon the occasion of Bishop Hay's death at Aquhorties in 1811, Menzies had been called to head the table at the funeral dinner. He made sure that the food would be served fashionably by bringing his own waiters from Aberdeen and acquitted himself 'very handsomely in the capacity of chairman'. Almost everybody was 'easy and happy' with his appropriate toasts, which were drunk 'in good humour'; several of those present, however, noted afterwards that the considerable expense had swallowed up much of the money destined for other purposes and that the Bishop, who died owning a wardrobe that would fetch 'scarcely twenty shillings', had been laid to rest in a grave which could not be located exactly because nobody had remembered to place an inscription over it.[66]

James Maxwell left Kirkconnell for Aberdeen in early December 1818 and arrived back home in early March 1819; he seems never before to have allowed himself such an extended holiday since the time he took over from his mother; he was not to have another.[67] When he had taken a few days at Buxton, it had been to seek relief from physical distress; when he had remained overnight at Swinburne Castle, as often as not it had been to await the drawing up of papers. Only steady, dedicated application to the management of his lands could have pulled him through the war years which had dropped friend after friend headlong into bankruptcy. James travelled with several servants. He was in no hurry. So, at Edinburgh, he treated himself to a shopping spree which ended with his buying fifty-six pounds of coffee and four half-kits of pickled salmon. At Aberdeen, he stopped long enough to select an Etruscan lamp and to supply himself with three hundred matches before going along the Dee to Blairs. His March return was just as leisurely. Edinburgh dinners at Mackay's were as sumptuous as they had been at the Crown in December, the bills revealing today a fine balance of food and port. James replaced his wardrobe from the skin out, hired a coach to attend him about the city, and, just before departing for Kirkconnell, went into Blackwood's for new silks as a gift to his wife.

The two cousins had two months and more together. Both getting too old and worn for the rugged life in the open which they had formerly enjoyed together, they rested content to visit such places as Aquhorties, to inspect estates and to oversee recent plantings of trees and new gardens, to entertain and be entertained, and to talk themselves to nodding on subjects of church and state. Because the time was near, even in William's view, for Elizabeth to begin her formal education, the cousins with William's blessing discussed what they might do for her. William would not have her locked out of the family; James and John would not have her recognized as a full and legitimate heir. The compromise which the cousins came up with during these winter months in front of the fire may have been arrived at through charity, but it led to a mutual affection between 'Eliza' and the lairds. Surmisedly, Maxwell and Menzies arranged that Elizabeth take her education abroad among the pupils of the Ursulines; factually, upon completing her studies, she would be allowed the opportunity of seeing if she was able to manage the household of the wifeless John Menzies. William could have paid the expenses of his daughter's education; a likely wager would be that his Aberdeen cousin did.

William was not blind to the fact that his brother's and his cousin's initial motive in harping upon the subject of Elizabeth's starting her education abroad was to protect his name as well as their own from scandalous rumors arising from his life with not only an illegitimate daughter but also that daughter's attractive, unmarried governess. He was too headstrong, too iconoclastic, to be bothered by tarradiddle; the important argument for him was what would be best for Elizabeth. Eliza was old enough for school; if the best education for her was to be found abroad, as it had been for himself and his brothers, then by all means let her go.

William's acquiescence gave James the right moment to reveal what had finally been decided upon at Blairs by way of helping to lift William's spirits upon the absence of his daughter. Two of the three years had run out on James's lease from Hyslop; the same years had given Dumfries a chance to talk of a new street cut between Buccleuch Street and the Nith along which William Holliday, the banker, Francis Short and Robert Threshie, the writers, Dr Harley, the surgeon, and Miss Margaret Maxwell of Munches already had lots for new town houses, all to be built in the finest Regency architecture. William was to have one of the two first homes completed.[68]

The time of William's removal to Castle Street, which only the generous interests of his brother and cousin could have made possible, was the day of Eliza's sailing for France and Miss Rennie's dismissal. The house into which he moved still stands as one of those making Castle Street the handsomest street by far in all Dumfries. John Wood's 1819 'Plan of Dumfries' shows homes only on the north side, the south side being vacant field all the way to the Nith. William's is at the eastern end, the second from Buccleuch Street. It rises today as it did when Wood surveyed it, three levels above a subterranean fourth for kitchen and laundry. Here the doctor lived the last fifteen years of his life, his sixties and early seventies, in such elegance as is suggested by a teak writing desk, blue moreen curtains, ribbon bell-pulls, 'a two-hundred piece dinner set of old Nankin China', and the folio first edition of Johnson's *Dictionary*.[69]

For attendance at the Infirmary, William had only a short drive by gig down the High Street, past Mrs Sweetman's real estate and St Michael's graveyard to Nithside; for calls at or about Kirkconnell, he would take Buccleuch Street to the Nith, cross to Maxwelltown, and turn south on the road to New Abbey.[70] As he drove, he could note that Dumfries was expanding and improving under the provostships of friends like William Thomson, that now there were not only new churches for Presbyterians but a church for Roman Catholics; not only the old Friars' Vennel but also a George Street and a Waterloo Street; not only the Old Bridge but also a New Bridge. Each year of living more in the past moved William at day's end, when he took the air, to turn his back upon the town and to go towards the Nith at the foot of Castle Street; for here the beauty of the stream on its way to passage between the merselands of Netherwood and those of Kirkconnell and here the solitude of the prospect of Lincluden beyond were unchanged.

Within a year of William's moving to Castle Street, his brother James at age sixty-one fathered an heir. It is true that Dorothy gave him not a son but a daughter to be baptized with the Christian names of herself and her mother-in-law. James, however, had anticipated such a turn by writing into his marriage contract at Cliffe that 'the Daughter or heir female so succeeding shall be bound and obliged to marry a Gentleman of the Surname of Maxwell or at least one who shall assume the same.' Dorothy Mary Maxwell was thus committed at birth in 1820 to continue the association of 'Maxwell' and 'Kirkconnell' if she chose marriage; but no provision binding an heir female could blunt the main point: if Dorothy Witham Maxwell did not bear a male child, her husband James and his brother William would be the last male heirs in the long, proud lineage with the right to bear the arms of the Maxwells of Kirkconnell.

The first four years of Dorothy Mary's life introduced a previously unknown serenity and happiness to the brothers' relationship. William and James were never more close, never more understanding of each other. Both thrived. In one January, James discharged his bond of £2,524 to John Syme and his bond of £1,260 to Dr John Gilchrist and still had enough money left over to draw £1,200 as cash for himself.[71] These years of prosperity made it possible for him to loan £12,000 to the Society for the Propagation of Christian Knowledge and, in behalf of the poor of Troqueer, to double the sum which he, as executor of Jean Baptiste Copleux, 'distributed amongst the poor Catholics of

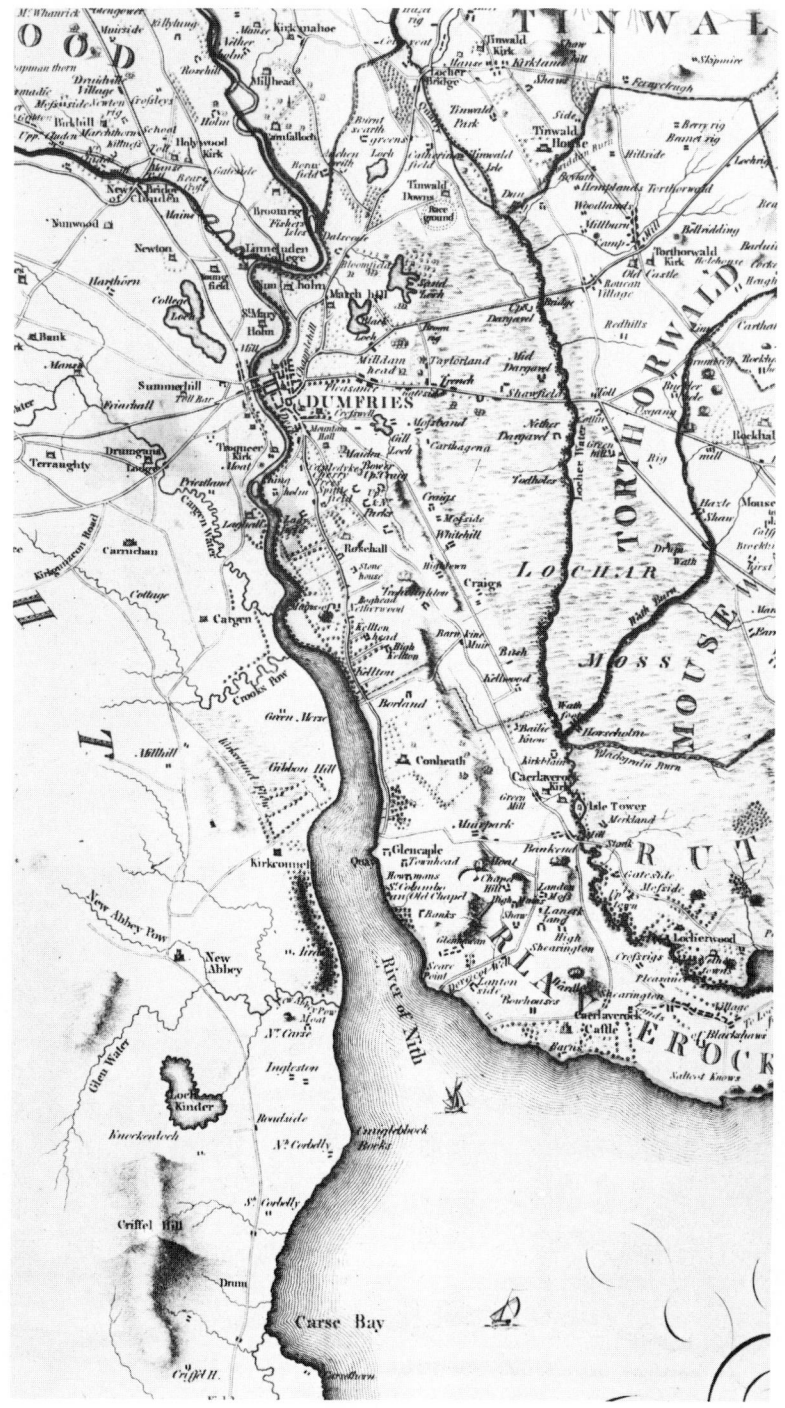

Plate 1. Map of Nithside,
from Crawford's *Map of Dumfries-shire,* 1804.

Plate 2A.　Sweetheart Abbey.

Plate 2B.　Kirkconnell.

Plate 3.   Dinant, a 19th century view by C. C. Stanfield.

Plate 4. The Dagger Scene, by James Gillray.

Plate 5A.   Mary Maxwell (mother).

Plate 5B.   James Maxwell (father).

Plate 6A.   John Syme.

Plate 6B.   James Maxwell (brother).

Plate 7. John Menzies, by Benjamin W. Crombie
(from *Modern Athenians,* 1882).

Plate 8.   William Maxwell (silhouette).

Terregles House Congregation'.[72] In the same period, William took from his extensive practice more money, not to mention more opportunities for more work than he knew what to do with.

John Fraser at the King's Arms, from whom the doctor hired a chaise for visits to Kirkconnell, might have been left to wonder from the frequency of these visits that the child Dorothy Mary did not know a day of good health;[73] but he did not realize that James's real object in calling out William was to show him the new clock for the nursery, to have his opinion of the latest pointer, or to ask him to sit for a portrait by John Allan, who had just finished painting Dorothy.[74] Nor did Fraser or anybody else other than William have to know that on any day James entered in his account-books an amount of interest like £83. 15s as due him by William on the furniture, the entry was sure to be followed by another entry specifying, 'By paid Dr Maxwell In full for his Trouble for Advice and Attendance to this date £83. 15s.'[75] Sometimes, as in this instance, the figures cancel exactly; more often, what James pays William for his services is double what the doctor owes; sometimes, a single day of the accounts shows only 'to pay Dr Maxwells fees £120'; no entry reveals that William ever returned to Dumfries one farthing out of pocket.[76]

Kirkconnell account-books for the years of Dorothy Mary's first governess, first 'piana from Bath', and first 'Dancing Master with Fiddler in Compliment' are the years of James's last illness and the years which foretell the passing of authority at Kirkconnell out of the hands of the Maxwells and into the hands of the Withams: the years 1824-1827. In 1823 Dorothy Maxwell started to board her mother and father at Kirkconnell for '£60 *p.a.*' When William, the father, died on 9 March 1825, Dorothy seems to have invited one of her father's sisters and her brothers Thomas and John to join her mother and herself at £45 a year. Then and there, the Reverend Mr Thomas Witham began to be the man to reckon with; for by then James was ready to make his last will, while living on whisky and brandy of his own prescription, the honey and eggs of William's, the drugs of Dr Fraser, and the bleedings of Dr Shortridge. William was coming to him as many as forty-four times in five months, both as attending physician and sorrowing brother.

James named his wife as his sole executrix on 4 May 1825;[77] two months later, he added a codicil to the settlement of his barony.[78] This codicil, dated 12 July 1825, is in two parts: the first specifies that Thomas Witham be 'Guardian & Tutor' of the heiress-daughter Dorothy Mary. Later developments point to John Menzies having been designated as well; the second specifies that William be given the possessions as listed in the Netherwood Inventory. The last legal action signed by James Maxwell, therefore, favored his brother. And not only William: 'I do hereby Direct . . . my Executor . . . to convey . . . the whole of the said Furniture . . . to my said Brother . . . and failing him I direct and appoint the said Furniture to be conveyed to my Brothers daughter Elizabeth Maxwell. . . .' For James to include Eliza in his last will and to recognize her there as his brother's daughter were the final tokens of a complete reconciliation and love between brother and brother.

James died on 5 February 1827, a few months before his sixty-eighth birthday. At Kirkconnell on the twentieth, Justice of the Peace Robert Gordon, as James's agent, opened the charter chest in the presence of the family priest and guardian Thomas Witham, his brother John, William Maxwell, and William's agent Robert Murray, writer in Dumfries. The doctor was to have his annuity; he and his daughter were to have the furniture. Evidently, the Withams objected to the latter; for Robert Gordon had to spell out in a paper which he docketed *'Private'* that it had been he himself who had drawn up the 'separate settlement': 'Some years ago Mr Maxwell gave from 6 to £700 for the Doctors furniture — He leaves the Furniture to the Doctor and failing him the Doctors Daughter RG.'[79] Only one of the inventories, which Gordon was obliged to produce in proving this separate settlement, is extant.[80] Here one learns for the first time of items like 'Painting of Castle' and '257.03 oz. silver plate'; and here one can read evaluations of hitherto unrecognized objects like '4 Dessicated Maps in Boxes', '150 odd Vol^s of old Books', and 'Staircase Clock and case'. Similar lists exist for the Kirkconnell inventories after James's decease: '1111 Books £70', '75 1/2 Dozen of Port wine £113', '18000 Bricks at Brickfield £22. 10s', and '2 Donkeys £1'.

William Maxwell lived seven years after James was buried at Sweetheart Abbey by the side of his father, mother, and brother. Only in the last of these years did his health so fail that he could not practise actively. Dr Fraser succeeded him as family physician at Kirkconnell soon after James died; but rather stubbornly and proudly Dr William went out to accept calls from such loyal, old retainers of his family as his brother's factor William Copland.[81] He had treated William's wife Mary in 1807 until her death, and James had trebled the customary funeral allowances. Now the doctor sat by Copland to relieve his pain and to allay his anxiety with assurances that the young peach trees had been planted, that the hay was, indeed, being tedded properly, and that his assistant had brought back the new bull from David Newall's unharmed. It is doubtful that the doctor stopped long with the Withams, who were now in sole possession of the mansion because Dorothy Maxwell had moved to York Place in Edinburgh so that she could be near Dorothy Mary. Even so, William had to listen to more of Father Thomas's talk about stipend, money for the poor, and payments to Dumfries priests James and Andrew Carruthers than his little patience could endure and more of the senior Mrs Witham's small talk of a mended 'umber aller', a 'gowan & Parasole', and ribbons, 'spung cakes', and lace than suited his tastes for guns and whisky.[82] Missing James, William had the solace of Eliza and John Menzies.

The Laird of Pitfodels appeared tireless at seventy-one to those who watched him standing at James's funeral and to Sir Walter Scott who, a week earlier, had borrowed Menzies' pamphlets on the Russian Campaign for his eight-volume life of Napoleon. Scott's journal for 30 January 1827 reads:

> Blank day in Court, being the Martyrdom. Wrought hard at *Bon.* all day, though I had settled otherwise. . . . About three, Pitfodels called. A bauld crack that auld papist body and well informed. He is very angry with the Irish demagogues, and a sound well-thinking man.[83]

Truth to tell, Menzies was feeling his age when Sir Walter returned his call; at least, the laird was ready to change his life-style. The time was right for him to begin turning over the bulk of his wealth to the Roman Catholic Church; to accomplish this purpose, as well as to control it, he would have to be in Edinburgh. He had discussed what he had in mind with Bishops John and Aeneas Chisolm as successive Vicars-Apostolic of the Highland District and with Bishop Alexander Cameron of the Lowland Vicariate; he presently dealt with the Chisolms' successor Bishop Ranald MacDonald, but even more fully and confidentially with Bishop Alexander Paterson in Edinburgh. The first step was to make over the estate of Blairs as a new seminary to replace both Lismore and Aquhorties. This move alone took two years: 1828-1830. Menzies was slow and deliberate, hesitant to let go. Because he desired to keep his own eye on professors and students and to make sure that the seminarians observed good manners and morals, he reserved the right to retain a suite of rooms. By the time he was fully ready to depart Blairs for Edinburgh, where in 1828 he had placed

Father Gillis strategically for his purposes, the motto of the students had become, 'Dinna anger the laird.'[84]

The new life immensely fitted Menzies' fancy. His house at 24 York Place was large enough for him to invite Bishop Paterson as permanent guest and Father Gillis as chaplain, master of ceremony, liaison officer, and part-time secretary, although officially he was listed as a curate of St Mary's. Menzies probably paid for the elegant, box-like pew built into St Mary's in 1830 under the direction of Gillis as Honorary Royal Chaplain to seat the abdicated French king Charles X and his grandson Henry, while their Cardinal de Latil was at the altar; and Menzies probably had his reward of being thanked at Holyrood, which had been offered the French by King William IV.[85]

Bishop Paterson was John Menzies' 'permanent' guest for nine months before he died on 30 October 1831. Not wishing just any Edinburgh undertaker or just any funeral, the laird immediately arranged that Gillis be in charge of the obsequies because only he was capable of organizing the *pompes-funèbres*.[86] Before Gillis was through, he had transformed a room in the clergy-house of St Mary's Cathedral into a *chapelle-ardente* to receive the coffin; adapted the cathedral with a platform and steps hung with black cloth and brightened with escutcheons; printed tickets of admission; dressed up men as gentlemen ushers with wands; engaged the Cardinal de Latil to assist at High Mass; and buried Bishop Paterson under an episcopal throne. So greatly did Gillis please his benefactor by all this, 'the most spectacular Catholic function staged in Scotland since the sixteenth century', Menzies put forward the thirty-year-old curate's name to Gregory XVI as the best successor to Paterson. Such mischief made the feelings of the Scots bishops run so high that they successfully advanced the name of Andrew Carruthers. Gillis, they argued, was too inexperienced; let him return to his native Montreal if he had to have a bishopric.[87]

Undaunted, Menzies placated those whom he had offended by promising to stand most of the cost of a new Chapel of Ease on Lothian Street; meanwhile, his head and Gillis's were together for something more challenging. Why not an Ursuline convent in Edinburgh, complete with beautiful chapel and excellent school for young ladies to be instructed by the sisters? Gillis could go to France to enlist Ursulines; Menzies could pick out the site, purchase it, and hire an architect. How completely the old Aberdonian, educated by Jesuits, and the young Royal Chaplain, who had made several retreats in France among the

Jesuits, could read the future lies in mystery. They may have foreseen that the crypt they designed for under the altar of St Margaret's would receive their corpses. Knowing Gillis, Menzies could have imagined that his funeral would be even more of a spectacle than that of the late bishop. Actually, it was.[88] When the laird died in 1843, spirits of wine burned in sepulchral urns and a small orchestra played Mozart's *Requiem* before the hearse went across Edinburgh to St Margaret's and the *sub altare* tombstone cut with JOANNES . DE . SALES . MENZIES / DOMINUS . DE . PITFODELS / QUEM . SUAE . GENTIS . ULTIMUM.

John Menzies was a little, round man of stomach and watch fob when he entered upon the last phase of his life by removal from Blairs to York Place, January 1831. No man to lend himself to such falderal as love levels all ranks, he credulously spent himself believing blood is thicker than water. Both William Maxwell's daughter Elizabeth and James Maxwell's daughter Dorothy Mary had as much of the blood of the Maxwells of Kirkconnell as ran in Menzies' own veins. Once Elizabeth had been educated, once she had returned for trial under Menzies (probably first at Blairs), the laird soon began to allow her every bit of the lovely disposition which her father did. Elizabeth became Menzies' 'Eliza' as she always had been her father's.[89] She went to Edinburgh with Pitfodels. It was she who saw to his household comforts in York Place and those of such guests as Paterson and Gillis; and it was she who later made a home for Menzies and his 'permanent guest' Bishop Gillis in Greenhill Cottage, adjacent to the new convent and school. Greenhill was even less a 'cottage' than Troqueer Holm; after the laird enlarged it, the gate-lodge and the gardens alone would have told the Bruntsfield passer-by that only a man of some affluence could live at the end of the lane.[90] Eliza was with Menzies to share all the excitement of these beautiful new surroundings and old enough to assume much of the care of moving across the city to a view of the Lammermuirs in the south. She is the 'Miss Maxwell' whom the *Edinburgh Directory* lists as being with Menzies to his death in 1843 and then with Bishop Gillis, still managing at Greenhill Cottage as she had for the laird, until her own death in ?September 1858. Gillis fell heir to her inheritance from father, paternal grandmother, and Menzies.

The day-to-day presence of Eliza, who had been sent out of the country to the Ursulines for proper Catholic education, and the immediacy of Dorothy Mary with her mother at 42 York Place may have given Menzies and Gillis their inspiration for establishing the

Ursuline school of St Margaret's. Menzies had enjoyed many years of supporting Catholic education of young men; but in advancing Catholic education of young women, he must have suffered more than a twinge of Pooh Bah's, 'I'm not in the habit of saying "How de do, little girls, how de do" to anybody under the rank of a Stockbroker. Oh, my protoplasmal ancestor!'

Neither the Reverend Mr Thomas Witham nor Dorothy Maxwell, as guardians of Dorothy Mary, stood up to the lordly authority exercised by John Menzies, the third guardian. James's daughter came to Edinburgh as having been infeft in 1827 with Kirkconnell and having been allowed a yearly £300. As long as she was with her mother at York Place, Menzies chose the curriculum she was to follow; but Elizabeth Maxwell, as her 'Betsy', was the one to escort her to her music master on George Street, to purchase her Italian books and guitar strings, and to help her argue her case before Menzies for a rosewood harp at ninety guineas.[91] Menzies, not Thomas Witham, gave the permissions to go to Kirkconnell or to accept an invitation to Swinburne Castle; but Betsy was the one to chaperone her every mile of the way. After Dorothy Mary lost her mother in 1835, Menzies provided the Edinburgh home; but Betsy was the one to console her even as she prepared her wardrobe for matriculation at St Margaret's that fall. There Menzies watched over Dorothy Mary's progress in such lessons as English, Astronomy, and Writing; but Betsy offered the most encouragement, gently introduced the advantages of her skills in French, needlework, and pianoforte, and sent over the freshly laundered white Sunday dress, the summer uniforms of buff gingham, and the winter uniforms of 'brown stuff'.[92] Both Menzies and Elizabeth were alive to celebrate Dorothy Mary's coming of age in 1841; of the two, however, only Elizabeth survived in 1844 to attend the wedding of the heiress of the Barony of Kirkconnell to her cousin Robert S. J. Witham. With this marriage, an expression of Thomas Witham's complete authority after Pitfodel's death, Burke's *Landed Gentry* first printed 'Maxwell-Witham' in the genealogy of the Maxwells of Kirkconnell.

To be with her father during the last years of his life, Elizabeth did not have to wait upon Dorothy Mary's going to Kirkconnell; Menzies would have seen to that. The silhouette of William, done for his daughter in 1831, his seventy-first year, shows sharp features and bushy eyebrows, but suggests neither the height nor large set of the earlier portrait by Allan.[93] At the end of a day of patients, the father was pleased to rest in the library before joining his daughter for their evening meal together. Announcements in the newspaper, that he had just put aside, of events like the deaths of John Syme and Dr Gilchrist and the elevation of William Thomson to the presidency of the Directors of the Gas Board would start enough recollections to last out their stroll to the Nith. Eliza was a good listener. If, however, she were the one to introduce a subject, William was the one to exhaust it. She might begin with an explanation of the sounds he had heard overhead when he had closed his eyes in the library: she had been packing for her holiday at Glenaladale in the country of Prince Charles's flight from Scotland.[94] Happy with his own memories of holidays in the same part of Scotland with Menzies, William drifted from stories about Pitfodels and then about Swinburne Castle, always to return to reality: the bonds that had held the Menzies, the Riddells, and the Maxwells together for almost one hundred and fifty years were all but cut through; in the new generation only the Riddells would preserve a line from male heir to male heir; save for himself, in a sense, the Maxwells of Kirkconnell would be no more; save for John Menzies, the Menzies of Pitfodels would be no more; and save for an infrequent visit into northern England by Dorothy Mary, more likely to the Withams at Cliffe than to the Riddells, there would be no word of Swinburne Castle. After seeing Eliza off the next morning, the doctor went back to his patients.

The plague which exacted a terrible toll from Dumfries in the closing months of 1832 broke William Maxwell. Although spared cholera himself, he had been so called upon as the leading physician of the community that he was left without an ounce of strength. What his colleagues expected to hear in January 1833 did not make the rounds of the Infirmary until November: Maxwell was most ill and not expected to recover. Menzies dispatched Eliza to make sure that everything that could be done would be. Cousin and daughter appear to have shared the view that nothing more important could be done for the sick man than to return him to the Catholic Church. William survived, barely. Out of danger, but still sick, very feeble, and apprehensive in his certainty that he had only a brief time left in which to live, he seems to have listened to his daughter and promised her that just as soon as he found the strength, he would accept Menzies' advice to go back to Edinburgh with Eliza for death as a Roman Catholic.

Spring brought William the energy he required to look after something else of consequence. He wished to provide Eliza with all the inheritance his resources could command. This he himself must arrange; for the nature of her birth, the changes at Kirkconnell which kept him at a distance from the Withams, and the uncertainties of where he stood legally with respect to some of his affairs threatened disadvantages for his daughter after his death. William was made restless in his belief that his home and everything in it which Eliza did not want for herself or Menzies for himself should be put up for sale, the sooner the better. It would be a seller's market. He knew those who could best conduct the auction and those who had the money to purchase fairly. He had the community's goodwill. That this sale began on the premises, Tuesday 20 May, signifies that William had had sufficient reserve strength two days earlier to travel to Edinburgh attended by Eliza. It means, also, that he could do nothing further in Dumfries to safeguard Eliza.

William Maxwell had almost six months of life in John Menzies' Edinburgh home before he succumbed. It was then and there that he reaffirmed his belief in the Roman Catholic Church. Every Catholic in Edinburgh could vouch that the priest Gillis was every bit the eloquent preacher that his reputation made him out to be; Menzies could vouch that his permanent guest had enough of that worldly wisdom of Chaucer's 'Frere' to succeed:

> Ful swetely herde he confessioun,
> And pleasant was his absolucioun:
> He was an esy man to yeve penaunce,
> Ther as he wiste to have a good pitaunce.

Knowing much of what William would wish to talk about, having ticked away at his own list of the sins which were bound to be confessed, John Menzies would not have entrusted the conversion to anybody but James Gillis.

This priest must have confessed worse sinners than William Maxwell who had dedicated more than forty years to alleviating the pain of his fellow men. Weeks before 13 October 1834, Gillis, therefore, could assure Bishop Carruthers and John Menzies that Maxwell had been fully prepared as a Roman Catholic to receive the last rites when the time came. Thus on the thirteenth Carruthers gave the blessing and made the sign of peace.

Newspaper accounts of the funeral and burial are as unapparent as the great circumspection by both Menzies and the Withams is apparent. Today one can walk oneself to a limp in the graveyards of Edinburgh and wherever they can be found along both banks of the Nith, yet never come upon a grave for Dr William Maxwell or a grave for his daughter Elizabeth. Menzies was enough of a traditionalist to insist upon interment at Sweetheart Abbey; on the other hand, he was more than enough of a moralist to demand an unmarked grave in Edinburgh. What does it matter? If William was not buried with his family before the high altar of Sweetheart Abbey, that is where one can come upon his spirit today; after that, at the gateway to Kirkconnell or at the Nith within sight of Lincluden's ruins.

Newspapers did remark the October passing 'At Edinburgh, on the 13th instant'.[95] On the twenty-second, the *Dumfries Times* printed the following:

> Dr. Maxwell — This gentleman died in Edinburgh the other day. His departure was not wholly unexpected for he was full of years and of a constitution far from vigorous. Indeed his recovery from a severe illness that affected him last winter was at the time altogether unlooked for. Dr. Maxwell was for many years at the head of the medical profession in the district, and was in consequence a person of much influence as well as interest in our locality, where his talents and success were long and intimately known. His fame was not, however, limited to Dumfries. His intimacy with Burns whose friend as well privately as professionally he was, and of whose last illness he was a faithful and affectionate soother in both capacities, has in some measure rendered the name of Maxwell literary property, while the liberal principles of the deceased, his visit to Paris in the early days of the first revolution, and the well known denouncement of him and his presumed designs by Burke, give him a permanent place in the political history of the country. We had hoped to lay before our readers some particulars of the Doctor's varied life, but our time and space forbid us to enter on the subject this week.

The very absence of any mention of Kirkconnell would have told any alert Dumfries reader of this notice that the editor's limitations of time and space were but as euphemisms for the family's dictum: 'Let the curtains be drawn tightly.' Much more important is that before leaving William Maxwell, the editor reminded his readers that the deceased had been given something still more for the helter-skelter of his final consciousness. So among the last thoughts drawn and rolled like stones on the shore had been thoughts of Robert Burns.

K

FROM ROBERT BURNS—

The deil cam fiddlin thro' the town,
　　And danc'd awa wi' th' Exciseman,
And ilka wife cries, 'Auld Mahoun,
　　I wish you luck o' the prize, man!'

— 'The Deil's Awa Wi' the Exciseman'

O steer her up, an' be na blate,
　　An' gin she tak it ill, jo:
Then leave the lassie till her fate,
　　And time nae longer spill, jo:
Ne'er break your heart for ae rebute,
　　But think upon it still, jo:
That gin the lassie winna do't,
　　Ye'll find anither will, jo.

— 'O Steer Her Up an' Haud Her Gaun'

Drumlanrig's towers hae tint the powers
　　That kept the lands in awe, man:
The eagle's dead, and in his stead
　　We're gotten a hoodie-craw, man.

— 'As I cam Down the Banks o' Nith'

Of a' the airts the wind can blaw,
　　I dearly like the west,
For there the bonnie lassie lives,
　　The lassie I lo'e best.

— 'Of A' the Airts'

—FROM ROBERT BURNS

We have gotten a set of very decent Players here just now.

— To Gilbert Burns

I too, Madam, am just now Revolution-mad . . . mine is the madness of an enraged Scorpion shut up in a thumb-vial.

— To Mrs Dunlop

Our book Society owe you still the £1 - 4 -

—To Peter Hill, Bookseller, Edin.

May our success in the present war be equal to the justice of our cause.

— To Samuel Clarke Jun[r]

I daresay this is the first epistle you ever received from this nether world. I write you from the regions of Hell, amid the horrors of the damned. The time and manner of my leaving your earth I do not exactly know, as I took my departure in the heat of a fever of intoxication.

— To Mrs Robert Riddell

CHAPTER SIX

Poet

Now steekit frae the gowany field,
Frae ilka favrite houff and beild;
But mergh, alas! to disengage
Your bonny buik frae fettering cage,
Your free-born bosom beats in vain
For darling liberty again.

—Robert Fergusson

William Maxwell of Kirkconnell had just begun his last year of medical school when the poet Robert Burns entered Edinburgh from Ayrshire to be lionized as the author of the Kilmarnock *Poems.* Both men in that fall of 1786 were still in their twenties; Burns, the elder by more than a year and a half. Auld Reekie, which he called 'the venerable, respectable, hospitable, social, convivial, imperial Queen of cities', so rung his ears with 'multiplied honors and repeated acclamations' of numerous and elegant meetings that he was 'downright thunderstruck and trembling in every nerve'[1] The very fact that the poet was the rage of that winter season assures us that Maxwell saw him at the height of his popularity. This was the hour, also, of Burns's highest genius.

The movement of Robert Burns towards and away from this central year and more of Edinburgh describes how the Scottish Enlightenment served that genius at the same moment it was shaping William Maxwell.[2] Here a first query might be: had Burns owed anything to the Enlightenment *before* he rode from Ayr to the Athens of the North? Even after allowances for Calvinist accents upon freedom and democracy, for Presbyterian commitment to popular education, and for native inspiration, still the answer would have to be that same Yes implied in the following statement from a *Times Literary Supplement* review of a work by David Daiches: 'In a way anyone who can understand all Burns' references here or appreciate every important theme, also understands the last stage of the Enlightenment, and every idea and sentiment of the French Revolution.'[3]

Probably Burns was never more right than in identifying his constituent elements as pride and passion. Where he uses the word *passion*, he usually insinuates the words *heart* and *instinct*. Burns composed his best verses confident in the truth of Soutar's

> When the mind would speak
> But the heart has nought to say,
> Wait for the hour . . .
> This is your power
> To curb the fretful brain and trust the blood.[4]

For daily life as well as for poetry, Burns gave his trust to passion. Thus he writes his early friend Captain Richard Brown of the ship *Mary & Jean*, 'Men of grave, geometrical minds, the sons of, "Which was to be demonstrated," may cry up reason as much as they please; but I have always found an honest passion, or native instinct, the trustiest auxiliary in the warfare of this world. — Reason almost always comes to me, like an unlucky wife to a poor devil of a husband — just in time enough to add her reproaches to his other grievances, (*Letters*, ed. J. D. Ferguson, I, 206).

Because of passion Burns could speak of himself as being among the harum-scarum sons of imagination and whim. Because of passion it is the language of the heart that abounds in the early letters, where phrases like 'genuine emotion' and 'real passion' leap to the eye in contexts borrowing sometimes from a work like Adam Smith's *Theory of Moral Sentiments*, but most frequently and directly from Mackenzie's *Man of Feeling*. As completely, however, as Burns allowed his heart to melt with sensibility, there was always more durable matter to remain. This Thomas Campbell called a 'flexible and universal sympathy',[5] this Coila recalls in her words, 'I saw thee eye the gen'ral mirth With Boundless love.'[6] Such benevolence Burns cultivated, such benevolence he turned into tolerance so that he could 'scan the failings, nay the faults & crimes of mankind . . . with a brother's eye'.[7]

Scotland apart, the objects of Burns's pride were first independence, second literary fame, and third common sense. All three elements distinguish such poems as 'Man was made to mourn', all three inform such a song as the last air in 'The Jolly Beggars' with its chorus of

> A fig for those by law protected!
>   Liberty's a glorious feast!
> Courts for cowards were erected,
>   Churches built to please the priest.

This poetry was compounded of clashes of will between father and son, factor and ploughman, Auld Licht and Moderate, monarchist and republican, dyed-in-the wool champion of the *status quo* and reformer. From Burns's point of view, pride and passion might incite such clashes, but only forces of the Enlightenment might introduce worthy accomplishments because of them.

Simply, Robert Burns was too bright a young man not to have seen the opening and then taken it. As a great and original genius, he was endowed with a mind able to perceive essential things quickly, to reason powerfully, and to judge clearly and sensibly. Denied the opportunity of continuing formal education, he turned to self-education through books and men as a means of sustaining his genius with fuel in proportion to its spark.

Precise records of what Burns read are uncommon to a degree of suggesting his scorn of pedantry. From what can be known, however, it is safe to assume a reading list far more extensive than the oft-quoted poetic disclaimer to have no pretence to learning would warrant. In the currency of books, Burns soon became a sharp borrower and an usurious lender so that by 1783 he could write, 'In the matter of books, indeed, I am very profuse' (I, 14). This testimony is borne out more generally by his brother Gilbert's asserting, 'No book was so voluminous as to slacken his industry or so antiquated as to damp his research.'[8]

Cheerfully Burns sacrificed every other consideration in order to read any book that would indulge the joy of his heart: to study men, their manners, and their ways. From what he learned of Rousseau and Locke came something of his concepts of liberty and education as well as his poem 'The Author's Earnest Cry and Prayer'; from Hutcheson, Beattie, and Mackenzie, his opposition to Hume's scepticism; from moderates, his deistic and Socinian bias; and from his reading as a whole, a new awareness of what he was about. This awakening he was to convey much later to Erskine of Mar: 'The uninformed mob may swell a nation's bulk; & the titled, tinsel Courtly throng may be its feathered ornament, but the number of those who are elevated enough in life, to reason & reflect; and yet low enough to keep clear of the venal contagion of a Court; these are a Nation's strength' (II, 171).

Through his own poetry as well as through his reading, Robert Burns was brought, ever more often after the year 1780, into companies of men who reasoned and reflected. Three such associations are to be identified readily as the western gentry, the Bachelors' Club, and the Freemasons. Many of the Ayrshire gentry had been educated in Edinburgh and Glasgow at the height of the Scottish accomplishment through the Enlightenment; some of these returned each winter to reside in the capital for the society of its clubs and assemblies; others like William Wallace returned to lecture as professors at the university. Because of the gentry, what was known in Edinburgh was soon known in Ayrshire. Burns's idea of founding a club in Tarbolton for unmarried young men who sought mutually to encourage one another in literary aspiration through debate may be taken as a concrete example of how the ways of the Enlightenment extended into the countryside. Subjects of discussion at Tarbolton probably differed not at all from the following topics entertained by the Mauchline Conversation Society, which Burns started on its way in 1786: 'Whether a Republican form of Government or a mixed Monarchy is best,' 'Which is most an object of desire, an enlightened understanding or a feeling heart.'[9] It was from the midst of preparing arguments for questions like these that Burns was 'entertained an apprentice' in the St David Masonic Lodge of Tarbolton on 4 July 1781. On October 1st he was 'passed and raised'; and in July 1784, he was made deputy-master. One could write much of the history of the Kilmarnock Edition with names drawn only from Ayrshire freemasonry: the poet, Burns; the patron, John Ballantyne; the dedicatee, Gavin Hamilton; the printer, John Wilson; and the principal disposer, Robert Muir.

These new associations heightened Burns's assurance and deepened his understanding of such cherished concepts as independence, equality, brotherhood of man, tolerance, common sense, and benevolence. These men, who made unobtrusive talent and worth their business, confirmed Burns in his belief that next to worth, learning was most to be admired in another and that another's worth might be measured by his learning, whether he be a William Muir or a Dugald Stewart. They also taught the poet something of the spirit of cosmopolitan intellectual fraternity. Their sympathetic understanding of his passionate urge for literary fame was a natural response of individuals who themselves had been taught to esteem, to seek, to foster, to patronize, and to encourage the identical fame.

Versatile, indifferent with regard to matters of mere opinion, Burns's new friends not only could suggest the books which he might read but, best of all, could provide him with a copy; thus, his reading that hitherto had been rather tangential and attenuate in terms of the Enlightenment became stiffer and more direct. The works of writers like Voltaire and Rousseau which were ordered for the Mauchline group must have been discovered as the books to read at about the time of the earlier Tarbolton group. Attracted and held by the exciting exchange of ideas, Burns enlarged his views, trained his mind, and improved his conversational abilities. One must remark that the tempo of this exchange correlates exactly with the tempo of his most memorable creativity.

Burns entered Edinburgh, 29 November 1786, independent, hopeful of literary fame, and warm with anticipation of response from this the stronghold of Scotland's Enlightenment. Seventeen months later, on 24 March 1788, he departed the capital, dependent, doubtful of poetic reputation, and frozen with indifference. Entering an Ayrshire ploughman inspired by native ground, he left a Dumfriesshire leaseholder. Entering a busy bachelor, he left a busier bridegroom. Entering a proud and passionate republican, he left a candidate for exciseman in the service of His Majesty George III. Entering a poet at the pinnacle of his most fruitful creating, he left a collector, reviser, and composer of Scottish songs, with only 'Tam o' Shanter' to add to his matchless poems. It would seem, therefore, that some reason exists to doubt Professor Snyder's declaration that Edinburgh 'made no alteration in [Burns's] soul-stuff . . . He was the same man in the spring of 1788 that he had been in the autumn of 1786, and his life went on much as it would have done had "Auld Reekie" never had the honor of welcoming him.'[10]

Not three months in Edinburgh, Burns requested and received permission of the baillies to erect a stone at the unmarked grave of Robert Fergusson. Probably he made time to stand at that grave in the Canongate parish cemetery to ponder what of Fergusson's fate might be his own. Before Fergusson's 'The Daft Days', composed in 1772, the literati had begun to line up solidly in favor of standard English as the language of poetry; by the time of his own 'The Twa Dogs', composed in 1786, they stood shoulder to shoulder in this their main insistence, despite the fact that not a single major work of imaginative literature had been gained thereby. That literary fame ascribed to the Scottish

Enlightenment was not to be bestowed upon dialect poetry, whether Fergusson's or his own. Fergusson had learned that the better a poet's vernacular verses, the more attention; and the more attention, the stronger opposition to what could be done best.

Soon and late in Burns's Edinburgh sojourn, the most respected voices of the Scottish Enlightenment advised against his using guid braid Scots. Burns arrived in Edinburgh prepared for some advice; but he could not have been prepared for the overwhelming agreement among those men he most admired, men of learning and of worth, who, having been honored with literary fame, could confer it upon others. Henry Mackenzie straightway drew the point in his *Lounger* for 9 December 1786. Burns had but one bar to fame: his language. 'Even in Scotland,' wrote the man of feeling, 'the provincial dialect which Ramsay and he have used, is now read with a difficulty which greatly damps the pleasure of the reader.' John Sinclair had developed the same subject in his *Observations on the Scottish Dialect* of 1782. James Beattie picked up from Sinclair in his *Scoticisms . . . designed to Correct Improprieties of Speech and Writing* (1787). Here Beattie's purpose was to put young writers and speakers on their guard against some of those Scots idioms which were likely to be mistaken for English. His concern was that provincial idioms were occasioning the decline of learning. 'Our tongue,' Beattie scolds, 'was brought to perfection in the days of Addison and Steele . . . Every unauthorized word and idiom, which has of late been, without necessity, introduced into it, tends to its debasement; and every attempt to discredit such words and idioms will be praised, or at least pardoned, by the judicious critick' (p. 5).

Handed along from Stewart to Dalzell to Walker, from critic to critic, Burns always found cause to recognize something of a kindred spirit, enlightened, seemingly, in all respects save that of poems in the Scottish dialect. Burns honored Hugh Blair as a 'truly worthy and most respectable character', confidentially observing that 'he is justly at the head of what may be called fine writing; and a Critic of the first, the very first rank in Prose; even in Poesy a good Bard of Nature's making can only take the pas of him.'[11] But it was Hugh Blair who judged 'The Jolly Beggars' as altogether unfit for publication, and it was he who gave Edinburgh's goodbye to Burns in May 1787: 'You have laid the foundation for just public esteem . . . you will not, I hope, neglect to promote that esteem, by cultivating your genius, and attending to such productions of it as may raise your character still higher. At the same time, be not in great haste to come forward. Take time and leisure to improve and mature your talents. For on any second production you give the world, your fate as a poet will very much depend.'[12]

No person of influence in Edinburgh could have wished Burns more success than Dr Blacklock. As poets, however, the two were poles apart. Blacklock referred to his own verses as his 'timid wing', and Burns admitted to James Johnson that they took 'sad hacking & hewing'. Blacklock's original poems of 1780 present not one word of Scottish vernacular, even his Edinburgh chairmen speak English undefiled. Here are only Scottish songs translated into English. Such self-description as 'I ne'er, for satire, torture common sense;/Nor show my wit at God's, nor man's expense' and such polite passion as

> WHY heaves my bosom up and down?
>   My pulse and nerves why stir so?
> In *Capricornus* is the sun;
>   But I would be in *Virgo*.

While under the timid wing of Blacklock, Burns received his first letters from Dr John Moore, London. Once again the poet came across much to admire: tolerance, benevolence, championship of liberty and freedom of the press, religion as the simple fair dealing of men with each other, and such licence as that given in the doctor's *Mordaunt:* 'The world is fertile in error; yet falsehood can flourish only for a time, because doomed to perish as discovered; whereas truth, when discovered, is immortal. Reason and experience are the discoverers of truth; therefore none should be precluded from the exercise of their reasoning faculties; nor is any subject so sacred that it ought not to be examined into.'[13] While admiring all of this in Moore, Burns must have known that it would be only a matter of time before the doctor came round to what Edinburgh had made a chief issue. In November 1787, Moore added the weight of his own experience on the question of what language was suitable for poetry:

> . . . you hint at your scarcity of English. I am far from thinking that this is the case. On the contrary I am convinced you already possess that language in an uncommon degree, and with a little attention you will become entirely master of it. In several of your poems there is a striking richness and variety of expression — for which reason I hope you will use it in most of your future productions. If there actually existed a language called the Scotch language, I should perhaps prefer it to the English. But

unfortunately there is no such thing. The Scotch is as provincial a dialect of the English as the Somersetshire or the Yorkshire. And therefore no serious work can be written in it to advantage.[14]

Some critics Burns could dismiss angrily as 'toothy' and 'self-conceited', others as 'spinsters who spin their thread so fine that it is neither fit for weft nor woof', and still others as 'systematic Fathers and Brothers of scientific Criticism'. Blair's strictures might be accepted or rejected, those of Glencairn deferentially regarded; nevertheless, it is apparent that during even the first weeks in Edinburgh something basic to all of the criticism was working its way well under the skin. Thus Burns wrote the minister Greenfield:

> Never did Saul's armour sit so heavy on David when going to encounter Goliath, as does the encumbering robe of public notice with which the friendship and patronage of some 'names dear to fame' have invested me. — I do not say this in the ridiculous idea of seeming self-abasement, and affected modesty. — I have long studied myself, and I think I know pretty exactly what ground I occupy, both as a Man & a Poet; and however the world, or a friend, may sometimes differ from me in that particular, I stand for it, in silent resolve, with all the tenaciousness of Property. — I am willing to believe that my abilities deserved a better fate than the veriest shades of life; but to be dragged forth, with all my imperfections on my head, to the full glare of learned and polite observation, is what, I am afraid, I shall have bitter reason to repent. (I, 59)

Before the end of 1786, therefore, Burns felt a threat to his grounds as poet which had been mounted by Edinburgh's learned. Concerned, he admitted himself to be 'as unfit to write a letter of humour, as to write a commentary on The Revelation of Saint John the Divine' (I, 60).

On 15 January 1787, the poet wrote more directly to Mrs Dunlop: '. . . in a most enlightened, informed age and nation, when poetry is and has been the study of men of the first natural genius, aided with all the powers of polite learning, polite books, and polite company — to be dragged forth to the full glare of learned and polite observation, with all my imperfections of aukward rusticity and crude unpolished ideas on my head — I assure you, Madam, I do not dissemble when I tell you I tremble for the consequences' (I, 69). Burns swells to the same theme in February letters to George Lawrie and John Moore. In early March he clearly indicates his having yielded ground, in a letter to Gavin Hamilton where reference is made to the songs 'The Lass of Ballochmyle' and 'Young Peggy': 'My two songs on Miss W. Alexander and Miss P. Kennedy were . . . tried yesterday by a jury of Literati, and found defamatory libels against the fastidious Powers of Poesy and Taste; and the author forbidden to print them under pain of forfeiture of character. — I cannot help almost shedding a tear to the memory of two Songs that had cost me some pains, and that I valued a good deal, but I must submit.' This letter concludes: 'My poor unfortunate Songs come again across my memory — Damn the pedant, frigid soul of Criticism for ever and ever!' (I, 78-79.) On the last day of April, Burns was still protesting, this time to Mrs Dunlop: 'Your criticisms, Madam, I understand very well, and could have wished to have pleased you better. — You are right in your guesses that I am not very amenable to counsel . . . I set as little by kings, lords, and clergy, critics, &c. as all these respectable Gentry do by my Bardship' (I, 86). Such scornful disavowal has been known to cover the fact of submission.

What has been traced for the spring of 1787 may be said to have held true through the summer of touring Scotland, the hectic second winter in Edinburgh, and the removal to Dumfriesshire, although during these twelve months, it seems, Burns promised himself that the very first respite for composition of poems — not songs — would be an earnest trial of writing verses which in the eyes of the Scottish Enlightenment could merit literary fame.

Songs were another matter altogether. A primary challenge of the Scottish Enlightenment was to contribute to the causes of antiquarianism. When Burns lodged in Edinburgh, none of these causes was being advanced more zealously than that of preserving Scottish folk-song. Sometime before 1780 enlightened groups in the capital were alive not merely to the richness of their heritage of national song but also to the unreliability of transmitting this heritage through oral rendition. An object in the founding of the Society of Antiquaries of Scotland (1780) was stated to be 'a complete collection of the undecorated, simple, melodious, or warlike airs of the Scots';[15] a paper read at the meeting of that society, 8 January 1782, was 'A Disquisition into the Origin of the Christmas Carrols still in use among the vulgar in Scotland'; and a major gift to the library of that society was three folio volumes of Walter M'Farlane's collection of Scottish music, some 785 airs. Such names in the records of the Society as William Smellie, Alexander Cunningham, William Creech, Charles Hay, John Syme, and Alexander Fergusson of Craigdarroch support the conviction that in many an Edinburgh drawing-room, at gatherings of the Freemasons, and at convivial meetings like those of the Crochallan Fencibles as well as in the shop of James Johnson the engraver, Burns heard men of culture discuss plans to publish the songs of Scotland. Nothing in Edinburgh could have amazed the poet more than to hear Scottish folksongs talked about with that attention hitherto reserved for Blair's *The Grave* or Home's *Douglas*, unless it was the proposal to collect and publish these songs. Probably nobody in the city could sing more of them or could bring to bear upon them more critical acumen, nobody held them closer to his heart, nobody had been more sustained or more inspired by them. His immediate responses were to include in the 1787 edition of his poetry more than twice the number of his Kilmarnock songs, that had been included, by and large, to fill up an empty space, and to commit himself to the enterprise of James Johnson.

From December 1786 to his death, Robert Burns edited Johnson's *Scots Musical Museum*; from September 1792 to his death, he busied himself also as principal contributor to George Thomson's *Select Collection of Original Airs*. Less than three weeks before his death, Burns wrote Johnson, 'I will venture to prophesy, that to future ages *your publication will be the text book and standard* of Scottish song and music' (II, 268). Why was it Johnson's work and not Thomson's that received the poet's accolade? Mainly because Johnson aimed at collecting and publishing Scottish folksong with as much authenticity as he could command, whereas Thomson sought merely to provide seemly songs for fashionable young ladies. Never at ease with Thomson, Burns opposed the editor whenever he suggested English elements in place of the natural Scottish. When Thomson asked the sacrifice of natural Scottish simplicity for English pathos, sentiment, or point, Burns replied, 'These English songs gravel me to death. — I have not that command of the language that I have of my native tongue. — In fact, I think my ideas are more barren in English than in Scottish. — I have been at 'Duncan Gray', to dress it in English, but all that I can do is deplorably stupid' (II, 268). And when Thomson asked for a refined air, Burns answered, '[Let] our National Music preserve its native features. — They are, I own, frequently wild, & unreduceable to the modern rules; but on that very eccentricity, perhaps, depends a great part of their effect' (II, 172). Paradoxically, the Scottish Enlightenment denied the Scots poet exactly what it insisted upon as the *sine qua non* for the Scots folksong collector and reviser: identity or Scottishness.

To the publications of Johnson and Thomson, Burns contributed more than three hundred songs. Again and again, one is reminded that he worked with materials handed down to him much as Homer and the

Beowulf poet had worked. In Edinburgh and afterwards in Dumfries-shire, enlightened antiquaries such as Robert Riddell, Charles Kirk-patrick Sharpe, Adam de Cardonnel, Robert Clapperton, and Francis Grose collaborated with Burns in his successful efforts to record Scotland's past. Paramount in these efforts were songs like 'John Anderson', 'McPherson's Farewell', 'The Battle of Sherra-moor', and 'Auld Lang Syne'. Incidental to these efforts were songs like 'Of A' the Airts', poems like 'Tam o' Shanter', the Glenriddell manuscripts, the defense of William M'Gill, and the Monkland Friendly Society, founded by Robert Riddell and Robert Burns to store the minds of peasants and artisans with useful knowledge and to raise its members 'to a more dignified degree in the scale of rationality' (II, 89). All were of the Scottish Enlightenment.

If there was any lesson that Robert Burns did not have to go to school under the Scottish Enlightenment to learn, that lesson was toleration, the brotherhood of man. Uncomfortable in Presbyterianism, yet a product of it, Burns brought to Edinburgh a reputation as a sharp-tongued critic of his national church. As long as religious nonsense remained the 'most nonsensical of all Nonsense' (II, 120), his satire would never be without a target; as long as Black Russel sought 'the wild-goose heights of Calvinistic Theology' (II, 60), the satirist could hunt fair game. Burns's love for his fellow man, his propensity to grant every man liberty to uphold his form of worship, his religious uncertainty, his romantic inclination towards 'old Popish grandeur' and 'the old Romish way', and his recognition that no church better than the Roman Catholic realized that 'ceremony & show, if judiciously thrown in, [are] absolutely necessary for the bulk of mankind' gave him more curiosity and desire than qualm for the hand of friendship which Bishop John Geddes first extended to him in Edinburgh.[16]

Geddes was in Edinburgh as the coadjutor for the Lowlands under Bishop Hay. His boyhood had been spent among Scots farmers and crofters; therefore he knew country life. Since those early years he had become a man of great learning as well as a wise man whose natural disposition to oblige had earned the tolerance of leading citizens towards Catholics. These citizens included Geddes in their supper parties; so it was that he met Robert Burns in the home of Lord Monboddo on a December evening in 1786 and was able to inform John Thomson, a Roman Catholic agent, 17 January 1787, 'One Burns, an Ayrshire ploughman, has lately appeared as a very good poet.'[17]

Geddes became a subscriber to the poet's Edinburgh Edition and caused such religious establishments as the Scots colleges at Valladolid, Douay and Paris, and the Benedictine monasteries at Ratisbon and Maryburgh to subscribe. Burns, in return, transcribed in the bishop's copy of the new edition some twelve additional poems and identified therein, through annotation, the subjects of his satires. Burns's letters make it plain that he and Bishop Geddes struck up a friendship which grew firm. In applauding the 'good sense and philosophy in persons of elevated rank' which made it possible for such a distinguished person as Professor Dugald Stewart 'to keep a friendship properly alive' with one so much his social inferior as a ploughman, Burns tells Mrs Dunlop of one more instance, 'a Popish Bishop, Geddes; but I have outraged that gloomy, fiery Presbyterianism enough already, though I don't spit in her lugubrious face by telling her that the first [foremost] Cleric I ever saw was a Roman Catholic.'[18]

Such esteem betokens something more than casual acquaintance. What seems true is that the poet and the bishop met not only in Edinburgh homes like that of Dr Gregory but also in the bishop's residence, probably part of the Roman Catholic property in Blackfriars Street. Any man who was later to reveal his sympathy for fellow men by composing a Latin ode in praise of the French Revolution could not have been a man with whom Burns was not forthright. Geddes learned of Jean; he may have been told of Jenny Clow and Meg Cameron. He discovered in Burns such serious moral and religious opinions as those which the poet touched upon in a letter to Alexander Cunningham:

> I hate a man that wishes to be a Deist, but I fear, every fair, unprejudiced Enquirer must in some degree be a Sceptic. — It is not that there are any very staggering arguments against the Immortality of Man; that like Electricity, Phlogiston, &c. the subject is so involved in darkness that we want Data to go upon. — One thing frightens me much: that we are to live forever, seems too good news to be true. (II, 13)

William Maxwell had the connections, the time, the place, and the interest to have made one with others like Dr Gregory, Robert Burns, and even Fr George Maxwell in a company which Bishop Geddes brought together for an evening in his Edinburgh home. It was not only through Fr George that the bishop was well aware of the Maxwells of Kirkconnell; he knew that they supported his bishopric generously, and he acknowledged personally James Maxwell's voluntary gifts of £100.[19] Geddes would have news of William's being close by at

Edinburgh University, of his studying medicine under Gregory, of his coming under the spell of the Scottish Enlightenment which was working also upon the poet, almost his same age. What the bishop acknowledged by letters to James and Mary, he may have acknowledged otherwise by an invitation which brought William and Burns face to face as his guests. But accounts of both Robert Burns and William Maxwell are already as full as eggs of such conjecture for one to fancy more.

After the winter of 1786-87, each week of Burns's residence in Edinburgh intensified an uneasiness that could not be dispelled by satisfactions like those from the First Edinburgh Edition, profitably published for Burns and William Creech, and sightseeing in the north and south of Scotland with William Nicol and Robert Ainslie. Burns was concerned for Jean Armour, he was concerned for making a living away from Edinburgh, he was concerned for having discovered that 'my numerous Edin^r friendships are of so tender a construction that they will not bear carriage with me' (I, 87). His restlessness of the period is evident in the parade of his affections for Jean and Mrs McLehose, for Meg Cameron and Jenny Clow; it is apparent in the quickness of his response to the opportunity of leasing Patrick Miller's Ellisland with its certainty of returning him to farming for which he had lost taste; and it is clear in the subservience of his efforts to be placed as an exciseman. The ensuing months that brought instruction in the Excise, inspection of Ellisland, and a Dumfries burgess ticket also brought 'Sylvander's' release from 'Clarinda', Jean's second pair of twins, Meg's court action to protect her expectant child, and Jenny's pregnancy. Small wonder the poet continued fretful! On 11 June 1788, when he finally had moved into the Ellisland home rented from David Newall and had started to farm Miller's stubborn soil on the west bank of the Nith above Dumfries, he still had not come to terms with himself, so that with the new life came fits of depression and drink induced by the mind's dwelling upon separation from native Ayrshire, marriage to Jean, hopelessness of profiting as farmer, probable service under George III, and impact of Edinburgh values.

The embitterment taken from Edinburgh would not wear thin. Thus, early in 1789 Burns wrote his 'much-honored Friend', the 'Venerable Father' Geddes, 'That acquaintance, worthy Sir, with which you were pleased to honor me, you must still allow me to challenge: for, with whatever unconcern I give up my transient connexion [with the merely, Great] those self-important beings whose intrinsic [worthlessness is

L

con]cealed under the accidental advantages of their [rank, I cannot lose the] patronising notice of the Learned and the [Good without the bittere]st regret.' Some of this rankling derived from Burns's return to poetry which he announced in the same letter:

> Thus, with a rational aim and method in life, you may easily guess, my Reverend and much-honored Friend, that my characteristical trade is not forgotten. — I am, if possible, more than ever an enthusiast to the Muses. — I am determined to study man and Nature, in that view, incessantly; and to try if the ripening and corrections of years can enable me to produce something worth preserving.—
>
> You will see in your book, which I beg your pardon for detaining so long, that I have been tuning my lyre on the banks of the Nith. — Some larger Poetic plans that are floating in my imagination, or partly put in execution, I shall impart to you when I have the pleasure of meeting with you; which, if you are then in Edin[r], I shall have about the beginning of March. (I, 298-300)

What Burns is reporting is that he had found his opportunity after the September harvest of 1788 to try dressing Coila after the fashion of the Scottish Enlightenment.

The poet loosely sketched plans for a major work modelled upon Alexander Pope's moral epistles and comprising a number of parts to be titled *The Poet's Progress*. The 'Epistle to Robert Graham, Esq., of Fintry', his first attempt, opens with the verses

> When Nature her great master-piece design'd,
> And fram'd her last, best work, the human mind,
> Her eye intent on all the mazy plan,
> She form'd of various parts the various man.

Ninety-three lines later Burns as stylishly concludes with triple rhyme and Alexandrine:

> That, plac'd by thee upon the wish'd-for height,
> Where, man and nature fairer in her sight,
> My muse may imp her wing for some sublimer flight.[20]

Having just cause to wonder what exactly he had done in attempting to compose neo-classical poetry upon the subject of Robert Graham's support of the bid for the Excise position, Burns sought the criticism of the writer William Dunbar: 'I inclose you a Poem I have just finished.

— It is my first Essay in that kind of Poetry, & I ask your Criticisms on it, both how far you think that such a species of poetic Composition seems to suit my Muse, & what faults you find, or emendations you would propose in it. — I am determined, from this time forth, whatever I may write, to do it leisurely & to the utmost of my powers, correctly' (I, 261).

The so-called Dumfries period of Burns's life is that from 1788-1796, the last eight years, the first three at Ellisland and the last five within the town proper. The poetry of these years lends credence to the idea that, as a result of some months in Edinburgh face to face with the Scottish Enlightment, literary fame through neo-classical poetry became Burns's fond wish to his dying days, even though before the departure from Ellisland it had lost more and more of its determination. All through the decline of the poet's last years, one comes upon heroic couplets sinking Burns 'in a prosaic mire' and, as he admits, beclouding his soul with 'gloomy presages'; such are, for example, the apostrophe to dullness, the characters of Creech and Fox, the pieces for the actor Sutherland and the actress Fontenelle, the elegy hammered out to honor Miss Monboddo, and the 'sheetful of groans' mailed to Mrs Dunlop. Where heroic couplets give way to this or that stanzaic form, the reader still finds Burns attending the same elocution classes of Dryden and Pope, as, for example, in 'A Mother's Lament', the sonnet on Glenriddell's death, 'Caledonia A Ballad', 'Sweet Sensibility How Charming', and the 'Address to the Shade of Thomson'. For each of these poems Burns had a critic or two, invited or uninvited. Dr Gregory wrote to correct the verses 'On Seeing a Wounded Hare'. The subject, Gregory offered, was 'pretty good', the stanza would not do, the language was 'coarse', 'inscrutable', and 'improper'; the professor-doctor-critic then promised Burns a copy of Ann Home's poems so that he might learn not to be so 'stiff and quaint'.[21] Whistling in the dark, Burns explained to Lady Elizabeth Cunningham, 'Whether I may ever make my footing good, on any considerable height of Parnassus, is what I do not know; but I am determined to strain every nerve in the trial. — Though the rough material of fine writing is undoubtedly the gift of Genius, the workmanship is as certainly the united effort of labour, attention and pains. Nature has qualified few, if any, to shine in every walk of the Muses: I shall put it to the test of repeated trial whether she has formed me capable of distinguishing myself in any one' (I, 289). By 1792 Burns had grown so charmed under the spell of the learned or else so wretchedly disheartened that he instructed Creech to

hand over all authority for editing the 1793 volumes to Henry Mackenzie, Dugald Stewart, and Alexander Fraser Tytler.

Always with fewer and fewer notable exceptions after Edinburgh,
Burns's poetry testifies to the truth of his own observation that he never
succeeded to any purpose when he composed from wish rather than
from impulse. Each wish was fulfilled only with more artificiality
succeeded by greater vexation, until one is tempted to interpret his
famous flyting as a curse upon himself as poet-poseur: 'Thou Eunuch of
language: thou Englishman, who was never south of the Tweed: thou
servile echo of fashionable barbarisms: thou quack, vending the nos-
trums of empirical elocution . . . thou blacksmith, hammering the
rivets of absurdity . . . thou pitch-pipe of affected emphasis . . . thou
baleful meteor, foretelling and facilitating the rapid approach of Nox
and Erebus' (II, 77).

Together with such vehemence came 'Tam o' Shanter' in fall of 1790,
a glorious exception to the rule, its genesis replete with irony. Here
Burns, momentarily returning to himself as he allowed for the songs,
pleased even his Edinburgh critics. Alexander Fraser Tytler wrote, 'I
am much mistaken if this poem alone, had you never written another
syllable, would not have been sufficient to have transmitted your name
down to posterity with high reputation.'[22] And Burns answered, '. . . to
have that poem so much applauded by one of the first judges, was the
most delicious vibration that ever thrilled along the heart-strings of a
poor poet' (II, 70). Deep in losing himself to the Scottish Enlightenment's challenge to compose poetry consonant with the ideals of
Alexander Pope, Burns had composed his masterpiece in responding to
the same Enlightenment's challenge to contribute to the causes of antiquarianism.

It had been the combination of Captains Francis Grose and Robert
Riddell of Glenriddell as antiquaries that had given Burns the occasion
to compose 'Tam o' Shanter'. Those who would have Riddell an antiquary without an idea, a musician without an accomplishment, a
painter without an ability, hood their eyes to fact. His importance to
Robert Burns at Ellisland and his wife's importance to Robert Burns as
mistress at Friars Carse have always been disparaged, even though
such testimony as the Glenriddell Manuscripts and Burns's choosing to
name his favorite daughter after Elizabeth Riddell argues otherwise. At
Friars Carse, Burns was encouraged in his work on Scottish song,
helped in collecting materials, given the chance to exchange thoughts
with Stephen Clarke, the Edinburgh organist who was providing the

pedal-bass for songs in the *Museum*. There was his release after long rides as exciseman and dreary chores as tenant; there was his escape from anxiety for Jean and their bairns Francis Wallace and William Nicol and from concern for the illegitimate children by Jenny Clow and Anne Park. There Burns could compose in the seclusion of the hermit-age. There he first met Grose and John McMurdo, factor of the Duke of Queensberry at Drumlanrig, renewed friendship with Alexander Fer-gusson of Craigdarroch, and talked republicanism with John Syme. Because Robert Riddell and his wife Elizabeth had opened their doors widely to the poet, the doors of other influential families at such places as Woodley Park, Dalswinton, Drumlanrig, Closeburn, Barjarg, and Arbigland opened.

And why not the doors at Kirkconnell? Would those doors have remained shut while those at Carruchan, Terregles, and Terraughty stood open? Anyone hastening to answer 'No' should add that he gives answer upon likelihood, not proof. James Maxwell's account-books for 1791 do show the entry 'To a bill paid Mr. Burns - - - £8. 3-.'[23] This Mr Burns could have been the Robert who farmed Ellisland or his cousin William whom he employed or, for that matter, anybody else named Burns. James had the poems of Robert Burns in his library; knowing James, one is sure that he would have been delighted to meet their author, very possibly handed on by Bishop Geddes in Edinburgh. Yet there is no record of their meeting. Similar uncertainty marks the question as to whether or not William Maxwell met Burns during the three years he was at Ellisland; here there seems even less probability than in the case of James, for William then was never *at* Kirkconnell, he was merely hovering there an instant before flying off to alight in Paris or London. At the least, however, William as well as James and Mary knew of Burns's moving to the Nith and heard about the poet's new life from close friends who were well informed.

William Maxwell was in Great Portland Street when Robert Burns gave up farming as a failure and left his Ellisland home in November 1791. The worse Burns's fortune as Nithside farmer had become, the greater had been his dependency upon the Excise as the only way of supporting himself and his family. The first years of active duty as a gauger had taken him out upon the country astride his horse; but then appointment to a Dumfries foot division, recommendation to the rank of examiner and supervisor, and consideration for an opening in the Port Division of Dumfries suggested the wisdom of living where his duties were more and more keeping him. Burns, therefore, rented from

John Hamilton the second floor of a tenement in the Wee Vennel (now Bank Street). The space was inadequate, indeed thoroughly cabined and confined for Jean and her three children, all under six years old, who had become used to Ellisland. Having John Syme on the ground floor as the local stamp distributor could have been compensation only to Robert; knowing how much of a compensation it was to her husband to have 'Stamp Office Johnie' so near at hand could have made Jean not altogether unhappy in her new surroundings.

Two of the subjects dearest to the heart of Robert Burns were Religion and Politics: the former had got him into hot water with superiors in the Church of Scotland; the latter was to get him into boiling water with superiors in His Majesty's Excise.

The poet's political beliefs had never been orthodox. They began with 'jacobitical partialities' fostered by pride in the tradition that ancestors on the father's side had fought under the standard of the Earl of Mar during the Fifteen. These beliefs took strength from Scots patriotism, sympathy for the underdog and almost any lost cause, rebellious spirit, and sentimentalism; they throve upon romance and tearful toasting of Queen Mary and Bonnie Prince Charlie. Sir Walter was right when he said to Lockhart, 'I imagine his [Burns's] Jacobitism, like my own, belonged to the fancy rather than the reason.'[24] Unlike Scott, however, Burns used Jacobitism, as in 'Charly, He's My Darling' and 'It Was A' for Our Rightfu' King', to nourish distaste for the Hanoverians, 'An idiot race, to honor lost.'[25]

Such opinion as the last might judiciously at any time be better kept to oneself or to a gathering of circumspect friends than broadcast under one's name. For it to travel abroad at the time of the American Revolution and the French Revolution, for it to have been written by an officer in the Excise spelled danger. Robert Burns was fully aware that the Dumfriesshire years were 'no laughing times', that his sympathies were to be threatened:

> But Politics, truce! we're on dangerous ground;
>   Who knows how the fashions may alter;
> The doctrines today that are loyalty sound,
>   Tomorrow may bring us a halter.[26]

Despite such awareness, the poet permitted his revolutionary fever to mount, idealistically and wilfully:

Here's freedom to them that wad read,
Here's freedom to them that wad write!
There's nane ever feared that the truth should be heard
But they whom the truth would indite.[27]

Instinctively from the first stanza, Robert Burns had made independence the first requisite of his poetry as Alexander Pope had known any true poet must: 'Poets, a race long unconfined and free, / Still fond and proud of savage liberty.'[28] The liberty which Burns imagines as a 'Highland filly' in the poem 'On Glenriddell's Fox' is spirited, all but unbroken, and dangerous to self and rider, if not savage:

A sturdy, stubborn, handsome dapple,
As sleek's a mouse, as round's an apple,
That, when thou pleasest, can do wonders,
But when thy luckless rider blunders,
Or if thy fancy should demur there,
Wilt break thy neck ere thou go further.[29]

In coming to the Nith from Ayr and Edinburgh, Burns already had praised the American Revolution for its examples of independence and liberty. His 'Address to Beelzebub' had hailed the deeds of Hancock and Franklin as his 'Ode for George Washington's Birthday' had daringly exposed championship of another patriot. 'When Guilford Good' had ridiculed Lord North while applauding the Boston Tea Party and the Declaration of Independence:

Then up they gat the maskin'-pat
And in the Sea did jaw, man;
An' did nae less, in full Congress,
Than quite refuse our law, man.[30]

Before Edinburgh, the poet had kept himself absolutely free so as to be able to write of the American Revolution or church elders just as he willed. After Edinburgh, he knew that quite the same freedom was even more necessary for the poetry he ached to compose. What was a Minister? 'An unprincipled fellow who by hereditary or acquired wealth obtains a principal place.' What is Politics? 'A science wherewith, by means of nefarious cunning, & hypocritical pretence, we govern civil polities for the emolument of ourselves & our adherents.' (II, 149 f.) What of Reform? 'My God! What a reform I would make among the Sons, and even the Daughters, of men! Down, immediately, should go Fools from the high places where misbegotten Chance has perked them up.' (II, 164 f.)

Politics as well as poetry tore Robert Burns in two at Ellisland and in Dumfries. Want of subject matter was never the trouble. Want of that full freedom which the poet had allowed himself after the death of his father in order to make the Kilmarnock Edition remarkable *was* the trouble. Here the dilemma: to be a poet was to keep oneself free. Yet being the poet of the Scottish Enlightenment cost freedom; being married cost freedom; being a father cost freedom, a little more freedom with every child; and being exciseman cost freedom. Suffering this dilemma, Burns protested to Alexander Cunningham, 'O, to be a sturdy Savage, stalking in the pride of his independance amid the solitary wilds of his desarts! Rather than in civilized life helplessly to tremble for a subsistence, precarious as the caprice of a fellow-creature. . . . I do not want to be independant, that I may sin; but I want to be independant in my sinning' (II, 78 f.).

Politics, specifically the French Revolution, cost Robert Burns the last farthing of his freedom to be poet. The year of the fall of the Bastille opened for the poet at Ellisland with his getting off a letter of gratitude for a recent gift of two fine pistols. The one whom he had to thank was 'Mr David Blair *Gun Maker St. Paul's Square Birmingham.*' Burns had met this volatile democrat at Robert Riddell's and was anxious to share his company again:

My dear Sir,

My honor has lien bleeding these two months almost, as 'tis near that time since I received your kind tho' very short epistle of the 29th Oct. The defensive tools do more than half mankind do, they do honor to their maker; but I trust that with me they shall have the fate of a miser's gold — to be often admired, but never used.

Long before your letter came to hand, I sent you, by way of Mr Nicol, a copy of the book [*First Edinburgh Edition*], and a proof-sheet of the print, loose, among the leaves of the book. These, I hope, are safe in your possession some time ago. If I could think of any other channel of communication with you than the villainous expensive one of the Post, I could send you a parcel of my Rhymes; partly as a small return for your kind, handsome compliment, but much more as a mark of my sincere esteem and respect for Mr Blair. . . .

I remember with pleasure, my dear Sir, a visit you talked of paying to Dumfries, in Spring or Summer. I shall only say I have never parted with a man, after so little acquaintance, whom I more ardently wished to see

again. At your first convenience, a line to inform me of an affair in which
I am much interested — just an answer to the question, How you do, will
oblidge. (I, 293)

Correspondents other than David Blair were keeping Robert Burns
informed of their liberal activities. One of them, Dr John Moore, wrote
of France; Helen Maria Williams, the doctor's protégé, sent a copy of
her poem on the slave trade. And it was William Roscoe's poem in
praise of the French Revolution that gave Burns reason to speak of 'my
friend Roscoe in Liverpool' (II, 282).

Any poet who had written of Great Britain as a place 'Where
hundreds labour to support/A haughty lordling's pride' would have
chosen his side confidently and quickly when the Bastille fell.[31] Burns,
therefore, was an enthusiastic votary of the French Revolution from its
beginning; and he soon made this upheaval his symbol of perfect
liberty and equality. Opposite him, he could find only men like Hugh
Blair who rallied fellow conservatives with such pious platitudes as,
'We love our country as the seat of true religion. Freed from the
dominion of Popish superstition and darkness which so long over-
spread the earth, here the light of the blessed reformation continues to
shine in its greatest splendour.'[32] Even such an opportunity as this, Burns
let pass. Dumfries friends like Syme, Riddell, and McMurdo knew the
poet's private views; correspondents like Mrs Dunlop did; visitors to
Dumfries like Dr James Currie did, when he came up to Dumfriesshire
from Liverpool to inspect the properties of Dumcrieff and Stakeford
which his former collegemate and present agent John Syme had
arranged for his purchase. But publicly Burns managed, for several
months, to contain himself because of apprehension that he might lose
his security. Thus he wrote Robert Ainslie, three months after the
Bastille, 'I know how the word, Exciseman, or still more opprobrious,
Gauger, will sound in your Ears. — I too have seen the day when my
auditory nerves would have felt very delicately on this subject, but a
wife & children are things which have a wonderful power in blunting
these kind of sensations. — Fifty pounds a year for life & a provision
for widows & orphans, you will allow, is no bad settlement for a poet'
(I, 364).

In October 1790, James Fisher, a country rhymester no more gifted
than Sillar or Lapraik, published a volume of his poetry in Dumfries.
The first eight lines of Fisher's riddle upon Robert Burns reveal that
Burns was not expected to throttle himself to death, £50 or no £50:

A BURN, like Jordan long ago,
Did a' its sides an' banks o'erflow;
Sae rapidly did rin this Burn,
It nearly did the kirk o'erturn,
An' a' the clergymen swoop doun;
The kintry a' did hear its soun';
Its waters raise sae high an' keen,
They very near had wet the King.[33]

Fisher's burn began to overflow again in 1792; in spilling its banks it did, indeed, wet George III, with 'Here's the last verse of the last chapter of the last Book of Kings.'[34] Even if Robert Burns did not offer this toast at a public meeting as alleged, even if he did not compose 'The Tree of Liberty', he certainly did step out of line as an exciseman in 1792. In late February of that year, the Dumfries excise office was notified of smuggling underway. Riding Officer Walter Crawford and his fellow officer John Lewars went to Annan, boarded the *Rosamond*, and confiscated contraband in the King's name.[35] Lewars, who had the inventory in hand, informed Burns that the contraband would go up for public sale on 19 April. The poet, recklessly but not illegally, purchased four carronades as, apparently, a present to the French people and an expression of his sympathy for their revolutionary government. In November, he subscribed to the *Edinburgh Gazetteer* owned by William Johnston, who was later imprisoned for treason. Burns's request to Johnston for any papers that he might already have published includes the following exhortation: 'Go on, Sir! Lay bare, with undaunted heart & steady hand, that horrid mass of corruption called Politics & State-Craft! Dare to draw in their native colors these "Calm, thinking VILLAINS whom no faith can fix" whatever be the Shibboleth of their pretended Party' (II, 131). Finally, Burns was in the audience at the Dumfries Theatre on the night when a riotous rabble drowned out the playing of 'God Save the King' with howlings for 'Ça ira'.

Charges impugning the loyalty of Burns, the republican, were lodged with John Mitchell, Excise Collector at Dumfries; Mitchell forwarded them to Robert Graham of Fintry, Commissioner of the Scottish Board of Excise, in Edinburgh; the Board directed William Corbet, General Supervisor of Excise, to conduct an inquiry at Dumfries. All this in early 1793. Burns himself admitted that his actions had given the Board 'great offence' and that Corbet had been ordered by the Board to 'document me — "that *my* business was to *act*, not to think; & that whatever might be Men or Measures, it was for me to be silent & obedient".' To save his skin as exciseman, the poet said that he knew nothing about William Johnston other than that he had ordered his paper and would countermand the order. Burns proposed that he was 'most devoutly attached to the most glorious British Constitution'. What is more, his assurance to Graham in a letter of 2 January 1793, 'I have set a seal to my lips,' suggests that the price for retaining his position with deferment of promotion was the same assurance. Corbet and Graham of Fintry only partly forgave Burns; the Earl of Mar coldly forgave him not at all.

So, one year before Great Britain went to war with France, Robert Burns became a gagged placeman, an admonished, degraded, fearful, humiliated placeman. After the war began, he dared not release 'the pestilential fumes of my Political heresies' save in a most private conversation with a most trusted friend or in a letter to such a long-standing confidant as Mrs Dunlop. Even then, as was the case with Mrs Dunlop, his views gave offence that caused him to be forsaken. Burns did not leave us without his own description of the corner into which he had backed himself by the end of 1793 to live out his life:

> Reasons of no less weight than the support of a wife & children have pointed out as the eligible, & indeed the only eligible line of life for me, my present occupation. — Still, my honest fame is my dearest concern: & a thousand times have I trembled at the idea of the degrading epithets that Malice, or Misrepresentation may affix to my name. — I have often, in blasting anticipation, listened to some future hackney Magazine Scribbler, with the heavy malice of savage stupidity, exulting in his hireling paragraphs that 'Burns, notwithstanding the fanfaronade of independence to be found in his works, & after having been held forth to Public View & Public Estimation as a man of some genius, yet, quite destitute of resources within himself to support this borrowed dignity, he dwindled into a paltry Exciseman; & slunk out the rest of his insignificant existence in the meanest of pursuits & among the vilest of mankind.' (II, 170)

The dilemma of Robert Burns during the Dumfriesshire years quickened his propensity to drink excessively. Too many biographers have ducked the issue by doggedly repeating that the age was one of heavy drinking; that somebody else's capacity as 'a three-bottle man' made Burns a neophyte in the sport of Bacchus; that it was endocarditis, not alcohol, that brought untimely death; that the poet could not have gone on writing excellent letters and composing excellent songs had he been given to drink deleteriously. Idolaters remedilessly applying whitewash support these biographers.

Robert Burns may or may not have died of endocarditis; whether or not he did has been made to depend upon one's susceptibility to twentieth-century diagnosis of eighteenth-century complaints, irregularly reported. Burns did not, it is a fact, enjoy good health: he did have a severe cold upon his moving to Ellisland; he did have indigestion and a broken arm upon his moving into Dumfries; he did experience thickening gloom and multiplying illnesses throughout his last years. His own admissions that 'hard drinking is the devil of me' and his own descriptions of how obviously it was punctuate this steady decline (II, 40). Let any doubting Thomas re-read, for example, the letters to Ainslie and Cunningham; the apologies to Clark, McMurdo and William Robertson of Lude; the verses 'Sent to A Gentleman [?Simon Mackenzie] Whom He Had Offended'. Could it be mere happenstance that just about the only spanking-new biographical evidence to come out of court records in the past thirty years is the account of 'a roar of Folly & Dissipation' by the crony excisemen John Lewars and Robert Burns?

Burns spoke of Lewars as his 'particular friend' and as 'a young fellow of uncommon merit — indeed, by far the cleverest fellow I have met with in this part of the world' (II, 320). For Jessie, John's young sister, Burns composed his death-bed song, 'O, wert thou in the cauld blast'; upon the subject of John, Burns composed 'The Hue and Cry of John Lewars' in which he imagines his fellow-exciseman stealing upon the bewitching Miss Woods, governess at Miss McMurdo's boarding school:

> But softly—I have it—her haunts are well known,
>   At midnight so slily I'll watch her;
> And sleeping, undrest, in the dark, all alone—
>   Good Lord! the dear THIEF HOW I'LL CATCH HER! [36]

In April-May 1792 both Lewars and Burns were being tied up in the *Rosamond* episode and its aftermath of carronades for France. Lewars had other trouble. His landlord Samuel Blount had taken court action on 2 April to make him and Jessie get out of their 'high Lodging, cellar and garret lying in the high street of Dumfries'.[37] Because the brother and sister had only until Whitsunday to abandon the premises, they had been spending the weeks after Blount's decreet in hunting for another place. John Syme, as agent for Dr James Currie, had offered them Stakeford, a home across the Nith from Dumfries where Currie's mother had been born.

On Friday night, 17 May 1792, John Lewars left his home, whether the lodging owned by Blount or Stakeford owned by Currie is not certain, to join Robert Burns and other friends for supper at William Hyslop's Globe Tavern in the High Street. Burns at this time was still living above Syme's Stamp Office in the Wee Vennel. The eating and drinking lasted the night through. Very early on the morning of Saturday, 18 May, Burns and Lewars made their way from the Globe down to the sands, presumably to walk off their intoxication. They came upon the rear gardens of neighboring homes inhabited by Wellwood Maxwell and Dr John Gilchrist. Maxwell had been a provost of Dumfries; at the time, he was a justice of the peace and land-tax collector for the county of Dumfries. Six legal papers as one hitherto unidentified packet of the Dumfries Burgh Records make plain what happened after the two excisemen came up to the J.P.'s property.[38]

One of the papers is docketed, 'Declaration of Jean Murdoch and Janet Anderson/1792'; each of the five pages is attested 'Jean Murdoch'. They read:

Dumfries 18, May 1792—
In the Petition
The Fiscal of Court
Ag.t
John Lewars Officer of Excise in Dumfries

In presence of John Baily John Lawson [Dumfries baillies] Compeared Jean Murdoch Servant to Wellwood Maxwell Esq. of Barncleugh who being examined declares that about five oclock this morning She & Janet Anderson also Servant to the said Wellwood Maxwell were washing Cloaths in M.r Maxwell's wash-house at the foot of his Garden in Dumfries. The said John Lewars and another person whom the declarant does not know were walking past on the road [Waterloo Street] betwixt the Gardens and Waterside. That the said John Lewars having seen the said Janet Anderson coming down the steps of M.r Maxwell's Garden, came to the Garden Door which was locked, and damned the said Janet Anderson why she locked the door, and ordered her to open it immediately, but she having made no answer, he immediately broke open the lock of the door and came to the Wash-house, upon which they asked him what he wanted there & desired him to go about his business, in place of which he cursed & swore and used such obscene indecent language, as she or no modest woman can mention. That the declarant told him if he came into the house and endeavoured to use any of them ill, that she would throw boiling water at him, & in the meantime taking a porringer full of hot water & holding it in her hand, she was then in hopes that he would have retired, but instead of that he took up a pig-full of suds which he threw at the declarant at the same time that she threw the boiling water at him. That little of the suds came upon her, which he observing threw the pig before mentioned at her also, which struck her upon the side, and then fell to the Ground, broke, that this was a Crock-pig which would contain about four or five pints. That he then flew to the declarant and laid hold of her, still cursing and swearing, and using such indecent language as she had not heard before, and insisted that she should go to the Correcting house for throwing water at him. That the other girl coming to her assist- ance he laid hold of her also, and pushed them against a Corner of the Wash-house, and swore he would put them in the boiling pot, That the Declarant's breast and neck and also her left arm are very much scratched and bruised by the grips & hurts, she so received from him, —

declares That immediately after the water was so thrown Lewars lifed up a Garden-how and came running to her and the other Girl, and swore by his Maker, he would knock her to Eternity, but the other girl griped the how, & pulled it out of his hand. That the Declarant desired the other Girl to go for her Master, but Lewars griped her also and knocked her head ag! the wall & kept betwixt them & the door, swearing if one of them stirred, he would put them into the boiling pot or into the fire, and that her sex only saved her from an untimely end. That about this time, the Man who was along with Lewars came up to the Wash house and asked the Declarant & the other Girl who was their master, upon which the declarant answered M! Wellwood Maxwell, and said that it was a poor thing in him to meddle with people's Servants, when they were doing no harm, while he durst not meddle with their masters whereto he replied. That if he was there, he would use him in the same manner, it made no odds to him, and wished her master were in hell, to which the Declarant replied She hoped there was a better place provided for him and he said he hoped not, That after some further altercation the other man got Lewars to go out, and begged the Girls to say nothing of what happened, declares That she thinks it may be about three quarters of an hour, from the time the lock of the Garden Door was forced up, untill the time that the other man got Lewars out of the Garden, and all this she declares to be the truth

/s/   Jean Murdoch
John Lawson[39]

John Lewars' declaration speaks of his getting 'very drunk' in William Hyslop's, of his 'walking up the Water-side early in the morning with M! Burns', of his forcing open the door, seizing the girl for her having thrown water upon him, and of his inability to recollect anything else owing to 'inebriety'. After some altercation 'Mr Burns got him taken away.' Lewars admits to being sorry for what had happened. 'It was entirely the effects of Drink.'

The declarations of John Lewars and Jean Murdoch had been taken on the eighteenth as part of the action introduced by the Procurator Fiscal David Newall, the same man from whom Burns had rented a home at Ellisland until his own farmhouse had been renovated. Basically, the case which Newall presented, undoubtedly upon the outraged insistence of Wellwood Maxwell, was one of assault. Newall requested that the Dumfries baillies apprehend Lewars and 'imprison him in the Tolbooth of Dumfries' under 'Arch.^{d} Dalzell Jailer';[40] he did not bring any action against Robert Burns or, indeed, even name him. On the same day, the baillies over the signature of their John Lawson granted Newall's petition, called for witnesses, and set Lewar's caution at 'Two hundred Merks Scots'. On the twenty-fifth of May, the baillies lawfully summoned the two girls and Lewars to appear before them the following day; their summons reveals that there had been a witness to the assault, one George Haugh, 'white Smith', i.e. tinsmith.[41] Lewars was not at home to receive the summons; so John Aitken, the sheriff substitute and municipal-court clerk, left it 'with his sister within his dwelling-house in Dumfries'.[42] This paper shows that Provost David Blair, not to be confused with the Birmingham gun manufacturer with whom Burns was still corresponding, and Baillies John Lawson, William Wilson, and Robert Jackson were to hear the case of criminal assault. It specifies, also, the charges as 'crimes of a heinous nature and severely punishable': 'Breaking or forcing open Garden doors when locked'; 'assaulting, scratching the breast and other parts, hurting and discolouring the haunch, and abusing'; 'Cursing, Swearing, and Speaking obscene and indecent language'; 'threatening murder'; and 'throwing pig-crocks'. Again, Newall does not mention Robert Burns by name, merely as 'the other person'.[43] The case called for the twenty-sixth was continued to the twenty-ninth. Then David Newall, with the consent of Robert Jackson acting for the baillies, resolved the issue: 'The pro^r fiscal, on account of several favourable circumstances to the def. which have come to his knowledge since raising this summons deserts this process pro loco et tempore.'[44]

What makes this binge unique is not its hilarious high jinks, but the extent of its documentation. Robert Burns had known other all-night drinking bouts, such as, for instance, the whistle contest at Friars Carse when Adam Fergusson 'bure the gree' for having drunk upwards of 'five bottles of claret' in the judgment of John McMurdo and Patrick Miller; but the poet's morning-after letters are more likely to dwell upon 'the horrors of penitence, regret, remorse, headache, nausea, and all the rest of the d——d hounds of hell that beset a poor wretch who has been guilty of the sin of drunkenness' than upon description of the good time had by all (II, 99).

What makes this garden party significant here is its pertinence to Burns's dilemma of the day. The poet was tightly wound with 'To be or not to be'. At one and the same time, therefore, he allows his independence to give vent to impetuous defiance of and spleen against a town personage, yet allows his self-control to extricate Lewars and his precaution to beg silence of the girls. This evening, night, and early morning with Lewars is of another bold pattern for the years 1792 and 1793: trouble and still more trouble. Later on, those like Wellwood Maxwell would see Burns's being brought before an Excise board of inquiry as not unexpected: anybody who would trespass through a forced gate might very well make one of a rabble who hissed the national anthem and cried out for 'Ça ira'. Alexander Findlater, Burns's immediate superior as Supervisor of the Dumfries Excise Office, would regard the affair as a black mark not only against his two officers but also against the reputation of the Service itself. A year before, Findlater had had to reprimand Burns for an instance of his 'carelessness or impropriety' as exciseman (II, 82); scarcely a month before, the supervisor had been presented with the questionable conduct of Lewars and Burns in the *Rosamond* case; now he had another public relations thorn as a result of actions by the same two officers; before the end of the year, he would have word of Burns's encouragement to Johnston and the bill of his one-night stand at the Dumfries Theatre.

How did Lewars get off Scot-free? What were the favorable circumstances? How did Burns keep his name out of the proceedings except for Lewars' identification of him as the other person? Perhaps Mr Short, John's advocate, reminded the baillies of the defendant's diligence in trying to improve himself by learning mensuration or of his providing his younger sister with a home or of his being distraught on account of Blount's eviction notice. Perhaps Short supplied the baillies with character references from Findlater and others. As a J.P., Alexander Fergusson alone had sufficient stature to quash any thought of entering Burns as a defendant. Newall himself had enough goodwill to favor him; David Staig, who had been provost before Blair in 1790 and would succeed him in 1792, would have been listened to as a sympathetic friend of the poet; Charles Sharpe at Hoddam and George Maxwell of Carruchan, two more J.P.s, might have added their voices; John Syme and John McMurdo had weight in Dumfries. And one must not forget Robert Riddell of Glenriddell. Any or all of these gentlemen would have stood up for Robert Burns in mid-1792. A year later some of them, the most influential of them, would not. That they would not is because the shoe was on the other foot: when Burns offended them through intemperate drinking, their story was Wellwood Maxwell's story. The disastrous culmination of Burns's turning to drink as a relief from his insoluble dilemma was the so-called 'Rape of the Sabines'. After this act of drunkenness, he could no longer number Robert Riddell and his wife Elizabeth among his friends.

On that evening at Friars Carse, Burns drank himself into incautiousness. Whoever proposed enactment of the Rape of the Sabines is a mystery, but it is no mystery that Burns cast himself in the male lead and Maria Riddell to star opposite him as the Sabine wife. All too realistically, this able-bodied subject of King Romulus seized his beautiful girl so as to break up the festival of Consualia in panic. Rough handling, violence, whatever: one has to allow for action sufficiently grave because anything less could not account for the drastic responses. Robert Burns's 'letter from Hell' was one. Maria's high disdain was another. Glenriddell's banishment of the poet from Friars Carse was another; Elizabeth Riddell's refusal to have anything more to do with Burns for the rest of her life, still another. Rachel Kennedy, Elizabeth's sister, informed James Currie of 'some circumstances of improper Conduct of Burns to Mrs Walter Riddell which she represented to Mr Riddell'. Rachel's own opinion (she had lived with the Riddells at Friars Carse) was that Burns 'at length became, I fear, a very dissipated and profligate fellow'.[45]

Robert Riddell never forgave Robert Burns. The sonnet which the poet composed on 21 April 1794, the day of the laird's death, was meant as a 'heart-felt tribute to the memory of *the man I loved*' (II, 239). What having to live without Friars Carse signified to Burns lies in his dedication of the first Glenriddell Manuscript, 27 April 1791:

At the Gentleman's request [Riddell's], whose from this time it shall be, the Collection was made; and to him, & I will add, to his amiable Lady, it is presented, as a sincere though small tribute of the gratitude for the many happy hours the Author has spent under their roof — *There*, what Poverty even though accompanied with Genius must seldom expect to

M

meet with at the tables & in the circles of Fashionable Life, his welcome has ever been, The cordiality of Kindness, & warmth of Friendship . . . let these be regarded as the genuine sentiments of a man who seldom flattered any, and never those he loved.[46]

The death of Elizabeth Riddell Burns in September 1795 gave Robert Burns double sorrow: the new grief for loss of his daughter and the old grief for loss of those after whom he had named her. Severely as Burns lamented the loss of the Riddells' friendship, he would have had cause to lament it even more severely if another man had not come into his life to offer him in friendship much of what Robert Riddell had offered.

FROM ROBERT BURNS—

The wan Moon is setting behind the white wave,
  And Time is setting with me, O.

                    — 'Open the Door to Me, O'

Entre nous, you know my Politics; & I cannot approve of the honest Doctor's
[John Moore's] whining over the deserved fate of a certain Pair of Personages.
— What is there on the delivering over a perjured Blockhead & an
unprincipled Prostitute to the hands of the hangman.

                    — To Mrs Dunlop

MAXWELL, if here you merit crave,
    That merit I deny;
  You save fair Jessie from the grave! —
    An angel could not die.

            'To Dr. Maxwell
    On Miss Jessie Staig's Recovery'

I understand that I am to incur censure by the Wine-Account of this District
not being sent in.

                    — To Mr John Edgar Excise Office Edin^r

—FROM ROBERT BURNS

> But pleasures are like poppies spread,
> You seize the flower, its bloom is shed;
> Or like the snow falls in the river,
> A moment white — then melts for ever.

— 'Tam o' Shanter'

Maxwell is my most intimate friend, & one of the first characters I ever met with; but on account of his Politics is rather shunned by some high Aristocrates; though his Family & Fortune entitle him to the first circles.

— To Mrs Dunlop

> No more of your guests, be they titled or not,
> And cook'ry the first in the nations:
> Who is proof to thy personal converse and wit,
> Is proof to all other temptations.

— 'To John Syme'

Dumfries, 18th July 1796

Do, for Heaven's sake, send Mrs Armour here immediately. My wife is hourly expecting to be put to bed. . . . I think and feel that my strength is so gone that the disorder will prove fatal to me.

— To Mr James Armour

CHAPTER SEVEN

Doctor to Poet

O, I wad like to ken — to the beggar-wife says I —
Hoo a' things come to be whaur we find them when we try,
The lassies in their claes an' the fishes in the sea.
— It's gey an' easy speirin', says the beggar-wife to me.

— Robert Louis Stevenson

The year 1794 entered unfortunately for Robert Burns. He had lost the Robert Riddells, he was to remain frozen in the glance of Maria until Glenriddell's death in April. In returning her commonplace book soon after Hogmanay, the poet notes his having forfeited her esteem:

> In a face where I used to meet the kind complacency of friendly confidence, *now* to find cold neglect & contemptuous scorn — is a wrench that my heart can ill bear. — It is however some kind of miserable good luck; that while De-haut-en-bas rigour may depress an unoffending wretch to the ground, it has a tendency to rouse a stubborn something in his bosom, which, though it cannot heal the wounds of his soul, is at least an opiate to blunt their poignancy.[1]

Early in the same January, Burns, desperately and secretly, went over the head of Alexander Findlater to Robert Graham of Fintry for the purpose of improving his place in the Excise at the expense of a poor fellow-officer, who like himself was 'burdened with a family of small children' (II, 229). His mind darkened with that melancholia conveyed in a letter to James Johnson: 'You should have heard from me long ago; but, over & above some vexatious share in the pecuniary losses of these accursed times, I have, all this winter, been plagued with low spirits & blue devils, so that I have almost hung my harp upon the willow-trees'

173

(II, 233). Without Robert Riddell in the present, the poet tried to bolster his spirits by summoning friends from the past, as he wrote Peter Hill in Edinburgh:

> For my part, 'I jouk & let the jaw flee o'er.' — As my hopes in this world are but slender, I am turning very rapidly, Devotee, in the prospect of sharing larger in the world to come. —
>
> How is old sinfull Smellie coming on with this world? for as to the other, I suppose he has given that up. . . . If you meet with my much-valued old friend, Colon^l Dunbar of the Crochallan Fencibles, remember me most affection[ately] to him.—Alas! not infrequently, when my heart is in a wand[e]ring humor, I live past scenes over again — to my mind's eye, you, Dunbar, Cleghorn, Cunningham, &c — present their friendly phiz; my bosom aches with tender recollections. (II, 232)

Drink was another dimension of this despair. Because of it, Burns felt obliged to beg understanding from Samuel Clark, Dumfries lawyer:

> I recollect something of a drunken promise yesternight to breakfast with you this morning — I am very sorry that it is impossible. — I remember too, you very oblidgingly mentioned something of your intimacy with Mr Corbet, our Supervisor General. — Some of our folks about the Excise Office, Edin^r had, & perhaps still have conceived a prejudice against me as being a drunken dissipated character. — I might be all this, you know, & yet be an honest fellow; but you know that I am an honest fellow, and am nothing of this. (II, 234)

February 1794 was a continuation of January misery which blasted constitution and frame 'with a deep incurable taint of hypochondria' (II, 234 f.). The three demons of 'Indolence, Business & Ennui' hung on (II, 236). But, strikingly, in the first week of March, came an uplifting. 'Thank Heaven,' Burns exclaimed to Alexander Cunningham on the third, 'I feel my spirits buoying upwards with the renovating year. — Now I shall in good earnest take up Thomson's songs' (II, 236). Why such dramatic change? The poet recognizes spring's renewal as a factor. He might have added that he had ridden out, once more, domestic and financial worries. Might he not have had the recent friendship of William Maxwell as a reason, too?

Maxwell gave Robert Burns his friendship in 1794. Only the *when* of it lies open to question. By September 1794, the poet was able to speak of Maxwell to Mrs Dunlop as 'my most intimate friend' (II, 259).

Whether he used 'intimate' as 'familiar' or as 'confidential', the inference to be drawn is one and the same: Burns and Maxwell had known each other for some time before that September. Early spring is most probable. One can propose for their meeting, without stretch of credibility, that the month was March; the place, the lawn between Ryedale and Troqueer Holm; the agent, John Syme, solid friend to both poet and doctor; the manner, man to man, not patient and physician although a definite possibility; the basis, mutual belief in the French Revolution, passionate but sworn to silence.

The Government had silenced William Maxwell; the Excise Board, Robert Burns. Such realities as the war with France and the Habeas Corpus Suspension Act, May 1794, warned them of their need to maintain silence. They were not alone. Their correspondents like Dr James Currie and William Roscoe had cut off their own tongues after rumblings from Pitt and evidence that *sedition* was so vague and loose that it was becoming punishable as a felony. Dr John Aiken justly represented the wise way of life which republicans were enjoining on themselves: 'We are fairly immersed in a bloody, expensive, and, I think, unjust war, and we must either lament its success, or rejoice in the calamities of our country. Such an alternative is enough to make one draw off entirely from political discussion and I do it, as much as the occasional effervescence of *libera indignatio* will give me leave.'[2] But what Aiken was not free to discuss in the market place, he did discuss in the homes of particular friends like Currie and Roscoe.

Similar private conversations with Dr Maxwell convinced Robert Burns that he had at last met his match for republicanism. The one could talk daggers, the other carronades; both could talk David Blair. Maxwell could not have had a more sympathetic, attentive listener; Burns could not have had a better informed mentor. The doctor knew that the French patriots' trial of Girondin deputies meant that the Revolution like Saturn was devouring its own children. He was able to throw light upon the *Noyades* and the *Mariage Républicain*, Bishop Hay's turning recruiting-sergeant for King George, Marmaduke Maxwell of Terregles' forming Scots Catholics into the tartan-outfitted 'Glengarry Fencibles'. Maxwell had seen the same Robespierre who was guillotined in July 1794; he was a friend of the same Horne Tooke put on trial in October. And Maxwell had seen before such sights as the Edinburgh trial of Watt and such spectators as Walter Scott behaving as he behaved: '. . . as I had provided myself with some cold meat & a Bottle of Wine I contrived to support the fatigue pretty well.'[3]

Robert Burns had no friend other than William Maxwell during the last two years of his life to whom he could speak so directly, so frankly in praise of France. He thought that he could enjoy something of the same freedom with his correspondent Mrs Dunlop; too late, he found that he could not. Mrs Dunlop did not have to be told, as George Thomson had to be, that the song 'Scots wha hae' had been composed in 'a rhyming Mania' only in part roused by Scotland's glorious struggle for freedom under Wallace and Bruce (II, 196); she would have known that its genesis lay as much in 'glowing ideas of some other struggles of the same nature, *not quite so ancient*' (II, 196). She tolerated the poet's view that liberty was his 'dear theme' as she did his quoting Rousseau's 'L'Homme est né libre' (II, 246); but in the meanwhile she let him know in certain terms that she considered his sympathy for French patriots distasteful. It was Burns's complete lack of circumspection or Aiken's *libera indignatio* that introduced the separation. Burns must have been proud to have seen Dr John Moore's quotation from 'Tam o' Shanter' in his *Journal during A Residence in France*; but when he wrote Mrs Dunlop of this book in January 1795, he was motivated not by elation, but by disdain. How could Moore whine for the deaths of Louis and Marie Antoinette? The king was 'a perjured Blockhead', the queen 'an unprincipled Prostitute' (II, 281). Maxwell had no more use for them; he, however, was a far cry from Mrs Dunlop. Thinking of her four sons and one grandson in the army and of her two daughters married to French royalist refugees, as Burns was not, she showed her displeasure by abruptly ending their correspondence, nor did she relent until Gilbert informed her that his brother lay dying.

The poet's views which so shocked Mrs Dunlop were substantially the same views shared with Maxwell in private evenings of speaking forthrightly of revolutionary France. It is doubtful that anybody else in Dumfries other than John Syme sat in to hear their full exposure; when, however, the political subject was a local election, others including Syme regularly participated. Burns's election ballads in support of Nithside Whigs show that the poet and Maxwell distinguished between politics of national reform and politics of the Revolution; they unhesitatingly spoke out on the former; they strove for secrecy on the latter. Candidates of the Establishment, nevertheless, made hay by associating all opposition to the Government with Gallicism. Their chief support came from a club of Anti-Gallicans known as the Loyal Natives, which brightened its image by such means as an annual dinner and ball on the King's birthday. One of their number, a laureate in residence, rendered in verse the suspicions being rumored:

> Ye Sons of Sedition, give ear to my song,
> Let Syme, Burns, and Maxwell pervade every throng,
> With Cracken, the attorney, and Mundell, the quack,
> Send Willie, the monger, to hell with a smack.[4]

Burns came right back with at least two epigrams, of which the following is the better known:

> YE true 'Loyal Natives' attend to my song:
> In uproar and riot rejoice the night long,
> From Envy and Hatred your core is exempt,
> But where is your shield from the darts of Contempt?[5]

Such answer, however, was ineffectual in removing the stings of suspicion.

The charge of seeing William Pitt to Hell was not so uncomfortable for Burns and Maxwell to live with as the taunt of sedition. Neither they nor their friends like the surgeon James Mundell and the attorney William McCracken, who was caught up with John Syme in the legal affairs of James Maxwell, were meriting the opprobrium of disloyalty in respect of the war effort; but just as long as they lived without an opportunity of demonstrating their allegiance to King George in the public eye, they would be regarded distrustfully. Their moment to take sides unequivocally was the formation of the Dumfries Volunteers.

The original Minute Book of the Volunteers tells many a story.[6] One of the simplest is that just about everybody who was anybody in Dumfries rallied round when Napoleon threatened invasion; one of the less obvious is just how many of the Dumfries liberals, who had incurred the wrath or suspicion of the Government and its friends, enrolled for the purpose of proving their loyalty. Among those who signed up at the very first meeting in January 1795 were the arch-conservative Wellwood Maxwell and the equally conservative George Duncan, cousin to Dr James Currie, and James Gray, Rector of Dumfries Academy. But, at the same time, such 'violent' democrats as John Syme, Thomas White, and James Mundell enlisted. Among those who signed up at the second meeting in early February were Alexander Findlater, the writer William Thomson, and the contractor Thomas Boyd, who had built Burns's Ellisland farmhouse. But, at the same time, the volatile John McMurdo enlisted; and so did John Lewars, whom Burns had introduced to George Thomson with 'His only fault is — D-m-cratic heresy' (II, 320). Simon Mackenzie soon joined; and the bookseller William Boyd, the innkeeper William Hyslop, and the surgeon John Harley — in short, almost every associate of Robert Burns whom one can name. And not excluding Robert Burns himself. The poet enlisted with John Syme at the first opportunity; thus, he marched with John Lewars, the two of them shoulder to shoulder with Wellwood Maxwell. The one and only notable name missing is that of William Maxwell of Kirkconnell.

Robert Burns never swallowed so much pride. He marched with the Dumfries Volunteers on the King's birthday. Four days later, he sat down to dinner at the King's Arms provided for the Volunteers by the magistrates at a cost to the town of £38. 4. 4 6/12;[7] that evening he drank to the King's health at the Court House, thus closing a long day reported in the local newspaper as one of 'utmost harmony'. Burns had to keep a straight face when Mrs de Peyster presented the colors with the sentiment, 'the Ladies will always find protection from the Royal Dumfries Volunteers'; and he had to maintain that face through the Reverend Mr Burnside's consecration of those colors with the prayer, 'We desire to pray even for our enemies.'[8] Robert Burns was more than just another Volunteer. He was a prominent Volunteer from inception of the force. He served on its Committee of Management, he argued in favor of having the Volunteers pay for themselves instead of appealing to public charity, and he composed the words to their signature tune which pleads for an end to the wrangling of 'snarling tykes', for boiling each 'sacreligious dog', and, in its last stanza, for remaining loyal to the Throne:

> The wretch that would a *Tyrant* own,
>   And the wretch, his true-sworn brother,
> Who'd set the *Mob* above the *Throne*,
>   May they be damn'd together!
> Who will not sing GOD SAVE THE KING,
>   Shall hang as high's the steeple;
>   But while we sing, GOD SAVE THE KING,
> We'll ne'er forget THE PEOPLE![9]

Burns knew the kind of person whom this 'beginning song of triumph' would most please (II, 294). He posted a copy to Robert Alexander Oswald, the son and heir of Mary Ramsay Oswald of

Auchencruive. Despite the fact that the poet had suffered the mother's 'iron pride of unfeeling greatness', despite the fact that she had been 'detested with the most heartfelt cordiality', he approached the son for his patronage by way of the song and its accompanying announcement, 'I have come forward with my services as poet-laureate to a highly respectable Political party, of which you are a distinguished member.'[10] Burns was every bit as sure of the one person whom his song would least please.

Robert Burns's reasons for joining the Dumfries Volunteers were not necessarily William Maxwell's reasons for not joining. One can lose oneself in fancied comparisons from the terms *integrity, independence, indiscretion, indigence,* and *inconsistency* so as to miss the hard fact that William Maxwell's response to Burns's enlistment was to give himself more fully and faithfully to the friendship, perhaps in recognition of a greater need. That Robert Burns could refer to this friendship as his 'most intimate' (II, 259) may reflect his gratitude for Maxwell's not only having understood his becoming a Volunteer, but even his having advised the step as one the poet must afford.

The two-year friendship of Robert Burns and William Maxwell was professional as well as private. It may have begun, as has been admitted, with Dr Maxwell's attending the poet during his distresses from hypochondria and drink, early in 1794. Nothing much is to be made of Maxwell's replacing Mundell at that time as doctor to Burns and his family beyond pointing out that the change in no way affirms the Loyal Natives' opinion of Mundell as a 'quack', but rather affirms that he was a surgeon, whereas Maxwell was a physician. During the period of his attendance upon Burns, Maxwell made his calls at the home near the southern end of the Mill Vennel (today Burns Street), which the poet had leased as more commodious than the first tenement. There the doctor went in June 1794 for the complaint which Burns described to Mrs Dunlop: 'To tell you that I have been in poor health, will not be excuse enough, though it is true. I am afraid that I am about to suffer for the follies of my youth. My medical friends threaten me with a flying gout; but I trust they are mistaken' (II, 246). Maxwell may have been called again in September, when Burns was 'so poorly' as to be 'scarce able to hold my pen' (II, 258). Generally, however, for 1794 and the first half of 1795, Burns's health was not the worst. He did note changes which gave him some concern, chiefly his beginning to feel 'the rigid fibre & stiffening joints of Old Age coming fast o'er my frame' (II, 281), but he was not seriously laid up. Even when he had need of

Maxwell in June 1795, when he could not leave his bed, good health had not, as he thought, flown from him forever, but merely for the time it took to recover from a complaint following 'the delightful sensations of an omnipotent Tooth-ach' that had seemed as though 'fifty troops of infernal Spirits' were 'riding post from ear to ear' along his jaw-bones (II, 302). The mortal sickness of Burns came in late 1795. He speaks of it in his January 1796 letter to Robert Cleghorn:

> Since I saw you [?August 1795], I have been much the child of disaster. — Scarcely began to recover the loss of an only daughter & darling child [Elizabeth Riddell Burns], I became my self the victim of a rheumatic fever, which brought me to the borders of the grave. — After many weeks of a sick-bed, I am just beginning to crawl about. (II, 315)

William Maxwell attended Burns throughout the course of this sickness which terminated in death; he had tended the daughter Elizabeth, the year before, to her death and the son James Glencairn, a year before that, to his recovery.

However inadequate Dr Maxwell's professional skills may be judged by twentieth-century practitioners, however much they may be denigrated, they were highly thought of by his patients and his respected colleagues. Friends common to poet and doctor had reason to be grateful for this physician. He had saved, for example, Maxwell Hyslop, son of William. And, according to Burns, he saved Jessie Staig. The poet wrote Mrs Dunlop in September 1794:

> Ah, my dear Madam, the feelings of a Parent are not to be described! I sympathised much, the other day, with a father, a man whom I respect highly. — He is a Mr Staig, the leading man in our Borough. — A girl of his, a lovely creature of sixteen, was given over by the Physician, who openly said that she had but few hours to live. — A gentleman who also lives in town, & who had studied medicine in the first [schools] — . . . Dr Maxwell . . . was at last called in; — & his prescriptions, in a few hours altered her situation, & have now cured her. (II, 259)

Burns enclosed his epigram on Jessie Staig's recovery, just as he did in his letter to George Thomson where he identified Maxwell as 'the Physician who seemingly saved her from the grave' by curing her of 'a fever' (II, 258). Was it Dr James Currie's cold-water treatment of fever that cured Jessie? William knew Currie and had read his *Medical Reports.*

Annoyingly, because of the need for recourse to correspondence, it is easier during the Dumfries period to learn more about Burns and Mrs

Dunlop at Stewarton in Ayrshire and George Thomson away in Edinburgh than about Burns and McMurdo or John Syme, all along the Nith. Because distance and separation were likewise not elements of the friendship between Robert Burns and William Maxwell, a record of letters is not extant. Dr Maxwell was too readily come upon for there to have been any need for writing; every day, he all but passed Burns's door on his way to the Infirmary; otherwise, Syme could have taken word from the poet and given it to his neighbor over the fence between Ryedale and Troqueer Holm. One is left, therefore, to depend upon one's knowledge of the characters of this doctor and this poet and upon knowledge of their mutual acquaintances as means of enlarging understanding of their friendship beyond the subject of their common sympathy for the struggles of the French citizens.

At first glance, a 'most intimate' friendship between these men does not seem possible. The one a Roman Catholic though out of the church; the other a Presbyterian though his church's sharpest satirist. The one a university graduate honed factual; the other all but self-taught, inspired in his genius of imagination. The one a native of Kirkcudbrightshire; the other of Ayrshire. The one born into an illustrious, well-to-do family; the other born ploughman of a ploughman who suffered public roup. The one a moderate drinker with a palate for such French wine as his elder brother stored at Kirkconnell; the other a tippler. The one a sportsman like Tam Samson and John Syme, the mortal foe of a 'birring Paitrick' or 'cootie Moorcock'; the other tenderhearted for mouse and Mailie.

Where the two seen farthest apart — in the church of their birth, for example — they may be seen closely together. Neither was happy with the creed or the public image of his church; both naturally rebellious, each became a more adept critic of his church through the Scottish Enlightenment. Again, instinctively, each loved his fellow men; each in his broad toleration made lasting friends of ministers in the other's faith. Both were romantics and, therefore, dreamy Jacobites and impracticable men of business. Burns was a first son who got up from his place to seat the second son Gilbert; Maxwell was born the second son and acted as one. Both studied mensuration, yet neither could take the altitude of money. Very poor heads for credit and debit, both could have paid more attention to such drill as Pumblechook's 'Seven times nine, boy.' Gilbert learned nothing new from Robert's disgust in farming Ellisland; James knew William was 'no Engineer' without being told.

Partialities and fondnesses linked Maxwell and Burns. Both young men were extramural lovers: Burns as a husband out of sight of Jean; Maxwell as a bachelor out of sight of Mary. Both like McMurdo and Cleghorn enjoyed songs and could remember the bawdy ones. Each was very partial to drama and an evening at the playhouse. In the Dumfries Theatre, Maxwell heard Fontenelle and Sutherland speak Burns's lines; doctor and poet sat in the audience when Mrs Kemble played in *Yarico*. Both men enthusiastically supported the plans and the subscription for a new theatre. Maxwell preferred reading the plays of Corneille and Molière; Burns preferred *Douglas* and *Macbeth*. Both loved books and read widely. Burns started circulating libraries in Ayrshire and Dumfriesshire; Burns and Maxwell subscribed to the public library in Dumfries. Both readers had the curiosity to know what the other had picked up, both owned books written by the lights of the Scottish Enlightenment which they lent freely. Burns penned these lines, for instance, in his poetic epistle to James Tennant of Glenconner:

> I've sent you here, by Johnie Simson,
> Twa sage philosophers to glimpse on:
> Smith wi' his sympathetic feeling,
> An' Reid to common sense appealing.
> Philosophers have fought and wrangled,
> An' meikle Greek an' Latin mangled,
> Till, wi' their logic-jargon tir'd,
> And in the depth of science mir'd,
> To common sense they now appeal,
> What wives and wabsters see and feel.[11]

Men as well as books kept Burns and Maxwell in touch with one another. In Edinburgh, William had known Creech and Geddes; from Dumfries, William went up to Edinburgh where he made purchases for his brother James in Alexander Cunningham's jewelry store. The Dumfriesshire families at Arbigland, Glenriddell, Carruchan, Parton, Terraughty, and Terregles, which had befriended Burns, were landed gentry for generations allied with the Maxwells of Kirkconnell. Syme, Lewars, White, Newall, the Curries, and the McMurdos served James Maxwell in one respect or another. From Syme, William heard of the experiences which this neighbor at Ryedale had had on his trip in Kirkcudbrightshire with Robert Burns; from the Burns family, whom he attended as physician, Maxwell had account of the same excursion. The French Revolution brought Burns and Maxwell to their acquaintance with Dr James Currie and William Roscoe in Liverpool and with David Blair in Birmingham. As a confirmed Jacobite, Maxwell would have known about what follows from Burns's letter to Blair, 25 August 1795:

> The following, my dear Sir, is the history of Lord Balmerino's durk which you now have. — In the year 1745 a Bailie in Glasgow (I once knew his name, but have forgotten it) who was a secret abettor of the Jacobite interest, sent some hundred pairs of shoes to the Prince's army, through the medium of Lord Balmerino; & that with many compliments to my Lord's personal character. — His Lordship, who was truly a brave, generous, worthy character, wrote back a grateful letter of thanks to the Bailie, & accompanied the letter with a present of his own durk. — This durk & letter came into the possession of a son of the Bailie, a dissipated worthless fellow, who sold the durk to a particular friend of mine for an anker of Ferintosh whisky. — My friend, who is a gentleman of the most undoubted probity, has often perused the letter; & well had it been for the interests of the durk, had my friend's chastity been equal to his Integrity! For one evening the devil & the flesh tempted him, in the moment of intoxication, to a house of a certain description, where he was despoiled of his durk, & that durk despoiled of its knife & fork, & silver mountings which had indeed been very rich; His Lordship's arms, cypher, Crest, &c. being elegantly engraved on several places of it. — My friend, after a diligent search, at last recovered his durk in this mutilated situation; & from him it came to me. (II, 410 f.)

Jacobitism, Balmerino's dirk, Glasgow, a gentleman of the most undoubted probity, a particular friend. Was the provenance from Balmerino *to* bailie *to* bailie's son *to* William Maxwell in Glasgow as a medical student commissioned to purchase Highland sheep for Kirk-connell or as an unplaced graduate searching a practice *to* Robert Burns, the doctor's most intimate friend and fellow Jacobite, *to* David Blair, as a gesture of gratitude for his present of matched pistols? If one is bold enough to conjecture that William Maxwell had given the dirk to Robert Burns, one must be willing to assume that Burns saw no offence to Maxwell in giving Blair the dirk which had been presented him as a particularly meaningful token of their friendship and that Burns did not name Maxwell as the gentleman of probity because he was fully aware that Blair and the doctor knew each other well and because the gentleman who had lived that wild night in Glasgow should be spared obvious embarrassment.

Jacobitism, the French Revolution, dirks, daggers, and David Blair were but several of the common grounds upon which the doctor and the poet stood with mutual friends. An index of Dumfries proper names to be found in Burns's letters for the years 1795 and 1796 would be a list, almost without exception, of places and individuals from the history of William Maxwell. Select a name at random. James Gracie, the Dumfries banker? He was born in New Abbey within a stone's throw of the ruins of Sweetheart Abbey. His daughter Betty came to Dr Maxwell, as one of his first patients, after she had aborted herself. James offered his carriage to bring Burns back from Brow, just days before his death. And Burns, in one of his last four letters, answered 'God bless you!' (II 329).

Intimate and extensive portraits by Robert Burns of evenings spent with his friends do not exist; what has come down has no more scope than the snippets in the journals, letters, and poetic epistles which concur in naming good food, good drink, good company, and good conversation as the main ingredients. Surely Maxwell invited Burns to Troqueer Holm for a game of backgammon and Syme invited both friends to dine at Ryedale. All three certainly shared suppers in Dumfries inns. Jean had the hospitality to have invited the doctor to stay on in the family home near the kirk gate of St Michael's and partake of dinner, and we do know that Burns was host to the doctor.

In August 1795, Robert Cleghorn of Saughton Mills came down from Edinburgh with a Mr Wight [?Andrew Wight of Ormiston] and a Mr Allan [?John Allan, who painted the portraits at Kirkconnell]. Burns invited William Lorimer to meet his guests at three o'clock dinner: 'I have two honest Midlothian Farmers with me, who have travelled three-score miles to renew old friendship with the Poet; and I promise you a pleasant party, a plateful of hotch-potch, and a bottle of good sound port' (II, 308). Evidently Allan did not make one of the party, perhaps because he was hard at work painting the laird's wife at Kirkconnell. Syme and Maxwell may have sat down at the table; we know Burns had them meet his guests, although we do not know what other entertainment he arranged or whether Syme and Maxwell returned his invitation by honoring those from Edinburgh. Two Burns letters to Cleghorn refer to the events. The first is of 21 August:

> Pray, has Mr Wight got the better of his fright, & how is Mr Allan? I hope you got all safe home. — Dr Maxwell & honest John Syme beg leave to be remembered to you all. — They both speak in high terms of the acquisition they have made to their acquaintance. — Did Thomson

[?George, the editor] meet you on Sunday? If so, you would have a world of conversation. Mrs Burns joins in thanks for your obliging, *very obliging* visit. (II, 309)

In January 1796, Burns announced to Cleghorn the death of Elizabeth and his attack of rheumatic fever. Then he wrote:

Thanks many thanks for my Gawin Douglas. — This will probably be delivered to you by a friend of mine, Mr Mundell, surgeon, whom you may remember to have seen at my house. — He wants to inquire after Mr Allan. — Best Compliments to the amiablest of my friends, Mrs Cleghorn, & to little Miss, though she will scarcely remember me, & to my thunderscared friend, Mr Wight. (II, 315)

Thus Dr Mundell joins Maxwell, Syme, and Lorimer as the possible Dumfries guests at Burns's August dinner.

One blushes to recall that story which Robert Chambers printed of Robert Burns and William Maxwell at the same board.[12] It is so very opportune, so much loaded with what one expects to be reported of the poet after the birthday dinners got underway — 'rich deep tones', 'glorious intelligence', 'brilliant wit', many verses repeated', 'matchless eyes', 'noble sentiment', 'no impure or obscene idea', everything but such hamely fare as, 'Man, stick in like a soo in a pratie pit, and no' sit there mumping like a rabbit.' But if one takes it *cum grano salis*, one can wring out grains of fact: the anecdote was sent to the *Glasgow Citizen* and published by that newspaper in January 1848. The contributor was John Pattison of Kelvingrove, nephew to Alexander Pattison of Paisley, who was active in promoting the subscription to the Edinburgh Edition. John Pattison, as a boy, had gone to Dumfries with his father. Upon seeing Burns on the steps of an inn, the father had invited him to four o'clock dinner and begged him to ask his friend Dr Maxwell to join them. The father sat at the head of the table, Maxwell at the foot, Burns and the lad opposite one another. After dinner, the company remained to talk until late at night or early morning. 'Both Maxwell and my father,' John Pattison recalls from his grammar school days, 'were highly gifted, eloquent men. The poet was in his best vein.' Which, translated, means, 'Robert Burns and Dr William Maxwell were the best of friends.'

Contemporary Scots poets, when on Rose Street, Edinburgh, have been known to express two views of Robert Burns: the one is that his reputation is much exaggerated, greatly exaggerated, scarce a word of it is true; the second is that he died from want of sympathy.

Against this second view, a thoughtful person might wish to measure the friendship of Robert Burns and William Maxwell. Truth is, the sympathy of William for Robert outlasted the poet's death, the winning of financial security for Jean and the children, and the erection of the mausoleum; it was laid to rest only when the doctor was laid to rest. Whatever the motives of such steadfast loyalty, monetary gain could not have been one; any medical man attending Robert Burns in 1796 knew that his services and prescriptions would be perforce gratis.

Robert Burns came to his death owing a 'rascal of a Haberdasher' (II, 327), who, the poet said, commenced a process that would put him in jail. Such a process has never been produced. The notoriously unreliable Allan Cunningham, however, named the haberdasher as a Mr Williamson who, in dissolving his partnership, had his solicitor Mr Sloan send out letters demanding that debtors pay up.[13] Burns's indebtedness seems to have been a matter of just over £7 owed on his Volunteers uniform. Foggy as the episode remains, Burns was alone at Brow Well on 12 July 1796 when letter or rumor of what the 'cruel scoundrel of a Haberdasher' had in mind arrived (II, 328). Distractedly, the poet wrote two hasty notes for money; his pride selected the two men from whom he begged. Family came first; so he asked £10 of his first cousin James Burness at Montrose (II, 327 f.). Indebtedness to him came second; so he requested half that amount of George Thomson at Edinburgh and, in the same breath, engaged himself to furnish 'five pounds' worth of the neatest song-genius' as payment (II, 328). No other letter refers to the haberdasher's bill or the fright aroused. The horror was a one-day horror, a day when Burns was absent from Maxwell and Syme, completely alone, dying. Either Maxwell or Syme could and would have allayed the poet's fears had the two friends known. Perhaps Burns dropped the subject because Maxwell did pay the debt. Or Syme or somebody else among Franklyn Bliss Snyder's extravagant 'at least a score of persons in Dumfries . . . would have gladly assisted him in any financial difficulty.'[14] Demonstrably, the friendship of William Maxwell for Robert Burns was never a £7 friendship. Let somebody else take the oath for Snyder's nineteen others, unnamed and unvouched for.

There is no more authentic narrative of Burns's last illness than that given by James Currie. Who were Currie's informants? He names Maxwell himself: 'The particulars respecting the illness and death of Burns, were obligingly furnished by Dr. Maxwell, the physician who attended him.'[15] So it was a doctor, Burns's own doctor who gave the specifics; and he was giving them to another doctor, another Edinburgh-trained physician who would know what was given, Liverpool's foremost practitioner who only incidentally was the editor and biographer for the posthumous edition. Either Maxwell wrote Currie, or Syme and Gilbert Burns took his account to Liverpool when they went there for a few days to answer Currie's questions and to hand over materials pertinent to the forthcoming volumes. Currie names John Syme as another informant. The closeness with which Syme observed Burns's sinking is apparent in his bulletins to Alexander Cunningham; he knew what he talked about. And Currie names Maria Riddell. She spoke with Burns on two successive days at Brow Well. She observed the 'stamp of death'; she was the one of whom the poet asked, 'Well, Madam, have you any commands for the other world?'[16] Like Syme and Gilbert, Maria went to Liverpool for the specific purpose of aiding Currie with his work on Burns.

Disagreement, therefore, does not arise from identifying the most reliable evidence; it arises from reading that evidence. 'Stomach disorder', 'headache affecting temples and eye-balls', 'violent and irregular movements of the heart' may, truly, confirm death by rheumatic fever which Burns himself acknowledges for January 1796. Currie mentions that the trouble of that January was a 'rheumatism' after intoxication and exposure to early-morning severe cold which began the end.[17] And Currie says that Burns had a 'predisposition to disease' and was 'liable to fever of mind and body' and was 'perpetually stimulated by alkohol'.[18] If one substitutes 'an habitual drinker whose drinking became more and more detrimental to his health' for 'perpetually stimulated by alkohol', Burns's letters alone would easily take to the mat anyone who argued otherwise.

Of the period February to April 1796, Burns admits in a letter to George Thomson, 'Almost ever since I wrote you last, I have only known Existence by the pressure of the heavy hand of Sickness; & have counted time by the repercussions of PAIN! Rheumatism, Cold, & Fever have formed, to me, a terrible Trinity in Unity, which makes me close my eyes in misery, & open them without hope' (II, 319). In May, he follows up to Thomson, 'I have great hopes that the genial influence of t[he a]pproaching summer will set me to rights, but as yet I cannot boast of returning health. I have now reason to believe that my complaint is a flying gout: — a damnable business' (II, 321). On the first of June, he speaks of 'the hand of pain' that 'has these many months lain heavy on me' (II, 322), of 'miserable health' (II, 323). By June's end, he is 'a victim of affliction', an 'emaciated figure' (II, 323). When he writes Thomson on 4 July, he is at Brow Well suffering 'precarious health', 'emaciation', 'loss of appetite', and 'inveterate rheumatism'; he had come to Brow because 'the Medical folks' had told him that 'his last & only chance' was 'bathing & country quarters & riding' (II, 324). He repeats in another letter, dated 10 July, that it had been 'The Medical people' who had ordered him to Brow if he valued his existence; on the same day, he writes his brother Gilbert that he is 'dangerously ill, & not likely to get better' (II, 326).

Burns leaves his correspondents with no doubt that his rheumatic pains were excruciating, as he leaves them with no doubt that more than one doctor had advised bathing at Brow as a last resort. Currie asserts that Burns was 'impatient of medical advice', that 'he determined for himself to try the effects of bathing in the sea.'[19] These assertions tend to imply that the Brow cure was not of Dr Maxwell's advising, even that Maxwell was set against such an alternative. Being left to come up with several names, no one of which may be Dr William Maxwell, a person might begin with the surgeon Alexander Brown as the 'Mr Brown' whom some biographers bring into the case.[20]

Syme wrote Alexander Cunningham on Sunday, 17 July, that he had strong hopes Burns would recover with 'the care & attention & advice he receives from Dr. Maxwell'.[21] But then the poet was at Brow against his physician's better judgment. When he arrived back in Dumfries the next day, Syme's hopes fled; for the poet was no longer able to stand upright, a tremor shook his frame, his tongue was parched, and his mind was 'delirious' whenever he was not roused to conversation.[22] On that Monday, Dr Maxwell told Syme that he, as physician, had no hopes; the next day Syme informed Cunningham that 'the hand of Death is visibly fixed upon him.'[23] The fever increased on Tuesday and again on Wednesday as Burns steadily lost strength. Thursday, 21 July 1796, John Syme wrote Alexander Cunningham, 'Burns departed this morning at 5 o'Clock.'[24] The church bells tolled on Monday as magistrates, citizens, neighboring gentry, the Dumfries Volunteers in full uniform, bands with drums muffled, and firing squad formed the funeral party between lines of the Cinqueport Cavalry and the Angusshire Fencibles.

Before publication in 1800, James Currie mailed John Syme his account of the poet's last minutes to ascertain if it could be supported in point of fact as remembered from their conversations in Liverpool.

Syme, evidently, asked Currie to suppress Burns's last exclamations out of delirium, and Currie did. What Currie originally mailed to Syme including what was suppressed follows here, as alleged and given by the self-interested contributor from holograph manuscript he claimed to exist but never identified through complete provenance and never saw fit to show:

> With all his failings, Burns was a most affectionate parent, and the fate of his infant family pressed heavily upon him in the latter days of his life. The subject brought with it many bitter reflections that unmanned his resolution and sunk his heart into despondence. The consciousness of his poverty was constantly present to his mind. 'Why,' said he to Dr. Maxwell, 'should you waste your precious time on me? I am a poor pigeon not worth the plucking. Alas! I have not feathers enough upon me to carry me to the grave!'
>
> And when his mind began to wander from the precincts of reason, the apprehension of want haunted his troubled imagination continually. At times he conceived himself as under confinement for debt; and under the convulsive motions which preceded his dissolution, considering himself as torn from his family to encounter the horrors of a jail, he called on his friends for assistance, exclaiming, 'Maxwell! Macmurdo! Syme! will none of you relieve me?' These were the last words he uttered.[25]

Let us grant that if the holograph material containing the above passage is unlocked and published, it will show that what has been given out of context is accurate both in and out of context. Where do we find outselves?

Delirium is a far more prickly field to walk barefoot in than a field of wheat just after mowing. True it is that Burns unreasonably feared incarceration for indebtedness some days before he died. But true it is that he was not jailed. True it is that anyone bent upon being paid does press for payment as long as the bill is unpaid. But true it is that nobody pressed for payment.

In the *Journal of the Border Tour*, May 1787, Robert Burns wrote, 'I am determined to live for the future in such a manner as not to be scared at the approach of Death.'[26] But he *was* frightened to death, not because of fear for retribution on himself in a life to come, but because of fearful concern for his wife and children having to live on unprovided for in the life he was leaving. This comes clear in his letter to the schoolmaster James Clarke, 26 June 1796:

> Alas, Clarke, I begin to feel the worst! — As to my individual Self, I am
> tranquil; — I would despise myself if I were not: but Burns's poor widow!
> & half a dozen of his dear little ones, helpless orphans, there I am weak as
> a woman's tear. (II, 323 f.)

Are deep-seated fears characteristic of delirium? Are evocations of
friends to combat those fears characteristic of delirium? First friends
first? If so, Burns's delirium was characteristic.

Maxwell or Syme or McMurdo could assure Robert Burns that he
would not be jailed for a debt of £7. But which of them in 1796 could
assure him or anybody else that the Burns family would be without
want? What they could guarantee was that they would make every
effort they could conceive to provide security in the present, in the days
to come, and in the long future to follow. Even as Burns raved, these
three friends were underway with their efforts. That is fact, not
delirium. Who owed what to whom? Jean christened the baby boy,
born to her on that Monday when her husband was buried, with the
name 'Maxwell' as token cancellation of old and new debts, her
husband's, her children's, and her own. No one understood better than
her husband the value of her currency, the only currency with which
she could repay Dr William Maxwell. That, too, is fact, not delirium.

The death of Robert Burns and the birth of Maxwell Burns filled Dr
Maxwell's life during the week of 18 July. Sentimental embellishments
of the hand-me-down sort creep into the poet's biography fifty years
later to speak of Maxwell; they tell of what a privilege it had been to
have cared for Burns and they would have it that 'Maxwell, a kind
physician, came often to gaze in sadness where no skill could relieve.'[27]
Alexander Cunningham comes closer to hitting the nail on the head in
his consolation to Syme the day before the death: 'To you and Dr.
Maxwell he owes much.'[28] Decisions of that week fell to Syme and
Maxwell. Before Thursday, Maxwell looked after the father and the
mother, while Syme began to move plans for aiding the family, which
he and the doctor had agreed upon. After Thursday, Syme consulted
with Gilbert about arrangements for the funeral, while Maxwell looked
after Jean. Both men composed a funeral invitation over the name of
the eldest son, the ten-year-old Robert.[29] Syme and Maxwell had help,
mainly from John and Jessie Lewars: she at the bedside and he out in
the streets seeing to details.[30]

Robert Burns did have periods of lucidity on Monday and Tuesday
of his last four days alive, and William Maxwell was near to share his

last clear thought. It seems that as he lay dying, Burns tried to think of ways by which he could show gratitude to this friend. He may have thought then of naming the unborn 'Maxwell'; he did think of a gift, his one material possession of any value, that was especially appropriate as a symbol of the friendship. David Blair had presented him with two handsome pistols. These the poet gave Maxwell. The doctor held on to them dearly during the next thirty-eight years. Upon his own deathbed, he gave them to his daughter Elizabeth, who, in turn, left them to her heir Bishop Gillis. On Tuesday, 19 April 1859, the bishop read a paper before the Society of Scottish Antiquaries in which he spoke of Robert Burns and the pistols which he, Gillis, was now bestowing upon the Society.[31] Linking the poet and the doctor, Gillis remembered the 'youthful enthusiasm' which had 'misled' William as a very young man to approach David Blair in Birmingham. From those days, Gillis continued, William had been led back to the religious convictions of his earliest years. He had, indeed, been at the scaffold in Paris that twenty-first of January, but he had not dipped his handkerchief in the blood: Maxwell had too much 'high breeding', 'exquisite sense of propriety', and 'deep and noble feeling' for such an action. William had returned to his native home 'to lay . . . the foundation of that high professional character which he subsequently perfected'.

Did not Robert Louis Stevenson once observe that the relation with the least root in matter is undoubtedly the airy one of friendship? The endeavors of John Syme and William Maxwell of late July 1796 prove Stevenson true. Little help might have been expected from Jean and the brother Gilbert; some from Patrick Miller, who with Syme and Maxwell had been appointed by the poet as his executors, and some from John McMurdo; none, at the moment, from Alexander Cunningham, who could only be kept up-to-date. The first imperative was relief for the family. Syme and Maxwell had decided upon two approaches as most promising: one immediate, the other distant; one, a public subscription of money, the other, publication of a posthumous volume of 'poetical remains'. Further avenues of charity were not overlooked; so Syme and Maxwell encouraged Thomas White to request a grant from the Royal Literary Fund in London.[32] Given manifest urgency, Maxwell and Syme sent off to newspapers an advertisement in such good time as to have it published the day after the burial. The *Edinburgh Courant* for Tuesday, 26 July, asks that contributions to aid the widow and children be taken to Sir William Forbes & Co. or to any Edinburgh bookseller and asks, in anticipation of a subscription volume, that poems and letters of Burns be directed to either Alexander Cunningham on George Street, Edinburgh, or John Syme, Ryedale, Dumfries.

How much money was subscribed and entrusted to Patrick Miller lies in doubt. The oft-repeated figure of £1,200, which is uncertified, appears to stretch the point,[33] James Currie's figure of £700 seems closer to actuality if one argues that the £100 or so which Currie collected in Liverpool probably matched all that was subscribed in Dumfries and half of all that was subscribed in Edinburgh.[34] Syme told Cunningham, 2 August, 'We have here got about £100 — Dr. Maxwell gave ten guineas — and will get more.'[35] If Scotland had continued the subscription as Maxwell started it off, £1,200 and double that amount would have gone to the poet's family.

Friends like Syme, McMurdo, and Miller did not dig so deeply into their own pockets as Dr Maxwell. They were, however, not unhappy to have White press his request in London and doubly happy to receive the £25 which the Royal Literary Fund announced in October. Nor did they mind trying to make Gilbert Burns knuckle under for what he owed his deceased brother's estate, always providing that they did not have to force the knuckling. John McMurdo elected William Maxwell for that unpleasant office.

John Syme disliked the 'stupid' citizenry of Dumfries and 'female gossips'; he liked shooting, gooseberries, and 'violently hopping dames'.[36] At age thirty-six, Gilbert Burns lived as though a violently hopping dame did not exist. Looking something like his older brother and writing a hand which bore striking resemblances to that of the dead poet, he despairingly worked the soil at Mossgiel even as he considered leasing a Dumfriesshire farm as one more start after one more ruinous failure. Robert's success in Edinburgh had brought Gilbert a loan for continuance at Mossgiel; but try as he could, the younger brother had not been able to cancel the debt. On his conscience he had such knowledge as the thought that nine days before death Robert had begged their cousin for £10 to save him from the horrors of jail in a note to which he added, 'I have been thinking over & over my brother's affairs & I fear I must cut him up' (II, 328). Gilbert owed £300; he could not keep up with even the interest on that sum, despite his deducting for the cheese and potatoes he supplied his brother's family.[37] With him at Mossgiel were his five children, his wife Jean, his sisters Agnes and Annabelle, his mother, for whom Robert had requested that an annuity of £5 be deducted from the loan, and 'dear bought Bess' for whom

Robert had specified a second annuity as another deduction. William Maxwell perceived Gilbert's inability to pay the debt and caught his despair; so he advised the executors not to pursue the matter. Syme reported to Cunningham, 7 March 1797, 'We do not think it proper to use vigorous measures in exacting payment of a £300 bill due by Gilbert Burns, who has fairly stated his present inability to discharge that debt. But I hope it will be secure in the end.'[38]

John Syme and William Maxwell closeted themselves with Gilbert before noon Tuesday, less than twenty-four hours after the funeral, for purposes which Syme immediately outlined to Cunningham:

> I am just now come from a private meeting, Dr. Maxwell and I with Gilbert Burns, the brother of the deceast, who goes home this afternoon, and will return about the middle of August. We have concerted — 1st, to seal up all his papers till then, when we shall look thro' them; 2d, To advertise next week in a proper stile that those who have been favoured with the correspondence or little pieces of Burns would be so kind as send them and copies of them, or allow copies to be taken exactly, to the following persons, viz. yourself and Professor Stewart in Edinburgh, but we mean you principally — to Messrs. Perry and Gray, proprietors of the Morning Chronicle, London, who are worthy men and were great friends of Burns, and to Mrs. Imley (formerly Woolstoncroft), a particular correspondent &c. of Burns and Mr. Robt. Aitken of Ayr, for Ayrshire — and to Dr. Maxwell and me for Dumfries &c.[39]

Gilbert returned to Mossgiel that afternoon, reimbursed for his outlay on mortcloth and bells. Two days later, Thursday, the twenty-eighth, a meeting of the Dumfries friends of Burns was called to be reported Friday by Syme to Cunningham:

> Yesterday about a dozen or 15 of friends met according to advertisement, Mr. Miller chiefly the acting member of the meeting, tho' not the most liberal subscriber. At this time about 70 guineas were subscribed, and I dare say as much more will be given by the other benevolent people here, and this I doubt will be the utmost. Perhaps it will be considered pretty handsome. A Committee was appointed to examine the MSS. to purge them of such personalities, or perhaps excrescencies of fancy, in point of religion and politics, as ought certainly to be sealed up at present. The rest are to be made into bundles and sent to you, to be laid before Professor Stewart and such others of his qualifications whom you and he shall chuse, that they may digest and prepare proper materials for being published. The sooner this is set about the better. The Committee are Dr.

Maxwell, Mr. McMurdo, Mr. Miller senior and junr., Mr. Wallace, writer here, one whom Burns loved and a clever liberal young fellow who will take all the drudgery &c. on him, and myself.[40]

The Dumfries Committee soon realized that one of their number would have to go to Edinburgh to fill in Alexander Cunningham; they chose William Maxwell. During the preceding February, Syme had already begun to praise Maxwell to the skies in his letters to Alexander Cunningham:

He [Robert Burns] and I dined tete a tete last Sunday in my Cabin — quite sober — only one bottle port betwixt us. I like this better than a debauch, even in an Inn. Yet when two or three are gathered together in the name of friendship and *nostri generis* — why, I would as soon have a bottle or a bottle and a half as a share of that quantity. We have a very superior young fellow here — Dr. Maxwell — who, to an uncommon if not wonderful science in Physic, adds the perfect manners and mind of a gentleman. You would be much attached to him. Without him and Burns I should find this place blank and dreary.[41]

Before Maxwell left for Edinburgh in early August, Syme extended this notice to Cunningham:

. . . let me not omit to tell you Dr. Maxwell is to be in Edinburgh next friday [5 August] — I shall give him a letter of introduction to you, and he says he will call upon you. Let me describe for a moment this superior Man. His address is such that you may at first think him stiff and affected. This is a natural cast arising perhaps from defect of articulation etc. But there is not a jarring atom in him — His manners are of the finest school, his liberality, humanity, and judgement — not to mention professional skill — are of the first kind. In short if there be a perfect man of virtue, he seems to me to be so — I have great pleasure in making you acquainted with each other — I wish heartily you would come out with him and take a peep into Burns' Cabinet — He returns on Tewesday.[42]

Thus Syme could come away from the days of Burns's last sickness, death, and funeral convinced of not only Maxwell's humanity but also his 'finest professional skill'. Syme could have had no greater praise of his friend, but he could reiterate to Cunningham his belief and Maxwell's that Cunningham should come to Dumfries to share the decision-making:

I wrote you a hasty page yesterday [Tuesday, 2 August]. This is to introduce Dr. Maxwell, whom I mentioned in my last. The opportunity of your obtaining from him all the information I can give you supersedes the incumbency of my writing you so particularly as I mentioned. You can converse him on every point, and as he and I agree on all circumstances, it will be the same as if you and I were consulting on matters. Last night we went to the house of the late Bard and opened his repositories — look'd thro' his manuscripts, which are pretty numerous but in utter confusion. We separated the papers in this manner — threw all *his* hand writings into one bundle, Letters *to* him into another — accounts and vouchers into a third, and so on. These particular bundles we are on a future occasion to examine and reduce into order to be sent you. . . .

As to publishing the list of Subscriptions here, we have not made up our minds on it — Dr. Maxwell and you may converse on its merits.

I have really a notion that you will take a trip hither in company with Maxwell. Would it not be a nice thing to have the opportunity of turning over all the papers of the Bard's. You could spend 5 or 6 hours a day in this occupation with singular gratification, you should have a room to yourself. This would not only accelerate the collection and arrangement, but be a proper thing. The Gentlemen of the Committee will cheerfully adopt you. Indeed, owing to their avocations etc., we cannot dedicate the necessary time due to the business, but must be convened on convenient occasions.[43]

Elsewhere in this letter, Syme talks about the extent of Burns's contributions to George Thomson's editions of Scottish song; such stress had been Cunningham's signal for inviting Thomson to write an obituary of Burns suitable for newspaper publication. Thomson did better than that; he sent an obituary to the *Edinburgh Courant* and then an article to the *London Chronicle*. His obituary asserts that although Burns had 'extraordinary endowments', they were 'accompanied with frailties which rendered them useless to himself and his family'.[44] Having found his stride, Thomson ran on in the *Chronicle*: Burns's talents were obscured and finally impaired by excess, he had failings as well as powers, he had exhausted his mind previous to his death. Others took the baton from Thomson with more of what Syme called 'damned, illiberal lies'; Burns had been everywhere caressed in Edinburgh; 'it is probable that he was not qualified to fill a superior station'; 'his manners were not such as to secure the permanent friendship of the respectable part of society'; he sank 'into a habit of low debauchery'; he finally fell a victim to excess; 'Mr Burns left a wife, and five infant children, without any resources but what they might derive from the generosity of the public; and a subscription has been since set on foot.'[45]

The worst fear of Syme and Maxwell was coming true: Burns had offended far too many of those people upon whose goodwill any Dumfries subscription or, for that matter, Edinburgh subscription must depend. What might be expected from the Earl of Galloway's wide circle of influence after

> WHAT dost thou in that mansion fair?
>   Flit, Galloway, and find
> Some narrow, dirty, dungeon cave,
>   The picture of thy mind.[46]

Commissary Goldie might or might not have found the following amusing:

> LORD, to account who dares thee call,
>   Or e'er dispute thy pleasure?
> Else why, within so thick a wall,
>   Enclose so poor a treasure.[47]

Maria Riddell could forgive Burns for having spoken in his poetry of her heart as 'rotten',[48] but her husband Walter would hate the poet who wrote

> SIC a reptile was Wat, sic a miscreant slave,
> That the worms ev'n damn'd him when laid in his grave;
> 'In his flesh there's a famine,' a starved reptile cries,
> 'And his heart is rank poison!' another replies.[49]

The butt of such verses does not rush forward to make a howling success of a subscription intended to promote the welfare of the author's family; moreover, the heart of the public does not vibrate with sympathy for a man eulogized as a débauchee who dies of his excess. To make matters still worse, Maria Riddell published her *Memoir*. She had written it within a fortnight of Burns's death as a defense of Robert Burns; she released it without having sought the counsel of Maxwell and Syme. Within a few hundred words, Maria's tribute admits that Burns was 'candid and manly in the avowal of his errors', that his had been 'the frolic of the flowing bowl', that he had 'irregularities' and 'frailties', 'frequent errors' and 'misfortunes', 'imprudencies that sullied', and such 'inconsistencies' as alternately exalt and debase one's nature.[50]

Originally Maxwell and Syme intended to emphasize the subscription and keep the posthumous volume as 'a nest egg'.[51] But sorting the poet's manuscripts in Dumfries; puzzling over Creech's, Johnson's, and Thomson's claims; receiving questions about probable editor and possible biographer; reading Maria's *Memoir*; hearing calumnious rumors; and observing how the poet's rights could be transgressed by those motivated only by self-protection compelled the executors to face up to the proposed publication before they wished. They were quickly learning that instead of gaining new materials through public advertisement, they were running the risk of losing some of the best materials in hand. Mrs Dunlop wanted return of her letters, and she had Gilbert Burns to protect her interests. 'Clarinda' asked for her letters through Robert Ainslie, whom she retained.[52] Maria sought control of whatever referred to herself. What Syme and Maxwell were discovering in 1796 was what Allan Cunningham admitted to Charles Kirkpatrick Sharpe in 1834: Robert Burns had written much that was 'pure, witty, and wicked, and Madam Public is squeamish'.[53]

Forward movement came from Syme and Maxwell, infrequently strengthened by McMurdo or the younger Miller. What was 'palpably useless' was burnt. But what was to be done with such personal items as 'Clarinda's' letters? The two executors first decided that, as gentlemen, they would seal the papers unread and return them to Edinburgh. Then they resolved to trust their honor and delicacy and read them. Impressed, Syme exclaimed, 'Heavens! were it possible to get his letters to that person. Avaunt the sacrilege of destroying them or shutting them up for ever from the Light!'[54] When Maxwell went up again to Edinburgh on Thursday, 18 August, one of his purposes was to inquire of Alexander Cunningham what chance there might be of obtaining from Mrs McLehose the letters she had received from Burns; another purpose was to discuss a more important development.

Syme and Maxwell had solicited the aid of Burns's Liverpool friends for the subscription. Chief among these were Dr James Currie and William Roscoe. The approach was through Currie, for both Syme and Cunningham had been fellow students of the doctor at the University of Edinburgh. Despite the fact that Currie on the day of the poet's death was up to the brim and a little bit over with publication of his *Medical Reports*, he gave his time to the subscription, willingly and most effectively. Before the Liverpool solicitation had run its course, the subject of the new edition to assist the family further had been introduced into the correspondence between Currie and Syme.

When it became apparent that Professor Dugald Stewart had no intention whatsoever of linking his name to a posthumous volume of Burns's work, Syme and Maxwell thought more and more of Currie as their man: he was a most respected Scotsman; he had already written memoirs and published them; as Roscoe's closest friend, he could rely upon assistance from the biographer of Lorenzo de' Medici; Currie and Roscoe knew the right publishers like Cadell & Davies; Roscoe had set up the Irishman John McCreery as his own printer in Liverpool; most tellingly, Currie saw that money was the object and that to get as much as possible, any editor-biographer of Robert Burns would have to remain aware that *delicacy* connoted *propriety* and *prudence*.

James Currie knew the poetry and songs of Robert Burns. He was well aware that Burns had wounded individuals and families in many a scathing satire or verse epistle, ill-tempered epigram, and coarse epitaph; Currie knew, also, that Burns had run counter to the times in his handling of such themes as religion, monarchy, revolution, and class. And he knew of the bawdry. When the main object was to make money through public subscription, no editor could touch such a song as 'When maukin bucks, at early fucks,/In dewy grass are seen, Sir' or the letter to Ainslie describing 'a thundering scalade' given Jean on 'some dry horselitter'.[55] After all, eight years later, Walter Scott dared throw off only twelve copies of *Sir Tristrem* 'without castration', even though he fumed, 'I can by no means think that the coarseness of an ancient romance is so dangerous to the public as the mongrel and inflammatory sentimentality of a modern novelist.'[56] And notwithstanding his vow of 1805 that he would as soon castrate his father as John Dryden, Scott finally judged that publication of an unexpurgated text of Dryden would be improper, that he would have to circumcise the Restoration poet 'a little'.[57]

Neither Currie in Liverpool nor Cunningham in Edinburgh had much spare time to devote to the posthumous edition. None of the principals in Dumfries, moreover, was more fully occupied with his own affairs than James Currie; but if he was willing to accept responsibility for the Burns, nobody else would object. Maxwell was at work establishing his new practice. McMurdo was a good man to have on one's side when a need arose for someone to throw weight around; however, he served the cause least of all. Late Chamberlain at Drumlanrig and late Provost of Dumfries, he was about to become 'McMurdo of Hardriggs'. He had married Jean, sister-german of David Blair, another Provost of Dumfries; two of McMurdo's relatives had married relatives of James Currie. John liked to help his own. Putting business in the way of the youthful writer William Thomson was one of McMurdo's interests, primarily because Thomson's wife was the daughter of John's uncle William, merchant in Dumfries. In 1794 McMurdo had seen to it that Thomson was appointed cautioner for the litigation of David Blair's will;[58] the posthumous edition was to prove another opportunity for boosting Thomson and, at the same time, for getting one's self out from under a load.

Like McMurdo, John Syme lacked stamina for a marathon. As he had grown to love gardens, shooting, and evenings among friends, he had come to detest the one thing that stood between him and such pastimes: paperwork. The Stamp Office, management of lands for clients like Currie, and loans to gentlemen like James Maxwell daily suffocated him under piles of paper, so that the prospect of one more heap, even if that heap was of Burns, brought him to his knees.[59] At heart, John Syme was a creature of comfort, 'a dauber at landskips', who saw in reverie a community of his best friends about him at Ryedale.[60] In projecting such a neighborhood, he encouraged McMurdo to buy land and William Maxwell to build his own cottage on the strip just south.[61] If Syme and not Maxwell had gone to Edinburgh, he would have looked first for the nearest oyster cellar. 'You and I,' he wrote Cunningham in late August 1796, 'must surely eat some oysters in a Closet together & open those shells which contain some confidential & secret pearls which ought no more to be exposed to common ears & eyes than the diamond in the dunghill.'[62]

Before the thirty-first of August 1796, Syme, Maxwell, and Cunningham had agreed that Dr James Currie should edit the papers of Robert Burns and write the biography and that they should so inform their man by way of an invitation baited with a holograph copy of the poet's autobiographical letter to Dr John Moore. In rising, Currie specified conditions: somebody, preferably Syme, was to come to Liverpool to talk things over, and those in Dumfries were to sift through the manuscripts and select those which were to be published.

Syme evaded responsibility for the sorting. 'You do it,' he wrote Cunningham. 'Let Currie and Roscoe do it,' replied Cunningham.

By the last day of September, William Maxwell and John McMurdo had half-heartedly agreed to do it, and Syme had assured Cunningham that he would 'spur them'.[63] All to little or no avail. Syme told Cunningham in early November that he was ready to dump everything into the lap of Currie:

> As to the MSS. From the desultory and continual occurrences of the Stamp Office, I found myself unable to sort or arrange the papers of the late Bard. I frankly said so to Dr. Maxwell and M'Murdo, and as I imagined they would be subject to similar avocations I suggested the alternative of sending them, as they were, to you or Currie. They did not approve of sending such an indigested chaos or mass. So they undertook to look over them and arrange them under the heads of originals, letters, etc. etc. This was in August. But still I find they have made little or no progress. I have prompted them frequently. And within this day or two I have spoken so decisively to them that I have every reason to believe they will set seriously to the task and accomplish it next week. I am extremely anxious that Currie should have them immediately, for the sooner the business be set about the better.[64]

Syme kept his spurs as dull to prick himself as he kept them sharp to prick Maxwell and McMurdo. Currie had already purchased a notebook in which he could enter his thoughts for a life of Burns when he wrote Syme on the last day of the year 1796 that he was unwilling, even with Roscoe's assistance, to take the responsibility of choosing what was to be published, that Syme must arrange and select, that those in Liverpool would find printer and publisher, and that Syme should come to Liverpool to sit in final council. Currie's long letter might just as well have been a brief Hogmanay greeting, for Syme had determined for himself what his next step should be. His reply to Currie arrived in Liverpool on 12 January 1797. Whatever its argument, this letter could have produced only the faintest ping compared to the loud bang of what it served to convey — 'the remains of poor Burns', 'the complete sweepings of his drawers and of his desk', 'the sheep not separated from the goats', 'the manuscripts of a man of genius, unarranged by himself, and unexamined by his family or friends . . . with all their sins on their head, to meet the eye of an entire stranger!'[65]

After January 1797, William Maxwell remained Syme's most conscientious helper in promoting the welfare of the poet's family. Cunningham, however, was happier with Maxwell's amiability than Syme was with Maxwell's aid. Syme's own attentions during this period seem more for damning Ayrshire as niggardly or for itemizing expenses of the Burns executorship than for lending Currie a hand. By mid-April he was ready to cry 'Mercy!' to Alexander Cunningham:

> I wish we could conclude the business now. I have some reason, tho' not I believe so much as you, to complain of the load — for neither Maxwell nor McMurdo, nor in short any one, lends me the least assistance; on the contrary, they augment my trouble by promising meetings and never performing them, thus occasioning me waste of time and loss of other engagements.[66]

Other letters between Syme and Cunningham for spring 1797 are more charitable to Maxwell and less waspish. They speak not only of Syme's, Maxwell's, and McMurdo's feeding with General Goldie on an Edinburgh turbot, the gift of Cunningham. Syme had had to own up to Cunningham on 13 March that 'Dr. Maxwell has been severely ill with a Quinzy — to which he is subject'[67] and it was more than a month later before he could report, 'Maxwell is now quite well — and busy at rearing his mother's Villa aside me.'[68] Understanding what William was building at Troqueer Holm and for whom is more difficult than understanding that he had at least one more reason for not maintaining the pace of efforts to help the family than anybody else had — namely, severe illness.

Syme had to admit that his going to Liverpool for consultations with Currie was inescapable; the solace he took was the resolve that every penny he had spent on the affairs of Robert Burns would be laid 'to the charge of the concern'.[69] Syme invited Cunningham to accompany him; but this associate declined, although he admitted that he would enjoy meeting his old friend Currie and that such an outing would contribute 'not a little to that felicity' of paying respects 'to Dr. Maxwell *en passant*'.[70] Syme turned elsewhere. Gilbert Burns was in Dumfriesshire looking for a profitable farm which he could afford, a farm which he had discussed in letters to Syme and Maxwell. So Gilbert was picked.

The Mail departing the George Inn, Dumfries, about seven o'clock of the Friday evening, 25 August 1797, could not have conveyed two more uneasy travellers than John Syme and Gilbert Burns.[71] They arrived in Liverpool, Sunday the twenty-seventh. Altogether, the two visitors had exactly seven workdays at Merseyside: Monday the twenty-eighth of August, through Sunday the third of September. Rather remarkably, Syme seems to have sustained from first to last a peevish, disagreeable, penurious, contrary mood of selfishness and vanity; whereas the simple, sentimental, sententious Gilbert reacted unpredictably with such winning touches as curiosity, civility, and affection.

The visit to Liverpool, documented by Gilbert's journal and Syme's lengthy letter to Cunningham of 10 September, introduced additional Burns materials, answered leading questions, and gave definition and incentive to what lay ahead of James Currie.[72] If the guests were awake to the realities of life in Currie's circle, they must have departed with some doubts that Roscoe could make time to share in the Burns enterprise by contributing a critique of the poetry, some awareness that Currie first had to complete the labor of his *Medical Reports* before freeing his leisure hours for the new edition, some satisfaction that a man like John McCreery, at the height of his Liverpool career as a master printer, was to contribute his skill and knowledge, and some hope that Cadell & Davies, aware of Currie's, Roscoe's, and McCreery's co-operation, would become the publisher. Syme had other awareness. He and Gilbert had just managed to survive a storm at sea on their return to the Nith:

> Such a scene of horror I could not conceive as I witnessed. Gilbert Burns was so sick and done up that he lay like brute matter in the hold. I sustained all the misery and distress of wakeful sense — Our ship became a wreck — unmanageable and drifting — her sails torn to atoms, ourselves at the mercy of the tempest. The Skipper got drunk from desperation. The crew at times raving wild and at times resigned to their fate. Dismay alone reigned — at length we providentially got into White-haven about one o'Clock of Wednesday, and took a chaise and reached Dumfries on Thursday night. We have recovered our fatigues. Burns has gone home and here I am as well as ever, tho' I have sustained, I think, as much suffering as my nature, I believe, could support. I have lost some cloaths, and upon the whole the jaunt has been a severe one in point of expense also. 'Tis a pretty Executry. But I will go through it if possible.[73]

The comparative silence following this account to Cunningham proves that the burden of those in Scotland had been shifted on to the back of James Currie in Liverpool. Breaking of this silence in early April 1798 marks the beginning of the last important contribution of

Burns's executors. Syme informs Cunningham of the event:

> A factor *loco Tutoris* is appointed to Burns family — Mr. William
> Thomson of Dumfries, a sedate and intelligent young man married to a
> Niece of McMurdo, will now attend to these affairs and free us from a
> heavy duty and burden. I shall *write* no more on the subject.[74]

This appointment meant that Thomson would relieve the executors
of having to carry out their decisions with respect to the poet's
children; the decision-making itself, however, remained their charge.
The election of Thomson signified, moreover, that the time had come
when the executors would have to enter negotiations with a publisher
for a contract on the posthumous volume or, rather, volumes, because
Currie now promised four: (1) the life, (2) the general correspondence,
(3) the poetry, and (4) the songs, together with excerpts from the Burns-
Thomson correspondence. Currie and Cadell & Davies had already
explored various possibilities, so that both sides were ready to see if a
settlement could be written. Even though the executors were more than
willing to designate William Thomson as their representative in a three-
way exchange, they found that realignment of the Scotland element
would be advantageous; thus, they determined that any agreement
should bear the approval of six persons: Maxwell, McMurdo, Syme,
Gilbert, Jean, and W. Thomson. This group then elected William
Maxwell secretary; it was he, therefore, who took the minutes of
actions through the time of McMurdo's death in 1803 and James
Currie's death in 1805.[75]

The reality of William Thomson's authority denotes a definite
change in the Scottish influence upon the affairs of Robert Burns.
Executors like Maxwell and Syme had been personal friends of the
poet; Thomson had not. Their voice of warm ·intimacy and
sympathetic understanding was not his voice of sober business and
frosty law. This solicitor could not have worn a bonnier feather than his
assignment to the family of Robert Burns; he displayed that feather
arrogantly. From the first, he threw himself about. In vain one looks
for amenities in his dealings, such as recognition of how others had
labored earnestly and — in the case of William Maxwell at least —
gratuitously towards success of the subscription or how Cadell &
Davies had responded magnanimously to promote the subscription on
the posthumous edition. As early as 14 May 1798, James Currie had
had more of Thomson than he could stomach. On that day he mailed
Cadell & Davies a letter marked 'PRIVATE' in which he objects to

having to negotiate through the man who was becoming the first among the 'friends of the family' advising Mrs Burns. Currie did not trust that what Thomson was stating as fact was, truly, fact: the view of the executors. It seemed to the doctor that Thomson's facts were far more likely the views of interested parties, such as the Scots booksellers anxious to pull the lion's tail. It had become important to Currie, therefore, to make his sentiments confidentially clear to the London publishers: he and he alone was to have the final say as to arrangement, size, number, etc. of the volumes; he and Roscoe were to act so that Cadell & Davies would acquire the copyright, if that was to be put up. No letter of Currie implies more disenchantment with the election of Thomson; and this is the first of his letters to show plainly that he and Roscoe, too, if he chose, were to insist upon having some authority in return for their pains.[76]

The effect of William Thomson's appointment, else, was to provide the executors with that excuse for which they had been reaching in order to extricate themselves from annoyances of 'heavy duty and burden'.[77] Jean had left everything in the hands of those her husband had designated. Gilbert had done very little before he lost his sea legs; he was to do not much more than sign his name afterwards. Never having done much but stand and wait, McMurdo was not to attend a meeting for much more than getting in out of the rain. Having done much, Syme and Maxwell were to have less and less to do. These executors had been asked by Currie to proceed with negotiating for the copyright; they answered with William Thomson. One can sniff the change in the air when Syme writes Cunningham, 29 May 1798, a month after Thomson was delegated authority. His letter does not serve to advance the reputation of Burns, the welfare of the family, the 'duty and burden' of Currie; instead, it indulges in gossip of revenue, leisure, presentation of a Burns tumbler to Cunningham, and John McCreery's address to William Roscoe upon the occasion of the printer's presenting his benefactor with a pen that had belonged to Burns.[78] Uncomfortably, one senses the day of interest in Masonic apron strings and bids on Highland Mary's locks.

James Currie's four-volume, posthumous edition of the works of Robert Burns did not appear until a little more than two years after the appointment of William Thomson as solicitor to the family and the executors. As attending physician of the Burns family during these years, Dr Maxwell shared with Jean the sadness of losing his namesake when Maxwell Burns died 23 November 1799. During these same two years, April 1798 through June 1800, Syme and Maxwell, as the chief executors of authority and commitment, were never without an issue demanding action or a concern ploughing their minds. Principles arising from day-to-day exigencies of the widow and the children had to be considered by the executors before Thomson could go to work on them. Where should the children be placed in school? Had the time now come for Gilbert to be held accountable for his debt? How was the money from the subscription to be placed? How much of that money should be allotted Jean? How much to each child? What distinctions, if any, should be drawn between the four boys born within wedlock and the two girls born without? All of these questions had to be answered at meetings of the executors: Syme and Maxwell customarily attending; McMurdo and Gilbert (now farming at Nithsdale) sometimes attending. To Syme and Maxwell, also, fell the onus of dealing with new materials and with those who had sent them in. And they were the ones having to find time to advance a second subscription: that for Currie's edition by which they expected the family to profit most of all. Simon McKenzie only complicated matters when he proposed a third subscription, to raise a monument to the poet in Dumfries.[79] Maria supported McKenzie's scheme; but Currie, Syme, and Maxwell successfully defeated it lest the two subscriptions still in progress be diminished. Finally, Maxwell and Syme had to arrange meetings, ever more often, to work out terms of an agreement with Cadell & Davies.

Negotiations on Currie's *Burns* started earnestly in June 1798;[80] they were complicated unnecessarily, first, by Thomson's bent to appear more knowledgeable than he was and, second, by Gilbert's removal to Lothian where he became manager at West Mains of Captain John Dunlop's property. The executors chose to approach Cadell & Davies by way of Dr James Currie. Their wish was to transfer the whole right to the posthumous edition for a sum of money to be arbitrated. The publishing house, having had more than a taste of the mess which had been made of the subscription for the new edition, countered by proposing that the executors conduct the subscription themselves, that they accept a number of sets of Currie's work for supplying subscribers, and that these sets together with a sum of money to be negotiated be the family's profit. Disagreement of that summer came on this matter of the subscription. Each party recognized how much of a worry any subscription was; Syme and Maxwell understood, even if Thomson could not be made to understand, that a subscription for a new edition of Robert Burns stood not a ghost of a chance for prospering in

Scotland as it might prosper in England, that previous records of Burns's friends in Ayrshire, for example, as compared with previous records of Currie and Roscoe in Liverpool, told where profit was to be wrung and won. So the main point was whether or not Cadell & Davies could be persuaded to conduct the subscription with Currie, Roscoe, and McCreery assisting in Liverpool, Maria in London, and the executors in Scotland. To James Currie belongs most of the credit for Cadell & Davies's conceding to the executors.

Before September, shape had been given to what would be terms of the final agreement: Cadell & Davies for sole copyright would give the family without charge five hundred sets of the first edition for subscribers and pay the family £250 as well; should there be a second edition, the family would receive an additional £200 in either cash or in books; should there be a third, £150 in cash or books.[81] Thomson returned this draft in March 1799 with 'such amendments as occurred to us to be proper'.[82] Because he had taken his time, Cadell & Davies paused to consider what might be done to protect themselves against a wave of piracy that was damaging the reputation of Robert Burns and, in some instances, drawing into print pieces that Currie's edition was to have published for the first time. Not until early 1800 could the parties agree on how that protective clause should read and settle enough differences for Edward Foss, solicitor to Cadell & Davies, to draw up the 'Deed of Agreement'. This deed, as two copies signed by Thomas Cadell and William Davies, went out from London to Scotland, 3 March. It begins:

> This indenture made the twenty fifth of February in the Year of our Lord one thousand and eight hundred BETWEEN William Maxwell Esquire Physician in Dumfries John McMurdo Esquire of Hardriggs and John Syme Esquire Collector of Stamp Duties at Dumfries the acting Trustees for the Family of the deceased Robert Burns sometime residing in Dumfries North Britain Gilbert Burns Farmer at Mossgiel only Brother and nearest Male Heir to the surviving Infant Children of the said Robert Burns Jean Armour the Widow and Mother to the said Children William Thomson of Moat Writer in Dumfries Factor loco tutoris appointed by the Right Honourable the Lords of Council and Session in Scotland to the said Infant Children.[83]

William Maxwell's minutes for the meeting of the Burns executors, called by Thomson for 22 March 1800, show that two important differences still awaited resolution: Cadell & Davies insisted that

Currie and Roscoe have complete authority to decide what was publishable, now and later; the executors insisted upon clarifying more specifically what works were being conveyed. What, for example, was to be done about George Thomson's claim that Burns had given him copyright to all his songs published in the *Select Collection?*[84] A last flurry of meeting-letters-meeting settled each point. Before 3 June, therefore, the principals in Scotland, beginning with William Maxwell, signed the deed, affixed their seals, and returned one of the duplicates with John Lewars and William Graham of Templand as their witnesses. The executors for their pains received ten shillings from Cadell & Davies; Jean and the children received approximately £1,300.

Before their signing, the executors had gone over Currie's life of Burns and approved it; after their signing, they helped distribute some of the 2,001 sets of the first edition in four volumes. From fall 1800 to fall 1801, demands of their execution tapered away to mere formality. They met to go over statements of what had been collected on the subscription sets, now in the number of 560, and to authorize William Thomson to open an account for this money in the Dumfries branch office of the Bank of Scotland; they met to give a reckoning of the one hundred sets that had been consigned to them and to unscramble the tangles of the Scottish booksellers like Forsyth in Ayr and Brash & Reid in Glasgow. They met in early January 1801 to support Thomson's request to Cadell & Davies for immediate payment of the £200 due on the second edition, which had been in sheets off McCreery's press by the month before, and to decide what was to be done with the Burns materials which Currie was beginning to return from Liverpool; and they met in October 1801 to seek promptly the £150 on the third edition, because 'The boys are becoming daily more expensive.'[85]

When Maxwell and Syme sat back breathing sighs of relief in January 1802, they had finished six and a half years of taking Jean and the poet's five children from utter poverty and bitter misery to financial security and peace of mind. Four of the offspring, two of the three boys and the two illegitimate daughters, lived beyond age twenty-one; after 1815, however, Thomson no longer had a minor in his custody. Jean Armour lived comfortably in Dumfries until she died there in March 1834, just before William Maxwell went up to Edinburgh for the last time.

William Maxwell, therefore, had the same thirty-three years as Jean Armour to live on after Cadell & Davies fulfilled their agreement to its last letter. Those years introduced no satisfaction with respect to himself and Robert Burns comparable to the satisfaction of the friendship and the satisfaction of the accomplishment on behalf of the poet's family, the proof of that friendship. In those years, Maxwell dissociated himself from those who honored Burns 'al of the newe jet'. Interest in what the poet had made of himself never failed this executor, but interest in what others were making of the poet in the new century never trapped him. Citizens of Dumfries stood an excellent chance of seeing the physician on his way down Burns Street to the family's front door; but they could not expect to be able to point him out in a gathering commemorating Scotland's poet.

William Maxwell had the desire to be with James Currie when the biographer came into Scotland to survey his lands at Dumcrieff and Stakeford in the company of his agent John Syme and to pay his respects to Burns's widow; on that occasion, the executor would have lamented with the editor that the reputation of Robert Burns had never before been so much at the mercy of court actions, acrimonious controversy, political chicanery, and real and spurious obscenity. Maxwell as well as Syme had both the curiosity and the responsibility to meet Cromek in 1807 and 1809 when this collector of Burns reliques came to Dumfriesshire. Probably Maxwell reserved to himself what he thought of Cromek's exclaiming, 'God help that Man who runs after Poets & their Productions!'[86] Even though the period of planning and erecting the Burns Mausoleum, the years 1814 and 1815, was the period of the Netherwood sequestration, William Maxwell accepted his appointment of January 1814 to serve on the Mausoleum Committee with the Marquis of Queensberry, the Earl of Selkirk, David Staig, John Syme, and the brothers Henry and Thomas Duncan, ministers of the Church of Scotland and Currie's relatives.[87] Maxwell, therefore, was one of seven who approved T. F. Hunt's design, arranged the ceremony of laying the cornerstone, 5 June 1815, and saw the construction to its completion in September. Along this way, he gave his money as well as his name to the public subscription; he is to be found among other subscribers, such as George Maxwell of Carruchan, James Gray, William Roscoe, and William Wallace Currie, the deceased biographer's eldest son. As physician, Maxwell was the one member of the special committee to have charge for the reinterment of 12 September; as friend, doctor, and executor, he was the one man to be in St Michael's churchyard next to Jean and Syme when the coffins of the father Robert and the son Maxwell were lifted. In 1820, Dr William Maxwell was one of the few alive who knew most of what it meant to hear that Gilbert Burns had repaid at last his debt to his brother with money received from Cadell & Davies for work on the eighth edition of Currie's volumes. On all such occasions and in all such enterprises relating to Robert Burns, Maxwell desired to participate.

The doctor remained in close touch with fellow associates of Robert Burns. During these years, James Maxwell of Kirkconnell was employing John Lewars from time to time and borrowing money of John Syme repeatedly.[88] William continued a loyal fried of Syme to talk of Burns, of peaches and nectarines, of removal from Ryedale, and of the Thursday morning desolation when Mrs Syme died because of 'a bad case of pregnancy'.[89] Maxwell called upon Syme for his services as land agent and upon William Thomson for his services as writer during and after the sequestration.[90] As physician, he may have attended both; as executor, he did join both. Their ways diverged only when it became a matter of putting on a Burns face for public appearance. One might argue that Thomson did so because he sought public office and that Syme did so because he depended upon public office for his livelihood; Maxwell did not do so, because his principles drew lines beyond which he could not pass.

The doctor never approved of those who were mouthy; thus, he tried not to place himself in any position that exposed him to such declaration as that of the Earl of Selkirk's speech, 'The Defence of the Country', given on 10 August 1807, shortly after Napoleon's destruction of the Russian army at Friedland:

> Who is there who can imagine without horror, our aged and beloved monarch weltering in his blood, — his place occupied by a heptarchy of French usurpers, the minions of the conqueror, — the family of our sovereigns, along with the sad remains of all that is now eminent and dignified in England, wandering as exiles in foreign lands, while the mansions of our nobility are parcelled out to French generals, and every thing that is desirable in England becomes the prey of a Frenchman.[91]

Such declamation because of Napoleon was one thing; similar declamation because of Robert Burns, quite another.

January had become an exceptional month in Scotland and the twenty-fifth an exceptional day before Napoleon left Waterloo. So it was that in January 1816, Alexander Boswell, son of the biographer, Francis Jeffrey, Walter Scott, and George Thomson were in that company which took place in MacEwan's Tavern, Edinburgh, to commemorate the birthday of Robert Burns. Accounts of the festivities reveal that Mr Boswell 'proposed the health of Mr. Geo. Thomson, to whose enterprise and exertions chiefly it was owing that the greater number of the exquisite lyrics of Burns had been produced. This toast was drunk with loud and prolonged expressions of approbation and cordial concurrence, to which Mr Thomson replied by a neat and modest address of thanks.'[92]

Dumfries found ways to improve upon Edinburgh.[93] On 25 January 1819, those who had come together to celebrate the anniversary agreed to open a subscription for purchase of a china punch bowl capable of holding three gallons, decorated with emblematic devices, and accoutred with silver ladle and a set of glasses. Peter Lawrie, John Syme, and Provost William Thomson were among those who subscribed; William Maxwell was not. A year later, Syme, as Vice President, announced that the contributors had formed themselves into the Dumfries Burns Club, that membership would be 10/6, that tickets for the annual dinner could be bought 'at the Bar of the Inn', and that the punch bowl would be lodged with the Secretary and used for the Club, but never 'for any other party or individual'. Six years later all was pat:

> Burn's [sic] Club — The admirers of Burns met in the Commercial Inn here [Dumfries], on Thursday last, the anniversary of the poet's birth. The company, though not so numerous as we have seen, was composed of a considerable proportion of the respected gentlemen of the town. According to previous arrangement, the chair was filled by John McDiarmid, Esq. and Mr. Harkness, Rector of the Grammar School, officiated as croupier — The dinner consisted of all of the substantials, and not a few of the rarities and delicacies of the season, among the former of which we ought to class the great 'chieftain of the pudding race', a well stuffed — well cooked haggis. On the removal of the cloth, and after the ordinary toasts, usual on public occasions, had been drunk with due marks of loyalty and respect, Mr. McDiarmid proposed the toast of the day, but we are sorry to have it not in our power to give it at length; suffice it to say that it did justice to the memory of the bard to whom it was dedicated, and much credit to the head and heart of the talented chairman. The surviving relatives, personal friends and patrons of the poet, followed, and in the course of the evening several bumpers were pledged to the living poets and poetesses of the day, and to the memory of those who have left us, prefaced with appropriate remarks by different members. A number of songs were also sung, and the meeting broke up a little past ten o'clock [dinner had started at four]. The dinner was excellent and the wines and spirits were of the best; both reflected

increased and increasing credit on Mrs. Williamson the landlady, and those in her employment. As usual the portraits of Burns and his 'bonny Jean,' and the bust of Sir Walter Scott ornamented Prince Charlie's Room, and the punchmaker of the Club was kept pretty constantly at work by the rapidity with which the china jugs, on this occasion denominated steam-packets, went round the table, until they came to the harbour of the huge bowl, by which time they were generally empty, and prepared for a fresh cargo. The evening was spent very happily throughout.[94]

What could be left? Only a quaich or nuggen carved from a rafter of Kirk Alloway. Anything else for the lifetime of Dr William Maxwell? When the Burns Mausoleum was opened in March 1834 to receive the corpse of Jean Armour, there were those who took a cast of the skull of Robert Burns.[95] Before William left Dumfries in May 1834 for Edinburgh and his October death, he could have bought a gilded copy of this cast on the High Street.

William Maxwell of Kirkconnell was not the man to be amused by such nineteenth-century antics. Would he not have been bemused, however, by what late nineteenth- and twentieth-century biographers of Robert Burns have said of William Maxwell? What of McDowall's assertion: 'Of the daggers that flashed in the imagination of Burke, there was neither evidence nor likelihood?'[96] What of the woman who writes, 'How any physician, even at that age, could recommend immersion in the Scottish seas is hard to explain. Perhaps it was the Parisian fashion of the day in therapy?'[97] What of the very recent biographer who explains, 'Burns' chief physician in his terminal illness was his friend Dr. James [sic] Maxwell, whose father, Kirkconnel [sic] Maxwell, had followed Prince Charles in 1745'?[98]

In 1896, one hundred years after the death of Robert Burns and the birth of Maxwell Burns, William Ernest Henley uttered a conviction by begging a question: 'It was while, or soon after, the enormities of the Terror were at their worst, that Maxwell became a chief associate of Burns. To some this seems a 'noble imprudence'. Was it not rather pure continence of self?'[99] May it not now be hoped that true answer has been returned Henley as well as Dr William Maxwell of Kirkconnell?

List of Abbreviations[1]

B.C.   *Annual Burns Chronicle and Club Directory.* 87 vols. Kilmarnock, 1892-

B.P.   The Besterman Papers

D.B.R.   Dumfries Borough Records

K.H.   Kirkconnell House

Letters   *The Letters of Robert Burns,* ed. J. DeLancey Ferguson. 2 vols. London, 1931

N.R.O.   Northumberland County Record Office

Poems   *The Poems and Songs of Robert Burns,* ed. James Kinsley. 4 vols. London, 1968

P.R.O., H.O. London Public Record Office, Home Office

[1]For full details see Selected Bibliography, pp. 241-8

Notes

INTRODUCTION

GENERAL NOTE

KIRKCONNELL HOUSE (cited as K.H.):
No record exists for what is at Kirkconnell House, save for a rough Old Register House (Edinburgh) inventory of papers in the Charter Chest of the Strong Closet off the Library. Papers, books, maps, letters, accounts, etc. lie in various places, all but completely disarranged, in some instances eaten away by vermin, in other instances all but ruined by dampness. Loosely speaking, one can say, however, that muniments, maps, charts, and the like are in either the Strong Closet or the Library; that account-books, daybooks, reckonings, receipts, and other business papers are in tin chests in the Attics; that church papers are in the Sacristy and corridors just off or under the Chapel; that personal correspondence is in the Tower Room; that curios, such as the bonnet worn by James Maxwell during the Forty-Five, are in the Tower Room; and that protraits, silhouettes, etc. are in the Gallery or the Morning Room. To be more specific would be to mislead.

1. See, for example, Maria Riddell's letters to James Currie for 23 Feb. and 9 Apr. 1799, *B.C.*, XXXIII (1924), 89 and XXX (1921), 105-106.

2. *Letters*, I, 316.

3. Ibid., II, 325.

4. *The Poetry of Robert Burns*, eds. William Ernest Henley and Thomas F. Henderson, The Centenary Edition (Edinburgh, 1896), II, 443 and William McDowall, *History of the Burgh of Dumfries*, 3rd ed. (Dumfries, 1906), p. 579, n.

5. See, for example, *Poems*, II, 941 and III, 1453. Professor Kinsley's naming Dr Maxwell 'James' probably follows J. DeLancey Ferguson's example in the *Letters*.

6. *The Life and Works of Robert Burns*, 4 vols. (Edinburgh, 1851), IV, 223.

7. Ibid.

8. See, for example, my 'Robert Riddell, Antiquary,' *B.C.*, II (1953), 44-67 and my *James Currie The Entire Stranger and Robert Burns* (Edinburgh, 1963), pp. 383-393.

9. *The Life of Robert Burns*, ed. William Scott Douglas (Liverpool, 1914), II, 171.

10. D.B.R., 'Diet Book 1793,' p. 30.

11. John Goldworth Alger, *Englishmen in the French Revolution* (London, 1889), p. 685.

12. *Johnson's Dictionary*, eds. E. L. McAdam, jr and George Milne (London, 1963), p. 31.

CHAPTER ONE

1. Here the genealogies have been cross-checked from various published and unpublished sources. For the Maxwells of Kirkconnell, I have consulted Fraser's *The Book of Carlaverock* (Edinburgh, 1873) as well as such items at Kirkconnell House as the family Bible, Dorothy Maxwell-Witham's copy of *The Office and the Masses for the Dead* (London, 1830), in which Dorothy, Dr William Maxwell's niece, entered facts about her relatives' deaths, and, lastly, her son's, Robert Maxwell-Witham's, table worked out in the late nineteenth century; for the Menzies of Pitfodels, D. P. Menzies' *The Red and White Book of Menzies* (Glasgow, 1894) as well as materials at Blairs College; for the Riddells of Swinburne Castle, a table worked out for me by the present head of the family, John Riddell, J.P., The Hermitage, Barrasford, Hexham, as well as the Riddell Family Papers now deposited at the Northumberland County Record Office, Mr Robin Gard, County Archivist.

2. J. S. Richardson, *Sweetheart Abbey*, Ministry of Works Official Guidebook (Edinburgh, 1951), p. 6.

3. 'Of the Warldis Instabilite,' *The Poems of William Dunbar*, ed. W. Mackay Mackenzie (London, 1932), p. 29.

4. *Guy Mannering*, Waverley Novels Border Edition (London, 1924), p. 9.

5. Alfons Bellesheim, *History of the Catholic Church in Scotland* (London, 1890), IV, 27-28.

6. Kirk Session Papers for the second half of the seventeenth century are full of such details.

7. William Fraser, *The Book of Carlaverock* (Edinburgh, 1873), I, 601.

8. Third Series (Boston, 1855), p. 124.

9. N.R.O., MS. 358/B346/1, 'List of prisoners delivered from the County Gaol, Middlesex,' docketed 'Ex'd 9 Junii 1716' and endorsed 'Mr. Thomas

Riddell.' Also, MS. 358/30 item 6, a contemporary copy of the indictment of Thomas Riddell for his part in the Fifteen, dated '1716' and *The English Catholic Nonjurors of 1715*, eds. Estcourt and Payne (London, 1885), pp. 145 & 206. In Estcourt and Payne one will find notices of other Roman Catholic families important in the history of the Maxwells of Kirkconnell, such as 'Scroop,' 'Widdrington,' and 'Witham.'

10. McDowall, *Dumfries*, p. 579.

11. The composition of this party is suggested by *A List of Persons concerned in the Rebellion . . . 7th May 1746*, Scottish Historical Society (Edinburgh, 1890). The main source for James Maxwell's participation in the Forty-Five is his own *Narrative of Charles Prince of Wales' Expedition to Scotland in the Year 1745*, Maitland Club (Edinburgh, 1841). The original manuscript of Maxwell's narrative is in the hands of the Maxwells of Carruchan line; an early nineteenth-century transcription from the original, which belongs to the Maxwell-Withams, is deposited at the Clydesdale Bank, Dumfries. I have worked with this transcription as well as the copy of the Maitland Edition in Houghton Library, Harvard University (Br 8023.5.52.9*). Other works, more generally helpful in understanding James Maxwell's part, are George Charles' *History of the Transactions in Scotland in the Years 1715-16, 1745-1746*, 2 vols. (Stirling, 1816); David Lord Elcho's *A Short Account of the Affairs of Scotland in the Years 1744, 1745, and 1746*, annotated by Evan Charteris (Edinburgh, 1907); Rupert C. Jarvis' *The Jacobite Risings of 1715 and 1745* (Cumberland County Council, 1954) and *Collected Papers on the Jacobite Risings*, 2 vols. (Manchester, 1972).

12. 'A Song Composed in the Year 1746', *Highland Songs of the Forty-Five*, ed. John Lorne Campbell (Edinburgh, 1933), p. 150.

13. *A Memoir of the 'Forty-Five'*, ed. for Folio Society by Brian Rawson (London, 1958), p. 74.

14. McDowall, *Dumfries*, p. 588.

15. *List of Persons*, p. 143.

16. Bishop Forbes, *Lyon in Mourning*, ed. Henry Paton (Edinburgh, 1895-96), II (1895), 310.

17. Dated 'Windsor, Aug. 21, 1746,' *Selected Letters of Horace Walpole*, ed. W. S. Lewis (New Haven, 1973), pp. 19-22.

18. Maitland Edition, p. 66.

19. Ibid., p. 108.

20. Ibid., p. 168.

21. Ibid., p. 191.

22. Scottish Record Office, Ref. RS 23/24, photostat of land conveyance in a charter under the Great Seal dated 29 Nov. 1750 and recorded in the *Commissariat Books of Drumfries* [sic], 21 July 1753.

23. Fraser, I, 601.

24. The family papers at N.R.O., N. Pevsner's *The Buildings of England:*

R

Northumberland, Penguin Edition (London, 1957), and a visit to the site are the bases for this description.

25. K.H., MS. docketed 'Contract of Marriage Betwixt M.[r] Maxwell of Kirkconnell and M.[rs] Mary Riddell-1758' and signed '21 Aug.[t] 1758'.

26. Such documents as N.R.O., MS. 358/40/29 (sub-title with 27, 28, 'Extract, Deed of Settlement of M.[rs] Maxwell of Kirkconnell, 1807'); MS. 358/45/2, '22.[d] November 1781, Bond . . . Tho.[s] Riddell Esq.[r] to M.[rs] Dorothy Riddell'; and a similar instrument (MS. 358/45/3) dated 'November 15.th 1790' indicate that Mary and her sisters were well provided for.

27. James b. 30 Aug. 1759; William b. 30 [?31] Aug. 1760; Thomas b. Dec. 1761.

CHAPTER TWO

1. K.H., MS. 'decreet for the Funeral Expences of umq.[le] James Maxwell of Kirkconnell M.[rs] Maxwell [?*abbrev. for Gentlemen*'] Maxwells &.[c] N 12 of Ap:X1763,' signed 'John Goldie of Craigmuie Commissary principal . . . Dumfries.'

2. 'In Prais of Wemen,' *Poems,* ed. Mackenzie, p. 83.

3. K.H., MS. *Account Book* [22 Nov. 1760-Aug. 1763]. Here are entries for the elder Gilchrist and for a 'D.[r] Young'; as an example, the entry for 20 May 1762 indicates that Gilchrist was paid £1. 1.

4. K.H., undated MS. docketed 'For M.[r] Thomas Maxwell.' After outlining the Contract of Marriage between James Maxwell and Mary Riddell, 21 Aug. 1758, and noting that both William and Thomas were to have £1,000 each, the unknown writer specifies that on 14 Jan. 1761 James, the father, had executed a Nomination of Tutors and Curators 'to his Three children'; the writer continues with a description of this execution. An accounting by the tutors dated 14 Mar. 1777 shows that Mary as well as John Maxwell of Terraughty and Adam Craik, the Younger, of Arbigland had been appointed tutors and that she together with the two gentlemen was serving out the tutelage.

5. Although the K.H. account-books and cashbooks for the period of the children's infancy are not all extant, there are enough of them, given in day-by-day entries of expenditure, to reveal particularly and intimately how each aspect of life was managed.

6. K.H., MSS. *Account Books* [1760-1763, 1768] kept by Mary Maxwell.

7. These maps are in the K.H. Strong Room. The same room contains plans of the various farmsteads and the detailed drawing 'A Map of the Mains' by John Tait.

8. K.H., MSS. *Account Books* [early 1790s]; these show the paternal relatives in Dumfries.

9. The above details of life in Dumfries are from issues of the *Dumfries Weekly Journal* for the period.

10. K.H., MS. *Account Book* [1763]; an entry for August shows that 6s. was spent 'To W^ms Expences home.'

11. 'Sugar Candy . . . 6d.' appears frequently in Mary's accounts.

12. Mary and her sons James and William all refer to this boyhood sickness. Early in Oct. 1792, for example, James reminded William from York, England, of 'your long and severe attacks some years ago' (K.H., MS. holograph copy). The case for stuttering rests primarily upon John Syme's statement to Alexander Cunningham, 2 Aug. 1796, 'His [*William's*] address is such that you may at first think him stiff and affected. This is a natural cast arising perhaps from defect of articulation etc' (*B.C.*, XI [1936], 36).

13. K.H., MS. holograph copy of letter, Mary to Mr Alexander Maxwell, London, 16 Sept. 1792.

14. K.H., MS. docketed 'For Mr Thomas Maxwell.'

15. K.H., MS. apparently in James' hand, which speaks of his having 'past the years of his pupillarity abroad' for his 'better education and Improvement' and of his having appointed his mother to be his 'Commissioner & Factor.'

16. K.H., MS. docketed 'For Mr Thomas Maxwell: The said William Maxwell was Ten years of age in August 1770 and Thomas Maxwell in December 1771. both lived with their Mother till 5th August 1771 when they set out for Dinant in Germany for their Education.' In the K.H., MSS. *Account Books* for the years of the boys' schooling abroad, Mary irregularly figured out expenditures for each of her sons so that she could report to Terraughty and Arbigland. Because James received more than his brothers, his account is generally given separately, whereas those of William and Thomas appear under such a heading as 'Acc! of Payments for W^m & Th^os Maxwell.'

17. *Records of the English Province of the Society of Jesus*, ed. Henry Foley, S. J., VII, Part 1 (London, 1882), 496-497.

18. Stonyhurst College Library, MS. D.I.4, 'Accounts: 1769-1797' and MS. D.I.5, 'liege School ledger, 1773-1790' as well as K.H., MSS. *Account Books* [1771-1773]. These sources provide such detailed information as the following: 'By bill from Mrs Mary Maxwell/Hugh Lawson on Harris & Co Sep! 29 1773/payable 70 days after date, for the use of Mrs Menzies at Dinant £72 for her, & £2 for Mr Jno Webber of Hammersmith's . . . £74' (Stonyhurst, MS. D.I.4, 4 Aug. 1773).

19. See, for example, *The Tour of Holland Dutch Brabant, the Austrian Netherlands and Part of France* (London, 1772).

20. Philip Thicknesse, *A Year's Journey through the Pais Bas* (London, 1786), p. 244.

21. Fraser, I, 601.

22. For my description of Dinant, I am indebted to such works as Henri Hachez' *Histoire de Dinant* (Bruxelles, 1932), Edouard Gérard's *Histoire de la*

Ville de Dinant (Namur, 1935), 'Siderius's' *Dinant* (Dinant, 1859), and the unpublished thesis of Danielle Gallez, *La Ville de Dinant et Ses Magistrats de 1772 à 1814* (June, 1969) to be found at the Archives de l'État à Namur, Rue d'Arguet, 45.

23. Archives Namur, MSS. *Archives Dinant*, trans. by me from undated MS letter, Pastor of St Michael to the Burgomasters, in file of miscellaneous papers relating to church/town affairs. The Dinant Archives are in the custody of Archives de l'État à Namur. I am especially obligated to Mrs A. Smolar, Assistant Archivist at Namur, for her bringing such items as the above to my attention when I was at Namur.

24. My accounts of the Jesuits at Dinant and Liége owe much to information in letters to me from Professor Roland Mortier, University of Brussels, and his student Mr André Botte. Otherwise, the following works have been helpful: Paul Bonenfant, *La Suppression de la Compagnie de Jésus dans les Pays-Bas autrichiens*, Académie Royale de Belgique, Mémoire, XIX. 3 (Bruxelles, 1925), 29 & 31; P. P. Brouwers, *Cartulaire de la Commune de Dinant*, VII, 1701-1792 (Namur, 1907), 195-197; Hubert Chadwick, *St Omer to Stonyhurst* (London, 1962); Fr Courtney, 'English Jesuit Colleges in the Low Countries, 1593-1794,' *The Heythrop Journal*, IV (1963), 254-263; F. Macours, 'Le Collège de Dinant après la suppression de la Compagnie de Jésus (1774-1794),' *Namur*, XXV (1950), 33-40; and A. Poncelet, *Histoire de la Compagnie de Jésus sans les anciens Pays-Bas*, 2 vols. (Bruxelles, 1926-1928).

25. Archives Namur, MSS. *Archives Ecclesiastiques Couvents Les Jesuits De Dinant, 15, Comptes 1752-1773*; see, for example, under 'Status habitualis collegii dionanttensis prima Maii 1773'; also, *Namur Ecclesiastiques*, MSS. 3750, -51, -52, and -53, especially 3752, 'Regitre appartenant aux Rvds peres Jesuits de Dinant commencant L'an 1746,' under years 1770 & 1771.

26. M. L'Abbé Maynard, *The Studies and Teaching of the Society of Jesus at the Time of Its Suppression, 1750-1773* (Baltimore, 1855).

27. K.H., undated MS. 'Acc.t of payments for W.m & Th.os Maxwell.' This MS. in Mary's hand covers the period 1762-1775. Another K.H. undated MS., scribbling by Mary, sums up expenditures for William and Thomas, Martinmas 1762-1776.

28. See, for example, [M. D'Alembert's], *Sur La Destruction des Jesuites en France* (London, 1756).

29. Bibliothèque historique de la Ville de Paris, holograph MS. Rés. 2034, f. 209; to Nicolas-Claude Thierot, 9 Jan. 1739 (Kehl, LIII. 142-4).

30. Foley, *Records*, VII, 496 f.

31. Compare, for example, what is said in *The Traveller's Vade Mecum through the Netherlands and Part of France and Germany* (Canterbury, 1782) with what Philip Thicknesse says in his *A Year's Journey through the Pais Bas* (London, 1786).

32. *Traveller's Vade Mecum*, p. 86.

33. My account is based upon the Stonyhurst MSS cited above and Stonyhurst MS. C.IV.2, 'Bruges Liége, Stonyhurst Letters, etc., 1615-1807'; also, K. H., MSS. *Account Books* for the period, Foley's *Records*, and Chadwick's *St Omer to Stonyhurst.*

34. One does not find after the Maxwell brothers' names such an entry as the following which pertains to the Riddell son: 'By Halfyears advances & extras — £20. 10. 10 up to Sept.' (Stonyhurst, MS. D.I.5).

35. Stonyhurst, MS. D.I.4, under 'Oct. 4 [1776]'.

36. Foley, *Records*, VII, 497.

37. K.H., MS. in Mary's hand, a series of calculations showing interest on the £1,000 each bequeathed William and Thomas by their father as set off against costs of their education, clothing, and aliment. A similar K.H. MS. shows various charges for William, 5 Aug. 1770-Mar. 1773, and from 28 Jan. 1774-28 Jan. 1776; the latter specifies that the accounts were 'attested by his uncle M.r George Maxwell.'

38. K.H., MS., two folio pages stamped 'SIX POUNDS': 'Inventory sequestrated Estate of William Maxwell Physician & Grocer in Dumfries,' 29 May 1816.

39. Stonyhurst, MS. D.I.4, under 'Jan. 30 [1778]'.

40. K.H., undated MS. in Mary's hand, 'Disbursements for my son William from 1 March 1776.' One item reads, 'To [?*one word*] Waistcoat breeches & Gun — £36. 4. 9 4/12.'

41. Carl Van Doren, *Benjamin Franklin* (New York, 1938), p. 564.

42. K.H., MS. undated letter, James Maxwell to his brother William, ca. late Sept. 1792, headed 'York en.d'

43. K.H., undated MS. ['List of dated Receipts of Payments by Mary to William for period 'Oct 1776' to 24 May 1783'] and MSS. *Account Books* [1777-1783].

44. K.H., MS., statement signed by Mary, John Maxwell of Terraughty, and Adam Craik of Arbigland, dated '14 Mar 1777'.

45. K.H., undated MS. in James Maxwell's hand, ['Debits of William']; here is notice of the 'Bond of Provision to W.m Maxwell,' dated '10 Aug.t 1783'.

46. See N.R.O., MS. 358/15/2, '22.d November 1781, Bond for £995 and Interest, Tho.s Riddell Esq.r to M.rs D. Riddell'; here Mary's sister is named 'Dorothy Riddell of Kirkconnell in North Britain Spinster'.

47. Mary's Troqueer properties are described in N.R.O., MS. 358/40/29, an extraction by Samuel Clark of Mary's will subscribed 4 July 1801. For the loan by William, see K.H., MS. ['Mary's Cash Book, 1776-1783'], under date.

48. Ibid., under dates.

49. Ibid., under date.

50. Ibid., entry for 2 July 1783.

51. D.B.R., 'Table of Customs & Duties Dumfries 5 Novr 1772.'

52. From an advertisement in the issue for 1 Sept. 1778.

53. Dated 'July 1778'.

54. *Dumfries Weekly Journal*, 14 Oct. 1777.

55. Ibid., 28 Apr. 1778.

56. Ibid., 16 Feb. 1778.

57. National Library of Scotland, MS. 29.5.8, 'Letters to George Paton,' III, 49.

58. Burke dwells upon the Catholic Question in 1792, the year of the Catholic Bill and of the French Refugees. His letters of this period, especially those to his son Richard, jr [see *The Correspondence of Edmund Burke*, eds. P. J. Marshall and John A. Woods (Chicago, 1958-1970), VII (1968), 9, 83, 94, et passim] speak of Catholics in Ireland as 'doomed to abject Servitude' and as having been 'undone past redemption' by 'outrageous' treatment of parliament. Such books as Bellesheim's *History* and Philip Hughes' *The Catholic Question 1688-1829* (London, 1929) describe the above 'deprivation' in detail.

59. Bellesheim, *History*, IV, 228.

60. *Dumfries Weekly Journal*, Feb. 1779.

61. Ibid., 14 July 1778.

62. K.H., dated 'Jany 29th [1779]'.

63. National Library of Scotland, MSS. 29.5.6, 'Gough-Paton Correspondence'; see, particularly, Gough to Paton for 8 & 29 June 1780, the bases for what follows.

64. Courtesy of Manchester Public Libraries, D. I. Colley, City Librarian. My source is a letter from David Taylor, Sub-Librarian, Local History Library, dated 2 May 1973, in which Mr Taylor cites references from the *Manchester Directory* for various years.

65. Robert D. Thornton, *James Currie*, passim.

66. I am grateful to Charles P. Finlayson, Keeper of MSS., Edinburgh University Library, for sending me photostat copies of the oaths or *sponsiones* and his description of how they might pertain to William Maxwell.

67. *The Speeches of The Right Honourable Charles James Fox in the House of Commons*, ed. A Barrister [pseud.], Third Edition (London, 1853), p. 675.

68. Thomas Percival, *Medical Ethics; or, A Code of Institutes and Precepts, adapted to the Professional Conduct of Physicians and Surgeons* . . . (Manchester, 1803), pp. 189 f.

69. I am grateful to J. Alan Howe, City Librarian, Central Library, Edinburgh, for helping me locate William in Edinburgh.

70. LXXII, issues for 25, 26, 27 Sept. 1792.

71. Edinburgh University Library, MS. 'Matriculation: 1762-1785' and

MS. 'Matriculation: 1786-1803.'

72. K.H., two copies of the thesis: one the presentation copy to James. I am indebted to Mr Charles P. Finlayson for sending me photostats of the title and dedication pages with his observations upon same.

73. 'Rerum ipsarum vera cognitio ex rebus ipsis est.'

74. Don Manuel Alvarez Espriella [pseud.], *Letters from England* (London, 1808), II, 239.

75. *Phillipps Studies,* ed. A. N. L. Munby, II (Cambridge, 1952), 8.

76. K.H., MS. letter from William to Corrie, dated 'Nicolsens St Feb. 22 1787'; undated MS. account in James's hand, 'William Maxwell my Brother [1783-1787]'; undated MS. account in James's hand, 'Cash advanced my brother'; undated MS. in James's hand, 'James Maxwell in Ac^t With William Maxwell his Brother [1787-1789]'; and MSS. ['Receipts'] signed by William for moneys he received from James by way of Corrie, 1784-1786.

77. K.H., undated MS. ['Debits of William'], two pages of computation in James's hand, and MS. holograph letter, William to James, dated 'Edin^r 17 August 1787'.

78. K.H., dated 'June 7th 1787'.

79. *Dumfries Weekly Journal,* Dec. 1787 and 27 May 1788; also, Dumfries Royal Burgh Museum, MS. 'Burgess Book,' for 27 Sept. 1786.

80. K.H., MS. copy 'last Will & Settlement of Miss Janet Maxwell with Statement of Accompt^s r^{cd} relative of her affairs & that of her Sisters who predeceased her. Examined 2 May 1815.'

81. *Dumfries Weekly Journal,* 22 Jan. 1788.

82. Ibid., 12 Aug. 1788.

83. K.H., holograph MS. dated 'Greenlaw 30th April 1787'.

84. *Dumfries Weekly Journal,* 29 Jan. 1788.

85. K.H., holograph MS. dated 'Edin^r 10 Septr 1787'.

86. K.H., holograph MS. dated 'Edin^r 25 Feb 1788'.

87. The date of William's departure and the allowances James made his brother are given in the following accounts kept by James: MSS. 'James Maxwell In Ac^t With William Maxwell his brother [1783-1789],' ['Debits of William, 1785-1788'], and 'Dr William Maxwell, [25 Mar. 1788-28 May 1789]'.

CHAPTER THREE

1. 'On the Feeling of Immortality in Youth,' *English Prose of the Romantic Period,* eds. C. F. Macintyre and Majl Ewing (New York, 1940), pp. 111 f.

2. K.H., MS. in James's hand, 'James Maxwell in Ac^t With William his Brother.'

3. This anecdote is attributed to Madame de Genlis by British travellers in France like John Moore and Arthur Young.

4. K.H., MS. in James's hand, ['Debits of William'], for period Whitsunday 1785 through 3 Nov. 1788.

5. Patrick Medd, *Romilly* (London, 1968), p. 73.

6. K.H., holograph MS.

7. K.H., MSS. ['Receipts']. Feb.-Aug. 1790; the first, for example, is dated 'Glasgow 3 Feb. 1790'.

8. K.H., MSS., two drafts of subscription by William at Kirkconnell written out, apparently, in James's hand; the first is dated '12 May 1789'; the second, '12 May 1790'. Herein William discharges James of the sum of £1,193. 10.

9. K.H., MS. holograph letter.

10. K.H., MS. ['Cash Book/James'], under 21 Oct. 1790.

11. D.B.R., MSS. *Misc. Papers, 1790-1799,* under '2 Augt 1790'.

12. N.R.O., MS. 358/45/16, 'Release of a Legacy'.

13. K.H., MS. [Account, 1790-1792, James Maxwell with William Robertson'].

14. K.H., MSS. [*Account Books* of James Maxwell].

15. K.H., MS. holograph letter, William to James, dated 'Jan. 10 1790'.

16. Ibid.

17. Blairs College, newspaper clipping docketed 'Feb 10 1932,' C. Sanford Terry's letter to an editor.

18. K.H., MS. holograph letter of 10 Jan. 1790.

19. See, for example, William's letter to the *Morning Post* (London) for Monday, 17 Sept. 1792.

20. K.H., MS. ['Inventory . . . 29 May 1816'].

21. Stanley Kunitz, 'The Class Will Come to Order,' *Selected Poems* (Boston, 1958), p. 111.

22. See *Gentleman's Magazine,* XCIII, Part the First (June, 1823), 569.

23. For Helen Maria Williams see Alger, *Englishmen,* pp. 68-75.

24. P.R.O., H.O., flyer titled 'A few Queries to the Methodists. . . .'

25. P.R.O., H.O., MS. 42.19.

26. Ibid., MS. ['Intelligence from Birmingham, 17 July 1791'].

27. George Chandler, *William Roscoe of Liverpool, 1753-1831* (London, 1953), pp. 384 f.

28. See my *Currie,* pp. 206 f.

29. P.R.O., H.O., MS. 42/21.

30. See my *Currie,* p. 208; this letter is dated Nov. 1792.

31. For such information, I am indebted to works like W. A. L. Seaman's *British Democratic Societies in the Period of the French Revolution,* University of London Doctoral Thesis, 1954.

32. D.B.R., MSS. *Misc. Papers, 1790-1799,* as 'Commission In Favour of John McMurdo 1790'.

33. P.R.O., H.O., MS. 42/21/618, holograph letter to Henry Dundas, 'Dalkeith House 27th Sep^t 1792'.

34. *The Correspondence of Edmund Burke*, eds. P. J. Marshall and John A. Woods, VII (1968), 177.

35. P.R.O., H.O., MS. 42/20, as reports dated 'Leicester May 23^d 1792' and 'Leeds 28th May 1792'.

36. *The Later Correspondence of George III*, ed. A. Aspinall, I (London, 1962), 602.

37. P.R.O., H.O., MS. 42/21/214.

38. *Horace Walpole's Correspondence with Hannah More*, ed. W. S. Lewis, XXXI (New Haven 1961), 372, dated 21 Aug. 1792.

39. P.R.O., H.O., MSS. 42/21/487, dated 'Stockport, August 25, 1792' and 'Manchester 26th Augt 1792'; also, MS. 42/23, dated 31 Aug. 1792.

40. *London Chronicle*, 8 Sept. 1792.

41. The *Sun* (London), 8 Oct. 1792.

42. Aspinall, *Later Correspondence*, I (1962), 615.

43. For both the Maxwells and Melbank, see George Stead Veitch, *The Genesis of Parliamentary Reform*, Reprint (London, 1964), p. 249.

44. J. Holland Rose, *William Pitt and The Great War*, Reprint (Westport, Conn., 1971), p. 94.

45. Lucyle Werkmeister, *A Newspaper History of England 1792-1793* (Lincoln, Neb., 1967), p. 142.

46. K.H., MS. holograph letter dated 'York Septr 26th 1792,' John Lawson to James Maxwell, and MS. 'Discharge by Dr Wm Maxwell 1 Oct. 1792 £500'.

47. For the meeting with Servan, see Seaman, *British Democratic Societies*, p. 219.

48. P.R.O., H.O., MSS. 42/22/567 and 42/23.

49. Ibid., MS. 42/22, ['Expences—Nov. 1792'].

50. *London Chronicle*, 14 Sept. 1792.

51. Ibid., 7 Sept. 1792, for example.

52. K.H., MS. one of a series of MSS (hereafter cited as 'Extracts'), possibly by James's writer Robert Gordon, whereby James wished to notify the Government through selections from the family correspondence that he disapproves of his brother's activities. What was extracted remains extant not only at Kirkconnell but also in the London Public Record Office (P.R.O., H.O., MSS. 42/22/25-28 & 50). Eight extracts are given. In addition, there is a letter from James to Nepean dated 'York 2^d Octr 92' and a letter from John Lawson, James's solicitor in York, to James, dated 'York Septr 26th 1792'.

53. Seaman, *British Democratic Societies*, p. 219; Seaman's source is French National Archives N° 74394.

54. P.R.O., H.O., MSS. 42/22/598 and 42/23/30.

55. Walpole, *Correspondence*, XXXI (1961), 377.

56. This account of the daggers is based upon the K.H. and P.R.O. 'Extracts' as well as various other papers in the P.R.O. cases 42/22 & 23; Burke's *Letters*, VII, 328-35; a photostat copy of a letter from J. Overton to

Edmund Burke, dated 'Birmingham Dec 21st 92,' provided me through the courtesy of John Bebbington, City Librarian, Sheffield; and Seaman's *British Democratic Societies*, pp. 219-222.

57. For a photostat copy of this article as well as for information bearing upon it, I am indebted to W. A. Taylor, City Librarian. Birmingham Public Libraries.

58. *London Chronicle*, 19 Sept. 1792.

59. P.R.O., H.O., MSS. variously for late Sept. 1792.

60. *London Chronicle*, 19 Sept. 1792.

61. The *Sun* (London), 12 Oct. 1792, from Wexford paper of 24 Sept. 1792.

62. Burke, *Correspondence*, VII, 223, dated 21 Sept. 1792.

63. Ibid., p. 215.

64. François Alphonse Aulard, *La Societé des Jacobins Recueil de Documents pour l'Histoire du Club des Jacobins* (Paris, 1889-1897), IV, 346.

65. Henry Redhead Yorke, *France in Eighteen Hundred and Two*, ed. J. A. C. Sykes (London, 1906), p. 71.

66. K.H., MS. 'Extract N° 2, Letter from Mr Maxwell to Dr Maxwell dated 13th or 14th September'.

67. K.H., MS. 'Extract N° 3, Dr Maxwell to Mr Maxwell, 14 September 1792'.

68. Burke, *Correspondence*, VII, 281.

69. *London Chronicle*, 17, 19, 20 Sept. 1792 and *London Evening Mail*, 19 Sept. 1792.

CHAPTER FOUR

1. K.H., MS. 'Extract N° 4, Mrs Maxwell to [Alexander] Maxwell, 16th Septem^{r} 1792'.

2. K.H., MS. 'Extract N° 5, Dr Maxwell to Mr Maxwell 17th Septem^{r} 1792'.

3. P.R.O., H.O., MS. 'Extract of a letter from Mr James Woolly to the R^{t} Honb^{le} Genl Conway dated Birmingham Novr 5th 1792'.

4. P.R.O., H.O., MS. 'Extract of a Letter from Birmingham, Sunday 30th Septem^{r} 1792'.

5. P.R.O., H.O., MS. 42/23/19, holograph letter dated 'Birmingham Septr 20 1792'.

6. P.R.O., H.O., MS. 42/21/590, holograph letter, J. Brooke, Birmingham, to Evan Nepean, London, 21 Sept. 1792.

7. Rose, *Pitt*, p. 64.

8. K.H., MS. 'Extract N° 6, Mr Maxwell to Mrs Maxwell'.

9. K.H., MS. 'Extract N⁰ 7 Mrs Maxwell to Mr Maxwell 19th September 1792'.

10. K.H., MS. 'Extract N⁰ 8, Letter Mrs Maxwell to Mr Maxwell 23^d September 1792'.

11. See, for example, N.R.O., MS. 358/45/16, 'Release of A Legacy of £1,000, Mrs D. Riddell to Sir John Lawson Bart. . . . For information about William Withers, I am grateful to O. S. Tomlinson, City Librarian, York.

12. K.H., holograph MS. dated 'York Septr 26th 1792'.

13. K.H., MS. 'Extract N⁰ 8, Mr Wither's opinion on Extracts . . . York 28th September 1792'.

14. K.H., holograph MS. dated 'Kirkconnell 30 Sep^t 1792'.

15. K.H., holograph MS.

16. *London Chronicle*, Sept. 27-29 and Oct. 2 1792; also, P.R.O., H.O., MS. 42/21, 'Rx from Mr Brook Watson 30 Sep^t 1792'. H.O., MS. 42/22/151 dockets this Watson letter 'Read by the King'.

17. K.H., MS. docketed 'Discharge by Dr Wm Maxwell 1 Oct. 1792 £500'.

18. K.H., holograph MS. 'York en^d'

19. P.R.O., H.O., MS. 42/22, docketed 'York 2^d October 1792 Mr Maxwell Rx5'.

20. See, for example, P.R.O., H.O. MSS. passim for Oct. 1792 and the *Sun*, 9 & 10 Oct. 1792.

21. *Correspondence*, VII, 218, to Lord Grenville, 19 Sept. 1792.

22. Ibid., pp. 220-224, to King George III, 20 Sept. 1792.

23. Ibid., p. 225, to brother Richard Burke, 10 Oct. 1792.

24. Ibid., p. 229, to Earl Fitzwilliam, 5 Oct. 1792.

25. Ibid., p. 271, to his son Richard, 17 Oct. 1792.

26. Ibid., p. 304, dated 28 Nov. 1792.

27. For the above statements see the issue for Tuesday, 9 Oct. 1792.

28. The *Sun*, 11 Oct. 1792.

29. For the above account see P.R.O., H.O., MS. 42/22/159-160, holograph letter, John Brooke, Birmingham, to Evan Nepean, Home Office, '17th Octr 1792'; H.O., MS. 42/23/80-83, 'Extract of a Letter from Mr James Woolley . . . Conway, dated Birmingham Novr 5th 1792'; and Burke, *Correspondence*, VII, 328-335.

30. 12 Oct. 1792.

31. P.R.O., H.O., MS. 42/22/385-386, holograph letter, A. Onslow to [?Evan Nepean], 15 Nov. 1792, and MS. 42/22/159-160, holograph letter, John Brooke to Evan Nepean, 17 Oct. 1792.

32. Veitch, *Parliamentary Reform*, pp. 227-228.

33. 25 Oct. 1792.

34. For the above exchanges see P.R.O., H.O., MSS. 42/22/185, holograph letter, Onslow to Nepean, 'Secret,' 26 Oct. 1792; holograph letter, Mr Newport, Dover, to Nepean, 5 Nov. 1792; holograph letter, Nepean to [John

Brooke, Birmingham], 6 Nov. 1792; and information 'M.ʳ Ketland of Birmingham,' 8 Nov. 1792. Also, H.O., MS. 42/23, ['Information from Liverpool, 21 Oct. 1792'].

35. Burke, *Correspondence*, VII, 328.

36. *The Parliamentary History of England . . . to 1803*, ed. W. Cobbett, XXX (1817), 188-189.

37. Burke, *Correspondence*, VII, 328.

38. Ibid., pp. 328 f.

39. For this cartoon see *The Works of James Gillray the Caricaturist with the History of His Life and Times*, ed. Thomas Wright (London, [1873]), facing p. 154.

40. Werkmeister, *Newspaper History*, p. 181.

41. Gillray, *Works*, p. 47.

42. Sheffield City Libraries, MSS. BK 1,854, item docketed 'M.ʳ J. Overton R.ᵗ Hon E.ᵈ Burke Birmingham Decb.ʳ 31.ˢᵗ 1792 Rights of Man Daggers,' courtesy of John Bebbington, City Librarian.

43. Burke, *Correspondence*, VII, 334.

44. Cobbett, *Parliamentary History*, XXX, 554-555.

45. [Melvin J. Lasky], *Encounter*, XLI, N.º 4 (Oct. 1973), 71.

46. John Moore, *A Journal during Residence in France Beginning of August to the Middle of December, 1792, A New Edition Corrected* (London, 1793), particularly the entry for 9 Aug. 1792.

47. Ibid., p. 123.

48. Yorke, *France*, p. 61.

49. See Alger, 'Englishmen and the British Colony in Paris, 1792-93,' *The English Historical Review*, eds. S. R. Gordon and R. L. Poole, XIII (London, 1898), 672-694.

50. Alger, 'British Colony,' p. 675.

51. Tuesday, 27 Nov. 1792.

52. Alger, 'British Colony,' p. 675.

53. See K.H., holograph MS. letter from James Maxwell to William, headed 'York end,' late Sept. or early Oct. 1792; also, Alger, 'British Colony,' p. 685; *The Despatches of Earl Gower . . .*, ed. Oscar Browning (Cambridge, 1885), p. 260; Veitch, *Parliamentary Reform*, pp. 227-228; and Rose, Pitt, p. 64.

54. Alger, 'British Colony,' p. 675.

55. Alger, *Englishmen*, p. 77.

56. Veitch, *Parliamentary Reform*, p. 227.

57. Yorke, *France*, pp. 64 f.

58. Alger, *Paris in 1789-94* (London, 1902), p. 346.

59. Leipzig 1911. See, also, Edgar Richter's *Konrad Engelbert Oelsner und die französische Revolution* (Leipzig, 1911) and Alger's 'British Colony,' p. 685.

60. For the following description of the execution I am indebted to John

Gifford's *The Reign of Louis XVI*, Second Edition (London, 1795); Moore's *Journal*; Saul K. Paslover's *The Life and Death of Louis XVI* (New York, 1939); and J. M. Thompson's *The French Revolution* (London, 1966).

61. For the anecdote see McDowall, *Dumfries*, p. 579.

62. *The Correspondence of George, Prince of Wales 1770-1812*, ed. A. Aspinall, II (London, 1964), 334.

63. Aspinall, *Later Correspondence*, II (1963), 3.

64. Ibid., dated 10 Feb. 1793.

65. Chadwick, *St Omer*, p. 381.

66. P. 195.

67. Sheffield Public Libraries, MSS. BK. 1,877, photostat of holograph letter through the courtesy of John Bebbington, City Librarian.

68. Miguel de Cervantes Saavedra, *The Ingenious Gentleman Don Quixote de la Mancha*, trans. Samuel Putnam (New York, 1949), II, 618-620.

CHAPTER FIVE

1. K.H., entry by Dorothy Mary Maxwell-Witham on the fly-leaf of her *Masses for the Dead*.

2. Peter F. Anson, *Underground Catholicism in Scotland* (Montrose, 1970), pp. 255 f.

3. K.H., MSS. *Cash Books, 1826-1827*.

4. *Dumfries Weekly Journal*, 1 June 1778.

5. Ibid., 18 Feb. 1796; also, D.B.R., MSS. 'Magistrates,' under dates 1 June 1792 and 7 Aug. 1793.

6. D.B.R., pamphlet, 'House of Correction Dumfries, October 7 1788, Rules'.

7. *Dumfries Weekly Journal*, 24 Oct. 1826.

8. James Webster, *General View of the Agriculture of Galloway* . . . (Edinburgh, 1794), pp. 38 f.

9. *Dumfries Weekly Journal*, 1 Aug. 1826.

10. D.B.R., MSS. *Miscellaneous Papers, 1790-1799*, 'Examination & Declaration of Doctors Gilchrist & Maxwell and Surgeons Copland, Nasby, Mundell &ca about the infectious disorder said to be prevalent in Dumfries. 27th June 1799'.

11. McDowall, *Dumfries*, p. [734].

12. In a letter of 5 Aug. 1972 from Miss Jean Maxwell, Dumfries. Ten years earlier Miss Maxwell had copied this from the original MS into her *Nithsdale Scrapbook*.

13. K.H., MSS. *Account Books*, under entries for 14 June 1804 and 12 Oct. 1808.

14. From a typescript of J. DeLancey Ferguson presenting his quotations from and notes upon the unedited Syme-Cunningham correspondence (hereafter cited as 'Ferguson *Manuscript*'), p. 32; also, National Library of Scotland, MSS. 1653-55, John Syme to Alexander Cunningham, 15 Sept. 1805.

15. See, for example, *Dumfries Weekly Journal*, 1 Sept. 1795.

16. Ibid., 20 July 1796.

17. K.H., MSS. *Cash Books, 1821-1826*, entries for 20 June and 31 Dec. 1821.

18. See *Rules and Regulations of the Dumfries and Galloway Horticultural Society*, Second Edition (Dumfries, 1814).

19. K.H., MS. holograph letter.

20. N.R.O., MS. 358/38/26, 'The last Will & Testament of Thomas Riddell Esqre.' One stipulation of these papers is that certain Swinburne lands are to be for 'the use of James Maxwell of Kirkconnell in North Britain esquire.' Furthermore, N.R.O., MS. 358/45/16, dated 'November 15th 1790,' shows James Maxwell as witness to a £1,000 legacy received by his aunt Dorothy Riddell.

21. N.R.O., MSS. 358/40/27 & 28, 'Settlement of Mrs Dorothy Riddell, 1793,' and K.H. MS. holograph letter, William to James, dated 'Dumfries 20 Feb. 1805'.

22. See, for example, K.H., MS. *Account Book, 1802*, under dates 15 June and 1 July; MS. ['List of Debts due by James Maxwell of Kirkconnell, 26 Mar. 1804']; Scottish Record Office, Ref. 18868, photostats of MSS. (1) 'Sasine Mrs Mary Riddell Kirkcudbright, 7 Dec. 1797,' (2) 'Sasine Dr William Maxwell Kirkcud^{ght}, 14 Apr. 1817,' and (3) 'Sasine D^{r} W Maxwell, 9 Apr. 1806'. Also, D.B.O., MS. 'Arrears, 1797-1799'.

23. Ibid.

24. K.H., MS. holograph letter.

25. K.H., MS. *Account Book, 1805*, under 24 and 28 Dec.

26. N.R.O., MS. 358/40329 (sub-title with /27, 28), 'Extract Deed of Settlement of Mrs Maxwell of Kirkconnell — 1807'.

27. K.H., MS. holograph letter dated 'Dumfries Sunday Jan [?1795]'.

28. For examples, see K.H., MS. 'Settlement by James Maxwell Esqr . . . . 12 July 1825' and K.H., MSS. letters from John Menzies to James Maxwell, 1816.

29. *Dumfries and Galloway Courier*, 1 Oct. 1816.

30. Ibid.

31. In a letter of 24 Feb. 1809 (K.H., holograph MS), William informed James that he 'purchased Netherwood yesterday'. For details about previous and subsequent ownership of the property, I am indebted to John Henderson & Sons, Solicitors, Bank Street, Dumfries; they represent the present owner, Mr John Maxwell. I am grateful to Mr Maxwell for having spent so much time with me when he took me about at Netherwood and answered my questions.

32. K.H., holograph MS.

33. D.B.R., MS. 'Decreet Martin ag.t Maxwell 1804'.

34. K.H., MS. *Account Book, 1805*, under 17 July; MS. 'Bond James Maxwell to M.r Thomas White 1793' as well as other bonds made out to the other lenders; and MS. ['Lists of Debts . . . 26 Mar. 1804'].

35. K.H., MS. holograph letter, William M.cMurdo to Hugh Corrie, 30 June 1800, and MS. holograph letter, Dr James Currie to James Maxwell, 22 July 1801.

36. K.H., MS. holograph letter.

37. K.H., MS. 'Nomination of additional heirs of Taillie'.

38. Dumfries Sheriff Clerk's Office, *Register of Deeds & Probative Writs*, Book 3, 'Bond and Disposi.tn by D.r Maxwell in Dumfries [29 Dec. 1814]'.

39. K.H., MS. ['Discharge, D.r William Maxwell to James Maxwell'], dated 23 June 1814 and docketed by Robert Gordon, James's writer, '23 June 1814. Immediately the Discharge was executed M.r Maxwell returned the Bill for £671-4/ in a present to his Br[other].'

40. K.H., MS. holograph letter, Robert Gordon to James Maxwell, dated 'Kirkcudbright 15 October 1814'.

41. K.H., MS. 'Poetry on the death of Mrs Maxwell of Kirkconnell, 10 March 1815'.

42. K.H., MS. holograph letter, D. Hamilton Craik to 'Doctor Maxwell Dumfries,' dated 'Arbigland 26th March 1815'.

43. K.H., MS. holograph letter, dated 'Dumfries April 14.th 1815'.

44. K.H., MS. holograph letter.

45. See *Dumfries and Galloway Courier* under dates 3 Jan., 7 Feb., 2 May, and 19 Dec. 1815.

46. Ibid., 26 Dec. 1815.

47. K.H., MS. *Cash Book, 1817*, under 'Jan.y 6'.

48. K.H., MS. holograph letter, John Menzies to James Maxwell, dated 'Abd.n 13.th May 1816'.

49. K.H., MS. holograph letter, John Menzies to James Maxwell, dated 'Abd.n 3.d June 1816'.

50. K.H., MS. holograph letter, dated 'Abd.n 3.d May 1816'.

51. K.H., MS. holograph note, William Reid to James Maxwell, dated 'Thursday 9 o clock P.M.'

52. K.H., MS. 'Inhibition Threshie — Maxwell 1817'.

53. K.H., MS., two folio sheets of stamped paper, subscribed by Robert Gordon at Dumfries 29 May [1816].

54. K.H., MS. copy of 'Obligation by Kirkconnell for the Rent of D.r Maxwell's House in Dumfries for four years from the term of Whit.y 1817'.

55. The preceding is based upon an inventory of William's effects which is attached to Gordon's conformation.

56. K.H., MS. holograph letter, dated 'Abd.n 12.th June 1816'.

57. K.H., MS. holograph letter, dated 'Blairs 7.th July 1816'.

58. See *Dumfries and Galloway Courier*, 27 Aug., 26 Sept., and 1 Oct. 1816.

59. K.H., MS. This decree was interponed 30 Dec. 1816.

60. K.H., MS., 'Horn and Poind Threshie — Maxwell 1816'.

61. K.H., MS. *Cash Book, 1817;* the payment to William is for 30 May, the Syme entry is for 25 Nov.

62. K.H., MS. 'Df.ᵗ Contract of Marriage between James Maxwell Esq and Miss Witham 1817'.

63. Scottish Record Office, Ref. 18868/2, 'Sasine D.ʳ William Maxwell Kirkcudᵍʰᵗ,' dated 5 Apr. 1817, and K.H., MS. 'Bond of Annuity James Maxwell Esqʳ to D.ʳ William Maxwell, Dated 1 Dec.ʳ 1818 Regᵈ 12 Mar: 1827'.

64. K.H., MSS., 'Janʸ 21ˢᵗ 1818 Inventory of Table and Bed Linnen' and 'Inventory of Silver Plate'. Also, *Cash Book, 1817*, and years thereafter.

65. This paragraph is based upon a visit to Blairs College, summer 1973, when Father Brennan showed me about and answered my questions about John Menzies.

66. Anson, *Underground Catholicism*, pp. 224 f.

67. The account of James's visit is based upon K.H., MS. ['Journey to and from Aberdeen 1818-19'], an itemized account of expenditures.

68. See D.B.R., MS. 'Police Assessment 1819,' under 'Castle Street 21'.

69. K.H., MS. ['Inventory and Appraisement of Furniture Bequeathed to Dr Maxwell'], dated '1828' and upon *Catalogue of Household Furniture, China, Earthernware, Glass Crystal, And a Valuable Library of Books To Be Sold by Auction at the House of Dr Maxwell, Castle Street, Dumfries, on Tuesday, The 20th May, and Following Days* (Dumfries, 1834).

70. This paragraph is based upon a photostat of John Wood's 'Plan of the Town of Dumfries and Maxwelltown' (1819) given me by Mr A. E. Truckell, Dumfries.

71. K.H., MS. *Cash Book, 1823*, under 'Janʸ 23'.

72. The loan is cited in K.H., MS., 'State of Debts owing by Mʳ Maxwell 18 January 1825,' under 'Loans'; the Copleux transaction is cited in K.H., MS., 'State of the Property left by the late John Baptiste Copleux — James Maxwell Esq Executor,' dated 2 June 1820.

73. See, for example, K.H., MS. *Cash Book, 1824*, under 'Dec.ʳ 15' and *Cash Book, 1825*, 'Janʸ 5'.

74. K.H., MS. *Cash Book, 1826*, after 'April 26'.

75. K.H., MS. *Cash Book, 1822*, for 'June 20'.

76. K.H., MS. *Cash Book, 1825*, after 'April 13'.

77. K.H., MS 'Minute at Opening of Repositories at Kirkconnell 20 February 1827'.

78. K.H., MS. 'Settlement by James Maxwell . . . Dated 12 July 1825'.

79. K.H., MS. holograph memorandum.

80. K.H., MS. 'Inventory and Appraisement . . . 1828'.

81. K.H., MS. *Cash Book, 1830,* after 'July 8'.

82. K.H., MS. *Cash Book, 1827,* entries for May.

83. *The Journal of Sir Walter Scott,* ed. W. H. Parker (Edinburgh, 1939-46), II, 15.

84. Anson, *Underground Catholicism,* p. [241].

85. Ibid., p. 255.

86. Ibid., pp. 256 f.

87. Ibid., p. 257.

88. Ibid., p. 268.

89. K.H., MS. holograph letter, John Menzies to the Rev Mr Thomas Witham, 5 Oct. 1838. Dorothy Maxwell-Witham called Elizabeth 'Betsy' (see K.H., MS. holograph letter, Dorothy to her uncle the Rev Mr Thomas Witham, 20 Mar. 1836). Elizabeth is the 'Miss Maxwell' listed in the *Edinburgh Directory* (e.g. 1840) as living with John Menzies and the Right Rev Dr James Gillis at 'Greenhill cottage'.

90. Edinburgh Room, Edinburgh Central Public Library, *Notes on the Lands of Greenhill* by John Smith.

91. K.H., MS. *Cash Book, 1833,* after '20 April' and '14 June'; also, K.H., MS. holograph letter, Dorothy Mary Maxwell to [the Rev Mr Thomas Witham], dated 'St Margaret's Convent March 20th, 1836'.

92. Anson, *Underground Catholicism,* p. 266.

93. The silhouette is in the Morning Room at Kirkconnell House; the Allan portrait, in the Gallery.

94. K.H., MS. holograph letter, Menzies to Witham, 8 Oct. 1838.

95. See, for example, the *Dumfries and Galloway Courier* for 22 Oct. 1834. Dorothy Mary Maxwell-Witham notes in her *Masses for the Dead,* 'Uncle Dr Willm Maxwell M. D. died at Edinburgh Oct 14th 1834'. Her son, Robert Maxwell-Witham, however, corrects her in his genealogical table, 'D^r W^m died in Edinburgh in the house of his relative John Menzies of Pitfodels on 13 Octr 1834'.

CHAPTER SIX

1. *Letters,* I, 67. Succeeding references to the *Letters* within this chapter are given within the text by volume and page only.

2. The following account is taken from my 'Robert Burns and the Scottish Enlightenment,' *Studies in Voltaire and the Eighteenth Century,* LVIII (1967), 1533-49.

3. The reviewer of *Robert Burns's Commonplace Book, TLS* for 17 Mar. 1966.

4. From 'Wait for the Hour,' *Modern Scottish Poetry,* ed. Maurice Lindsay (London, 1946), p. 68.

s

5. Houghton Library, Harvard University, *MS.* Eng. 1140.

6. 'The Vision,' *Poems*, I, 112.

7. *Robert Burns's Commonplace Book, 1783-1785*, eds. James Cameron Ewing and Davidson Cook (Glasgow, 1938), p. 7.

8. T. G. Snoddy, 'Robert Burns,' *B.C.*, III (1954), 21.

9. 'Mauchline Conversation Society,' *B.C.*, III (1954), 38.

10. Franklin Bliss Snyder, *The Life of Robert Burns* (New York, 1932), p. 291.

11. *The Life and Works of Robert Burns*, ed. Robert Chambers & rev. William Wallace, II (1896), 86.

12. Chambers-Wallace, II, 97.

13. Ed. W. L. Renwick (London, 1965), p. 97.

14. William Wallace, *Robert Burns and Mrs. Dunlop* (London, 1898), pp. 33 f.

15. William Smellie, *Account of the Institution and Progress of the Society of Antiquaries of Scotland* (Edinburgh, 1782), p. 17.

16. Robert D. Thornton, *Selected Poetry and Prose of Robert Burns*, Riverside Edition (Boston, 1966), p. 193.

17. Anson, *Underground Catholicism*, p. 192.

18. James M'Gloin, 'Robert Burns and "The Popish Bishop,"' *B.C.*, XXIV (1949), 22.

19. K.H., MS. holograph letter dated "Ed.ʳ 21ˢᵗ May 1793'.

20. *Poems*, I, 425 & 428.

21. Chambers-Wallace, III, 74 f.

22. Ibid., III, 255.

23. K.H., MS. *Account Book, 1791*.

24. John Gibson Lockhart, *The Life of Sir Walter Scott* (Edinburgh, 1903), IX, 230 f.

25. *Poems*, I, 348.

26. Ibid., 'Epistle to Mʳ Tytler,' I, 333.

27. Ibid., 'Here's a Health to them that's awa,' II, 663.

28. 'Essay on Criticism,' *The Best of Pope*, ed. George Wiley Sherburn (New York, 1940), p. 71.

29. *Poems*, II, 815.

30. Ibid., I, 49.

31. 'Man Was Made to Mourn,' *Poems*, I, 117.

32. Hugh Blair, *Sermons* (Dublin, 1801), V, 71.

33. James Fisher, 'A Riddle,' *Poems on Various Subjects* (Dumfries, 1790), p. 157.

34. See, for example, Chambers-Wallace, III, 379.

35. See Henry W. Meikle's 'Burns and the Capture of the Rosamond,' *B.C.*, IX (1934), [43]-51.

36. *Poems*, II, 826.

37. D.B.R., MS., 'Summons of Removing 1792,' dated 2 Apr. 1792.

38. D.B.R., MSS. *Miscellaneous Papers: 1790-1799,* 'Crim^{le} Sum^s The Fiscal Ag^t Jno Lewars 1792'.

39. Ibid., 'Declaration of Jean Murdoch and Janet Anderson 1792'.

40. Ibid., a grant of warrant dated 18 May 1792.

41. Ibid., 'Execution The Fiscal Ag^t Witnesses 1792'.

42. Ibid., as the fifth of the six items which constitute the action.

43. Ibid., 'Crim^{le} Sum^s The Fiscal Ag^t Jno Lewars 1792'.

44. Notices of both these actions are appended to the summons.

45. Thornton, *Currie,* p. 297.

46. Desmond Donaldson, *The Glenriddell Manuscripts of Robert Burns* (Wakefield, 1973), preceding p. [1].

CHAPTER SEVEN

1. *Letters,* II, 230. Succeeding references to the *Letters* within this chapter are given within the text by volume and page only.

2. Betsy Rodgers, *Georgian Chronicle Mrs Barbauld and Her Family* (London, 1958), p. 120.

3. *The Letters of Sir Walter Scott,* ed. H. J. C. Grierson, I (1932), 34.

4. Chambers-Wallace, IV, 133.

5. *Poems,* II, 732.

6. I am indebted to A. E. Truckell, Curator, Dumfries Royal Burgh Museum, for his help in going over this MS. deposited at the Museum.

7. D.B.R., MS. 'Supply Ledger,' under 8 June 1795.

8. For the account of this celebration of the King's birthday see *Dumfries Weekly Journal,* 9 June 1795.

9. 'The Dumfries Volunteers,' *Poems,* II, 764-766.

10. See 'Dweller in yon dungeon dark,' *Poems.* I, 446 f.

11. *Poems,* I, 225.

12. Chambers-Wallace, IV, 244 f.

13. Allan Cunningham, *The Works of Robert Burns* (London, 1834), I, 337.

14. Snyder, *Life,* p. 427.

15. [James Currie], *The Works of Robert Burns,* First Edition (Liverpool, 1800), I, 226, n.

16. Ibid., p. 223.

17. Ibid., p. 221.

18. Ibid., pp. 220 f.

19. Ibid., p. 222.

20. See, for example, Chambers-Wallace, IV, 271.

21. [James Cameron Ewing], 'Correspondence of John Syme and Alexander

Cunningham, 1789-1811,' *B.C.*, X (1935), [39]. This is the first of seven parts (hereafter cited as 'Correspondence' and by part, e.g. 'Correspondence-I'. Professor Ferguson's quotations from and notes on this correspondence before it was edited by Ewing are cited as 'Ferguson, *Manuscript'*.

22. Currie, *Works*, I, 225 f.

23. 'Correspondence-I,' *B.C.*, X (1935), 40.

24. Ibid., p. 41.

25. [James Cameron Ewing], 'The Death of Burns His Final Moments: His Last Words An Unpublished Account,' *B.C.*, XVI (1941), 18-19. In a footnote (p. 20), the late Mr Ewing wrote, 'The letter may be reprinted in full in a future volume of the *Burns Chronicle.*' It never has been; thus, one is left bemused by such criticism of Currie as editor.

26. Ed. J. DeLancey Ferguson in Robert T. Fitzhugh's *Robert Burns: His Associates and Contemporaries* (Chapel Hill, N. C., 1943), p. 118.

27. Professor [John] Wilson, *The Genius and Character of Burns* (New York, 1845), pp. 219 f.

28. 'Correspondence-I,' *B.C.*, X (1935), 41.

29. A printed copy is at the Dumfries Royal Burgh Museum, dated 'Dumfries, 23ᵈ July, 1796'.

30. D.B.R., MS. docketed 'Proposals by J. Lewars for Publishing a Map of the Town & Borough Roads of Dumfries 1796/16 May 1796. Read in Council to lye on the table'.

31. K.H., 'A Paper on the Subject of Burns' Pistols: Read at a Meeting of the Society of Antiquaries, On Tuesday the 19ᵗʰ Day of April, 1859 by The Right Rev. Bishop Gillis' (Edinburgh), inscribed 'To R[obert] Maxwell Witham of Kirkconnell With Bishop Gillis's Compliments'.

32. See James Cameron Ewing's 'The Literary Fund and Robert Burns,' *B.C.*, IX (1934), [68]-71.

33. Snyder, *Life*, p. 437.

34. Currie, *Works*, I, 232.

35. 'Correspondence-III,' *B.C.*, XI (1936), 36.

36. 'Correspondence-VI,' *B.C.*, XV (1940), 20.

37. Ferguson, *Manuscript*, p. 26.

38. 'Correspondence-IV,' *B.C.*, XIII (1938), 48.

39. 'Correspondence-II,' *B.C.*, X (1935), 47.

40. Ibid., p. 49.

41. 'Correspondence-I,' *B.C.*, IX (1934), 62.

42. 'Correspondence-III,' *B.C.*, XI (1936), 36.

43. Ibid., pp. 36-37.

44. *Edinburgh Evening Courant*, 23 July 1796.

45. For Syme's comment see 'Correspondence-III,' *B.C.*, XI (1936), 38; for an example of how others took up from Thomson see *The Universal Magazine of Knowledge and Pleasure*, C (London, 1797), 412-413, which is quoted above.

46. *Poems*, II, 696.

47. Ibid., II, 825.

48. Ibid., II, 769, under 'Fragment-Epistle from Esopus to Maria'.

49. Ibid., II, 734.

50. National Library of Scotland, 5. 505, 'Candidior,' pseud. This is a photostat of Maria Riddell's essay as it was originally published in the *Dumfries Weekly Journal;* the date of publication is not shown.

51. 'Correspondence-III,' *B.C.*, XI (1936), 35.

52. Thornton, *Currie*, pp. 333 f.

53. [Duncan M'Naught], ' "Correspondence of Charles Kirkpatrick Sharpe" (Blackwoods), 1888,' *B.C.*, XII (1903), 58.

54. 'Correspondence-III,' *B.C.*, XI (1936), 40.

55. For the first see *Poems*, II, [761]; for the second, *Letters*, I, 200.

56. *Letters*, I, 221.

57. Ibid., I, 284.

58. Old Register House, Edinburgh, *Com. Dumfries Testaments*, XVII.

59. That Syme and his father before him had business with those at Kirkconnell is made clear again and again by the household account-books and by such papers as Syme's bill to William McCraken, 25 Apr. 1816: 'To drawing a bond and disposition by James Maxwell of Kirkconnell Esquire to you for £2,500 at 10/6 per £100'.

60. 'Correspondence-I,' *B.C.*, IX (1934), 54.

61. 'Correspondence-III,' *B.C.*, XI (1936), 42. In a letter of 16 Nov. 1972, Miss Jean Maxwell, Dumfries, points out that John Lewars as well as Syme and William lived near Troqueer. Miss Maxwell cites as her source J. G. Hamilton-Starke's 'Troqueer in the Olden Time,' *Transactions of the Dumfries and Galloway Antiquarian Society, 1894-95.*

62. Ferguson, *Manuscript*, p. 2.

63. 'Correspondence-IV', *B.C.*, XIII (1938), 44.

64. Ibid., p. 47.

65. Duncan M'Naught, 'Dr. Currie and his Biography of Burns,' *B.C.*, XXVIII (1919), 22.

66. 'Correspondence-IV,' *B.C.*, XIII (1938), 50.

67. Ibid., p. 49.

68. Ibid., p. 51.

69. 'Correspondence-V,' *B.C.*, XIV (1939), 78.

70. Ibid., p. 79.

71. For the date and circumstance of departure see Gilbert Burns's *Journal of a Trip to Liverpool*, an unpaginated manuscript held at the Burns Cottage, Ayr. Through the courtesy of the Trustees of the Burns Monument, Ayr, I have a microfilm copy of the original (hereafter cited as 'Gilbert, *Journal*').

72. 'Correspondence-V,' *B.C.*, XIV (1939), 82-85.

73. Ibid., pp. 84 f.

74. 'Correspondence-VI,' *B.C.*, XV (1940), 19.

75. National Library of Scotland, MS. 1655, ['Minutes of the Trustees for 22 March 1800 in the hand of Dr William Maxwell'].

76. B.P., holograph letter, pp. 48-52.

77. 'Correspondence-VI,' *B.C.*, XV (1940), 19.

78. Ibid., pp. 19 f.

79. See James Cameron Ewing's 'Maria Riddell's Letters to Dr James Currie, 1796-1805-II,' *B.C.*, XXX (1921), 105-106, dated 'Kew-Road, Richmond, 9th April, 1799' and 'IV,' *B.C.*, XXXIII (1924), 89, as well as Ewing's 'Two Letters of Maria Riddell,' *B.C.*, XXI (1946), 43.

80. See B.P., pp. 54-56, Cadell & Davies to Dr James Currie, 31 May 1798, and B.P., pp. 56-61, four estimates on the edition of Burns which remained in the office files. An account of the negotiations continues in the Besterman Papers from these points.

81. B.P., p. 75.

82. B.P., p. 80, holograph letter, William Thomson to Cadell & Davies, dated 'Dumfries 1st March 1799'.

83. B.P., photostat of the 'Deed of Agreement' from the original in the Cowie Collection.

84. B.P., p. 80.

85. For the above see B.P., p. 187, holograph letter, William Thomson to Cadell & Davies, 23 Sept. 1800; p. 194, holograph letter, William Thomson to Cadell & Davies, 9 Oct. 1800; pp. 218-220, holograph letter, William Thomson to Cadell & Davies, 'Dumfries 6. March 1801'; and p. 244, holograph letter, William Thomson to Cadell & Davies, 18 Oct. 1801.

86. B.P., p. 409, holograph letter, Robert Hartley Cromek to Cadell & Davies, dated 'Allerton [William Roscoe's Liverpool home] 12th Feb. 1808'.

87. James R. Wilson, 'The Story of the Mausoleum,' *B.C.*, VI (1900), [5]-27, an excellent account based upon the minute book of the Mausoleum Committee, a group of seven selected from the twenty-three patrons of the subscription. See, also, the *Dumfries Weekly Journal* account of Tuesday, 11 Jan. 1814.

88. The K.H. account-books for 1815-1822 show a number of transactions like '1815 June 7 Borrowed of John Syme Esqr—£500'.

89. 'Correspondence-VII,' *B.C.*, XVII (1942), 10.

90. William Thomson lived to become Provost of Dumfries and, in or around 1826, President of the Dumfries Gas Company.

91. *Substance of the Speech of the Earl of Selkirk in the House of Lords, Monday, August 10, 1807, on the Defence of the Country*, Second Edition (London, 1807), p. 42.

92. *Dumfries and Galloway Courier*, 30 Jan. 1816.

93. *Dumfries Weekly Journal*, 18 Jan. 1820. See, also, *Robert Burns and Dumfries 1796-1896*, comp. Philip Sulley (Dumfries, 1896), p. [36].

94. *Dumfries Weekly Journal,* 30 Jan. 1827.

95. Chambers-Wallace, IV, 295 and Sulley's *Robert Burns,* pp. [22]-35.

96. McDowall, *Dumfries,* p. 579.

97. Catherine Carswell, *The Life of Robert Burns* (London, 1930), p. 443.

98. Robert T. Fitzhugh, *Robert Burns* (Boston, 1970), pp. 377 f.

99. William Ernest Henley, 'Robert Burns: Life, Genius, Achievement,' *The Poetry of Robert Burns,* The Centenary Edition (Edinburgh, 1897), IV, 340, n.

Selected Bibliography

The following selected bibliography is offered to indicate where I have searched anew outside the familiar pales of Ferguson's *Letters*, Snyder's *Life*, and the *Burns Chronicle* and to show any reader where he might start searching hopefully. By and large, the items listed below describe those sources which I have found particularly useful for this work, but never before in the past thirty years have had cause to footnote in a barrage of scholarly articles.

Every mention of Kirkconnell, here and within the text itself, is a recognition of Mrs Bettina M. G. Maxwell-Witham of Kirkconnell House. Among those who have patiently helped me previously and again now, I have cause to remember the late Mrs M. G. Brown of Castle Douglas; Charles P. Finlayson, Keeper of Manuscripts in the Edinburgh University Library; and A. E. Truckell, Curator of the Dumfries Royal Burgh Museum, who, as spiritedly as ever, told me of late that I was the first person to ask about Dr William Maxwell in the hundred years that he and his father before him have been curator in Dumfries.

Of those to whom I have gone for the first time in the cause of this book, I wish to thank Miss Jean Maxwell of Dumfries; Miss Rosamond Meredith, Archivist, Sheffield City Library; Mrs A. Smolar, Assistant Archivist, State Archives at Namur; W. A. G. Alison, City Librarian, Glasgow; William B. Davidson, Sheriff Clerk, Dumfries; R. M. Gard, County Archivist, County of Northumberland; Ian D. Grant, Assistant Keeper, Scottish Record Office, Edinburgh; John Henderson & Sons, Solicitors, Dumfries; David Hope, Photographer, Dumfries; R. E. Hutchison, Keeper, Scottish National Portrait Gallery; Roland Mortier, Professor at the University of Bruxelles; John Riddell of Swinburne Castle, Justice of the Peace; W. A. Taylor, City Librarian, Birmingham; O. S. Tomlinson, City Librarian, York; and F. J. Turner, Librarian, Stonyhurst College. And I wish to recognize here the full co-operation of the staffs of the following institutions: the British Museum, the Edinburgh Room of the Edinburgh Public Library, the Harvard University

Libraries, the National Library of Scotland, the Public Record Office in London, and the Yale University Libraries. Were I to be wholly frank, I would state that the only doors closed to me have been those watched by the Roman Catholic authorities in Edinburgh who have custody of the Menzies Papers and several Kirkconnell papers. Finally, I am grateful to both the State University of New York and the John Simon Guggenheim Memorial Foundation: the former for a combined Research Fellowship and Grant-in-Aid, the latter for a generous contribution toward the cost of illustration.

I.

MANUSCRIPT COLLECTIONS
&
PUBLIC RECORDS

ABERDEEN

Blairs College.
Although the Menzies Papers are 'somewhere' in Edinburgh, having been sent down from Blairs, this college library has many of Menzies' own books; other parts of the college contain other possessions of John Menzies of Pitfodels.

ALLOWAY

Burns Museum.
Holograph of Gilbert Burns's journal of trip to Liverpool, August-September 1797.

BLACKBURN and ACCRINGTON

Arundell Library, Stonyhurst College.
Records of the English Academy at Liége, e.g. 'Liége School Ledger 1773-1790'.

DUMFRIES

Ewart Public Library.
Here are the most complete files of the local newspapers.

John Henderson & Sons, Solicitors.
Netherwood Deeds.

Royal Burgh Museum.
Burgess Book. Dumfries Volunteers Book. Burgh Records, such as Diet Books, Entailed Estates, Processes, Protests, Services.

Sheriff Clerk's Office.
Some Sheriff Court Records, the remainder at the New Register House, Edinburgh.

EDINBURGH

Edinburgh Room, Edinburgh Public Library.
John Smith's notes on Greenhill.

National Library of Scotland.
MSS. 1653, 1654, & 1655. MS. William Maxwell's minutes as secretary of the Burns trustees, 22 March 1800. MS. 22.4.11(94), holograph letter, James Currie to Robert Anderson, 7 July 1800.

New Register House.
v. Scottish Record Office (Edinburgh).

Old Register House.
Births & Deaths, excluding those for Roman Catholics.

Scottish Record Office.
Some Sheriff Clerk Records. RS 3/580 & /1048, 23/24 & /27, as testaments, etc. of the Maxwells of Kirkconnell. 'Register of Kirkconnell Charter Chest.'

Manuscript Rooms, University of Edinburgh.
Album Academiae Jacobi VI Regis Scotorum . . . ab anno 1762, ad annum 1786. 'List of Students 1774-1784.' 'List of Members of the Royal Medical Society 1737-1811.' 'Matriculation: 1786-1803.'

KIRKCUDBRIGHTSHIRE

Castle Douglas, Sheriff Clerk's Office.
Some Sheriff Court Records, the remainder at the New Register House, Edinburgh.

Kirkconnell House.
Charter Chest. Account Books. Cashbooks. Daybooks. Catalogue of Household Effects. Catalogue of Library before Dispersal. Correspondences. Executorship Papers. Holograph Copy by Dorothy Mary Maxwell of James Maxwell's *Narrative.* Marriage Contracts. Papers on Salmon Fishing. Great numbers of other miscellaneous documents and papers.

NAMUR

Archives de L'État.
Archives Dinant. Cartulaire de Dinant. Commune Dinant. Couvents Les Jésuites de Dinant. *Ecclésiastiques,* 3740, 3750-56.

NEWCASTLE

County Record Office, County of Northumberland.
Papers of the Riddells of Swinburne Castle.

NEW PALTZ, NEW YORK

The Besterman Papers in my possession: (1) Theodore Besterman's tran-
script of the Earnock Manuscripts, National Library of Scotland, MSS.
1653-1655 together with my microfilm copy of these MSS; (2) photostats of
letters et al. from Cowie and Hornel Collections, City of Liverpool Public
Libraries, and Office Files of Cadell & Davies; and (3) photostat copy of
Contract between Executors of Robert Burns and Publishing House of
Cadell & Davies.

LONDON

Public Record Office.
HO 42/20-23.

SHEFFIELD

Sheffield Public Libraries.
Edmund Burke Papers.

YORK

York Public Libraries.
'Civic Officials and Parliamentary Representatives of York.'

II.

BOOKS, PAMPHLETS, ARTICLES

Actes de la Commune de Paris pendant la Révolution, eds. Sigismond Lacroix
et René Farge. Second Series: VIII. Paris, 1914.

Alembert, Jean Le Rond d'. *Sur la Destruction des Jésuites en France.* London,
1756.

Alger, J. G. 'The British Colony in Paris, 1792-93,' *The English Historical
Review,* eds. S. R. Gardiner and R. L. Poole, XIII (October, 1898), 672-694.

— *Englishmen in the French Revolution.* London, 1889.

— *Paris in 1789-94.* London, 1902.

Another Traveller . . . by Coriat Junior. 2 vols. London, 1767.

Anson, Peter F. *The Catholic Church in Modern Scotland 1560-1937.* London,
1937.

— *Underground Catholicism in Scotland.* Montrose, 1970.

Archives Parlementaires, eds. J. Mavidal, E. Laurent, et al. Series I, 1787-1799. 82 vols. Paris, 1879-1913.

Aulard, F[rançois A[lphonse]. *La Société des Jacobins Recueil de Documents pour l'Histoire du Club des Jacobins de Paris.* 6 vols. Paris, 1889-1897.

Bellesheim, Alfons. *History of the Catholic Church in Scotland.* 4 vols. London, 1890.

Bonenfant, Paul. *La Suppression de la Compagnie de Jésus dans les Pays-Bas Autrichiens.* Académie Royale de Belgique Mémoire, XIX, 3. Bruxelles, 1925.

Boyce, Edmund. *The Belgian Traveller.* 5th edn. London, 1827.

Buchez, P. B. and P. C. Roux. *Histoire Parlementaire.* 40 vols. Paris, 1834-1878.

Burke, Edmund. *The Correspondence of Edmund Burke,* eds. P. J. Marshall and John A. Woods. 9 vols. Chicago, 1958-1970.

Carlyle, Thomas. *The French Revolution: A History.* 3 vols. London, 1870.

Caron, P. *Manuel Pratique pour l'Étude de la Révolution Française.* Paris, 1912.

Catalogue of the Society Library Dumfries taken M,DCCC,II. Dumfries, 1803.

Charles, George. *History of the Transactions in Scotland in the Years 1715-16 and 1745-46.* 2 vols. Stirling, 1816.

Chassin, Ch[arles] L[ouis] and L[eon] Hennet. *Les Volontaires Nationaux pendant la Révolution.* 2 vols. Paris, 1899-1902.

Curvers, Alexis and Georges H. Dumont. *Les Délices du Pays de Meuse.* Bruxelles, n.d.

Daniel, Lr P. Ch. *Les Jésuites Instituteurs de la Jeunesse Française.* Paris, 1880.

Dick, C. H. *Highways and Byways in Galloway and Carrick.* London, 1819.

Directory to the Church Service for the Catholic Laity in Scotland, The. Dundee, 1834.

English Catholic Nonjurors of 1715, The, eds. Estcourt and Payne. London, 1885.

Foley, Henry, S. J., ed. *Records of the English Province of the Society of Jesus.* I-VII.2 (1877-1883). London.

Fox, Charles James. *Memorials and Correspondence of Charles James Fox,* ed. Lord John Russell. 4 vols. New York, 1970.

Fraser, William. *The Book of Carlaverock.* 2 vols. Edinburgh, 1873.

Gallez, Danielle. *La Ville de Dinant et Ses Magistrats de 1772 à 1814.* Unpublished thesis. Namur, June 1969.

George III. *The Later Correspondence of George III,* ed. A. Aspinall. 5 vols. London, 1962-1970.

George, Prince of Wales. *The Correspondence of George, Prince of Wales 1770-1812,* ed. A. Aspinall. 8 vols. London, 1963-1972.

Gérard, Edouard. *Histoire de la Ville de Dinant*. Namur, 1935.

Gifford, John, et al. *The Reign of Louis XVI*. 2nd edn. London, 1795.

Gillray, James. *The Works of James Gillray the Caricaturist; with the History of His Life and Times*, ed. Thomas Wright. London, [1873].

Godechot, Jacques. *The Counter-Revolution*, trans. Salvatore Attanasio. New York, 1971.

Gould, Robert Freke. *The History of Freemasonry*. 6 vols. London, 1883-1887.

Gower, see Leveson.

Hachez, Henri. *Histoire de Dinant*. Bruxelles, 1932.

History and Proceedings of the Lords and Commons during the Second Session of the Seventeenth Parliament of Great Britain, The. London, 1792.

Hughes, Philip. *The Catholic Question: 1688-1829*. London, 1929.

Jarvis, Rupert C. *Collected Papers on the Jacobite Risings*. 2 vols. Manchester, 1972.

— *Jacobite Risings of 1715 and 1745, The*. Cumberland County Council, 1954.

Kints, E. *Les Délices du Pays de Liége*. 3 vols. 1738-1766.

Gower, Earl [George Granville Leveson]. *The Despatches of Earl Gower English Ambassador at Paris from June 1790 to August 1792 to which are added the Despatches of Mr Lindsay and Mr Monro and the Diary of Viscount Palmerston . . .*, ed. Oscar Browning. Cambridge, 1885.

List of Persons concerned in the Rebellion . . . 7th May 1746, A. Scottish Historical Society. Edinburgh, 1890.

McDowall, William. *History of the Borough of Dumfries*. Edinburgh, 1867.

McKerlie, P. H. *History of Lands and Their Owners in Galloway*. 5 vols. Edinburgh, 1877-1879.

Macours, F. 'Le Collège de Dinant après la Suppression de la Compagnie de Jésus (1773-1794),' *Namurcum*, XXV (1950), [34]-40.

Marmol, Ferd. del. *Dinant*. Dinant, 1888.

Martin, A. and G. Walter. *Catalogue de l'Histoire de la Révolution*. 5 vols. Paris, 1936-1955.

Massey, William. *A History of England*. 4 vols. London, 1863.

Maynard, M. l'Abbé. *The Studies and Teaching of the Society of Jesus at the Time of Its Suppression 1750-1773*. Baltimore, 1855.

Medd, Patrick. *Romilly*. London, 1968.

Menzies, D. P. *The Red and White Book of Menzies*. Glasgow, 1894.

Miller, John. *Popery and Politics in England 1660-1688*. London, 1973.

Moore, Dr John. *A Journal during a Residence in France Beginning of August, to the Middle of December, 1792. A New Edition Corrected*. 2 vols. London, 1793.

[Oelsner, Konrad Engelbert]. *Bruchstücke aus den Papieren Eines Augenleugen und Unparteiischen Beobachters der Französischen Revolution*. Frankfort, 1794.

— *Flucht, Verhör und Hinrichtung Ludwigs XVI nach der Schilderung eines*

Deutschen Beobachters. Leipzig, 1911.

Padberg, John W. *Colleges in Controversy.* Cambridge, Mass., 1969.

Palmer, R. R. *The Age of the Democratic Revolution.* 2 vols. Princeton, 1959.

Parliamentary History of England . . . to 1803, The, ed. W. Cobbett. 36 vols. London, 1806-1820.

Parliamentary Register for the History of Parliament and Debates of the House of Commons, ed. J. Debrett, 45 vols. London, 1780-1796.

Paslover, Saul K. *The Life and Death of Louis XVI.* New York, 1939.

Richter, Edgar. *Konrad Engelbert Oelsner und die Französische Revolution.* Leipzig, 1911.

Rose, J. Holland. *William Pitt and the Great War.* London, 1911.

Rudé George. *Hanoverian London 1714-1808.* Berkeley, 1971.

Scott, Sir Walter. *The Journal of Sir Walter Scott,* ed. W. M. Parker. 3 vols. London, 1939-1946.

— *Tales of A Grandfather.* 4 vols. Boston, 1853-1855.

Seaman, W. A. L. *British Democratic Societies in the Period of the French Revolution.* Unpublished thesis. University of London, 1954.

Shaw, J. M. *Surnames of Kirkcudbrightshire, Dumfriesshire.* Galloway Historical & Antiquarian Society, 1893.

'Siderius.' *Dinant.* Dinant, 1859.

Smith, Charles. *St. Patrick's Church: Edinburgh.* Edinburgh, 1956.

Soboul, Albert. *The Sans-Culottes,* trans. Remy Inglis Hall. New York, n.d.

Southey, Robert. *New Letters of Robert Southey,* ed. Kenneth Curry. 2 vols. New York, 1965.

Sulley, Philip. *Robert Burns and Dumfries.* Dumfries, 1896.

Sydenham, M. J. *The First French Republic 1792-1804.* London, 1974.

Taylor, J. *Great Historic Families of Scotland, The.* 2 vols. London, 1887.

Thicknesse, Philip. *A Year's Journey through the Pais Bas.* London, 1786.

Thornton, Robert. *James Currie the Entire Stranger and Robert Burns.* Edinburgh, 1963.

— *James Currie's Robert Burns a Publishing History of the First Edition 1797-1800.* Unpublished manuscript.

— 'Robert Burns and the Scottish Enlightenment,' *Studies in Voltaire and the Eighteenth Century.* LVIII, 1533-49. Genève, 1967.

Tour of Holland Dutch Brabant, the Austrian Netherlands and Part of France. London, 1772.

Traveller's Vade Mecum through the Netherlands and Part of France and Germany, The. Canterbury, 1782.

Veitch, George Stead. *The Genesis of Parliamentary Reform.* Reprint. London, 1964.

Walpole, Horace. *Selected Letters of Horace Walpole,* ed. W. S. Lewis. New Haven, 1974.

Walzer, Michael, ed. *Regicide and Revolution,* trans. Marian Rothstein.

London, 1974.

Webster, James. *A General View of the Agriculture of Galloway.* Edinburgh, 1794.

[Wemyss], David, Lord Elcho. *A Short Account of the Affairs of Scotland in the Years 1744, 1745, 1746, with Memoir and Annotation by Evan Charteris.* Edinburgh, 1907.

Werkmeister, Lucyle, *A Newspaper History of England 1792-1793.* Lincoln, Neb., 1967.

Yorke, Henry Redhead. *France in Eighteen Hundred and Two.* ed. J. A. C. Sykes. London, 1906.

III.

NEWSPAPERS AND PERIODICALS

ANCIEN MONITEUR
ARIS' BIRMINGHAM GAZETTE
DUMFRIES AND GALLOWAY COURIER
DUMFRIES WEEKLY JOURNAL
EDINBURGH EVENING COURANT
EDINBURGH GAZETTEER
GENTLEMAN'S MAGAZINE
LONDON EVENING MAIL
LONDON MORNING CHRONICLE
LONDON POST
LONDON PUBLIC ADVERTISER
LONDON SUN
WILLIAMSON'S DIRECTORY (Edinburgh)

Index